THE
Chinese
Cook
Book

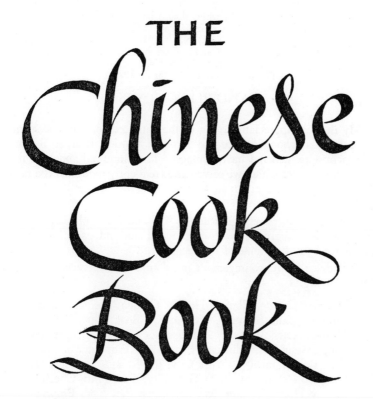

WALLACE YEE HONG

Charlotte Adams, Consulting Editor

CROWN PUBLISHERS, INC. • New York

Library of Congress Catalog Card Number: 52-5688
ISBN: 0–517–506602
Fourteenth Printing, March, 1978

ACKNOWLEDGMENTS

My deepest appreciation goes to the hundreds of customers and good friends who patronize the Ho Lee Garden Rest at Boston, Massachusetts, which I have managed. They inquired about all the varieties of dishes which we served and frequently requested the recipes. Day by day I accumulated hundreds of recipes, and hence my book.

I sincerely express my gratitude to Mr. and Mrs. John C. Knight of Lynn, Massachusetts, who encouraged me and gave invaluable assistance by testing some of the recipes.

For advice and encouragement my thanks and appreciation go to the following:

YEE KAY-CHONG, Chef of Ho Lee Garden, Boston, Massachusetts; CARL SHAPIRO, of Shapiro's Book Shop, Boston, Massachusetts; WONG JEN, Proprietor of Gamsun Restaurant, Boston, Massachusetts; DAVID YEE, Proprietor of May Yee's Restaurant, New York City; JOE K. YEE, Manager of Ding-Ho Restaurant, New York City; TAO TING, Chef of Cathay House, Boston, Massachusetts; BEN YEE, Proprietor of Ben Yee Restaurant, New York City; GEORGE YEE, Manager of Dragon Restaurant, Washington, D. C.; KING L. YEE, Proprietor of Casino Royal, Washington, D. C.; WALTER YEE, Host of Ruby Foo's Den, Boston, Massachusetts.

For helping with reading and typing of the manuscript I am sincerely indebted to Misses Ida Levy, Elizabeth Hooper, Elizabeth Brierly, Kathleen Johnson, Eleanor Annese, Mrs. Josephine Hubbard, Mrs. Anni Chin Yee, and Mr. Joe Lee.

FOREWORD

Chinese cookery is a combination of surprise, mystery and gustatory delight. It is difficult to describe in terms of our American culinary art, yet it isn't difficult to accomplish if you use oriental cooking methods. Just as an alchemist prepares his concoctions with exact quantities in a certain sequence, so does the Chinese chef. Chinese cookery is also extremely versatile and can be quickly adapted to whatever ingredients are at hand.

A visit behind the scenes in a Chinese kitchen will amaze you with the variety of dried ingredients and condiments on the shelves. Every kitchen you visit will disclose more and more of them. The diversity seems endless, yet each has its proper place in the preparation of a dish which will please the palate. Leftovers or fresh meat of any kind can be combined and blended with the correct seasonings in the proper order to result in a dish of gustatory delight.

Chinese cookery produces some of the most expensive dishes known in the world, yet can provide menus which are healthful, very satisfying to the appetite and extremely economical. To cook these oriental dishes in the home isn't difficult, and they will be quite successful if you follow the formulae, instructions and methods of preparation accurately. And that, simply, is the basis of successful Chinese cooking. Practice makes perfect, and the more you practice cooking these dishes yourself, the more delighted you will be with the result.

Another reason for attention to Chinese cookery is that the Chinese really make eating a serious business. When the food is in the center of the table and each has his bowl of rice, the host makes the first move, then all attend to the business at hand. As each one becomes satisfied, he leaves the table and washes his hands.

When we realize that the following recipes use condiments and ingredients with many, many years of history and custom behind them, the best advice for every reader is to realize that cooking is a very serious business—from the point of view of health, taste, and to fit the individual pocketbook. Many of the ingredients listed in this book may seem expensive, but are, on the contrary, very economical because a little goes a long way. When you decide to embark on an exploration of Chinese cooking, obtain only the best ingredients from reliable sources and accept no substitutes. The use of a single item in a recipe which is adulterated or of very inferior grade will result in an unsatisfactory dish. With some proper ingredients on hand, embark on an excursion into the intricacies and delights of Chinese cooking. Use the recipes in this book as your compass and follow the course exactly. The result will more than repay you. You will find that preparing and consuming real Chinese food is very satisfactory business for the health and the appetite.

A book could be written as introduction to a genuine Chinese cook book and still leave much unsaid. But if this foreword induces the reader to approach the preparation of a meal seriously and use the Chinese recipes properly, then the satisfaction which each diner will experience at the table will repay you in health and economy.

JOHN C. KNIGHT

CONTENTS

INTRODUCTION

To win the heart of your husband—satisfy his stomach.
To uphold the love of your dearest ones—serve them a
   good variety of food.
To expect your children to grow strong—give them
   appetite.

—Confucius

For thousands of years cooking has been regarded as a fine art in China—almost a science. The Chinese kitchen is, in effect, a kitchen laboratory—in which the weights and measures, the order in which the ingredients are put together, and the timing are exact. Chinese cookery is something that cannot be learned from reading a recipe—which should be used as a guide only—but must be practiced with patient and painstaking care.

Nevertheless, we feel that in this book we have arranged the various cooking procedures in such fashion that anyone can follow them, even a novice in the kitchen. We have been assisted by numerous famous chefs in leading Chinese restaurants all over the eastern part of the United States—and many of the recipes have been tried and tested in the homes of our friends and customers.

Although at first glance it may seem that many of the ingredients are strange and rare, it will be noted that there are various familiar substitutes for many of the Chinese ingredients. If the ingredients are not available in your neighborhood, write to any of the sources listed on page vii.

There are actually only three basic seasonings which are really necessary to obtain the subtle flavor so characteristic of Chinese cooking: two kinds of soy sauce (heavy and light) and seasoning powder (scientifically known as monosodium glutamate). Since relatively small quantities are used with each recipe, a reasonable supply will last a long time and prove to be quite economical.

Follow the recipes closely, step by step. We know you will be successful—and we hope you will find this new way of cooking both interesting and educational and that you will enjoy cooking these dishes as much as your family will enjoy eating them.

WALLACE YEE HONG

April, 1952

Sources of Special Chinese Ingredients

CALIFORNIA

Yee Sing Chong Company, 950 Castelar Street, Los Angeles
Shew Jung Company, 924 Grant Avenue, San Francisco

ILLINOIS

Sun Wah Hing Trading Company, 2246 Wentworth Avenue, Chicago

MASSACHUSETTS

K. S. Lung, 54 Beach Street, Boston
T. H. Lung, 9 Hudson Street, Boston
Sun Sun Company, 74 Beach Street, Boston
Tai Kwong Company, 60 Beach Street, Boston

MICHIGAN

Lun Yick Company, 1339 Third Avenue, Detroit

NEW YORK

Mandarin Food Product Corporation, 13 Bowery, New York
Mon Fong Wo Company, 36 Pell Street, New York

OHIO

Sun Lee Yuen Company, 1726 Payne Avenue, Cleveland

PENNSYLVANIA

Yick Fong Company, 210 North 9 Street, Philadelphia

Recommended Chinese Restaurants

CALIFORNIA

LIME HOUSE, 708 New High Street, Los Angeles
TAO LEE YON, 816 Washington Street, San Francisco

D. C.

CASINO ROYAL RESTAURANT, 14th and H Streets, N.W., Washington
DRAGON RESTAURANT, 1329 G Street, N.W., Washington

ILLINOIS

TAI DONG RESTAURANT, 2206 Wentworth Avenue, Chicago

MASSACHUSETTS

CATHAY HOUSE, 70 Beach Street, Boston
CHINA HOUSE, 146 Boylston Street, Boston
GAMSUN RESTAURANT, 21 Hudson Street, Boston
HO LEE GARDEN, 2 Hudson Street, Boston
RUBY FOO's DEN, 6 Hudson Street, Boston

MICHIGAN

NEW LIFE CHOP SUEY, 13991 Gratiot Avenue, Detroit

MISSOURI

LUCKY INN, 3018 Easton Avenue, St. Louis

NEW YORK

BEN YEE's RESTAURANT, 131 West 52 Street, New York
DING-HO RESTAURANT, 105 West 49 Street, New York
MAY YEE's RESTAURANT, 125 West 45 Street, New York
PACIFIC RESTAURANT, 30 Pell Street, New York
RUBY FOO's DEN, 240 West 52 Street, New York
TOY WAN RESTAURANT, 194 Canal Street, New York

OHIO

NANKING RESTAURANT, 720 Euclid Avenue, Cleveland
FAR EAST RESTAURANT, 2801 East Main Street, Columbus

PENNSYLVANIA

CATHAY TEA GARDEN, 1221 Chestnut Street, Philadelphia

RHODE ISLAND

PORT ARTHUR RESTAURANT, 123 Weybosset Street, Providence

SOUP

In Cantonese cooking, especially, a "base" soup stock is everything. A good Cantonese chef must first learn to make "base" soup stock. Then he must learn to make "common" Super Soup Stock. This Super Soup Stock is used in all cooking except sweet and sour dishes. Most families in Canton have such soup on hand, for use when unexpected guests or relatives call. Noodles, macaroni or vegetables may be added, if desired.

---

1. SUPER SOUP STOCK (*Shang Tong*)

A. 3 gals. water in large soup kettle
B. 3 lbs. pork neck bones, disjointed
C. 5 or 6 lbs. fowl, disjointed
D. 1 or 2 Virginia ham bones or skin
E. 1 left mouth fish (Chinese dried *do how* fish)
F. 1 doz. pieces dry ducks' feet or wings
G. not over 4 lbs. of three to six kinds of vegetables, such as celery, turnips, carrots, broccoli, scallions, soy bean sprouts, onions, or any vegetable *except* cabbage and cauliflower

COOKING

1. Bring A to boiling point.
2. Add B, C, D, E, F. Bring to a boil. Lower heat two thirds.
3. Add G and boil one hour.
4. Drain off soup stock. Remove meat from bones. Add desired quantity of stock to meat and vegetables for soup to be served immediately. Put leftover stock in refrigerator for use in Chinese or American dishes.

Note: Let soup stock stay in refrigerator overnight. Then pour off clear broth into glass jar for future use.

[1]

2.   CHICKEN SOUP WITH DROPPED EGGS
(*Don-Far Guy Tong*)

A. 8 cups super soup stock, in pot ready to cook
B. 1 cup meat (chicken, pork, beef, veal, or ham), chopped fine
C. ½ cup celery, chopped fine
D. 2 water chestnuts, peeled and chopped fine
E. 1 teaspoon seasoning powder (or 2 bouillon cubes)
F. 1 teaspoon cornstarch mixed with 4 tablespoons cold water
G. 3 eggs, beaten
H. salt and pepper to taste

COOKING

1. Bring A to boiling point.
2. Add B, C, D and boil for 10 minutes.
3. Add E.
4. Add F slowly; stir thoroughly.
5. Add G slowly, stir thoroughly. Turn off heat at once.

Serves 6.

3.   CHICKEN NOODLE SOUP (*Guy Mein Tong*)

A. 8 cups super soup stock, in pot ready to cook
B. 2 lbs. fresh noodles (or ½ lb. dried egg noodles), any length you desire; 5 or 6 inches is usual style
C. 1 cup cooked chicken, shredded
D. 2 teaspoons seasoning powder
E. 2 teaspoons peanut oil
F. 2 teaspoons soy sauce
G. a few drops of sesame oil (optional)
H. salt and pepper to taste
I. 1 whole scallion, chopped fine

PREPARATION

Put B in boiling water and boil for 5 minutes. If dried noodles are used, boil for 10 minutes. Rinse with cold water and drain well.

COOKING

1. Bring A to boiling point.
2. Add B, C, D, E, F, G, H and boil 5 minutes.
3. Sprinkle I on top of each serving.

Serves 6.

4. CHICKEN NOODLE SOUP, Gam Lo Style
(*Gam Lo Mein*)

A. 8 cups super soup stock, in pot ready to cook
B. 1 lb. fresh egg noodles (or ½ lb. dried noodles)
C. 2 teaspoons seasoning powder
D. 2 teaspoons soy sauce
E. few drops of sesame oil (optional)
F. salt and pepper to taste
G. 1 or 2 slices each of three of the following roast meats: chicken, Chinese pork, duck, beef, veal or ham
H. 3 hard-boiled eggs, cut in halves, or sliced with egg cutter
I. 2 heads fresh scallions, chopped fine

PREPARATION

Put B in boiling water and boil 5 minutes. Boil 10 minutes if you use dried egg noodles. Rinse in cold water and drain.

COOKING

1. Bring A to boiling point.
2. Add B and boil 5 minutes.
3. Add C, D, E, F and stir well.
4. Put G all around on top of the noodles in each soup bowl. Add H in center. Sprinkle I over top.

Serves 4.

5. NOODLE SOUP, Chop Suey Style
(*Chop Suey Yoka Mein*)

A. 8 cups super soup stock, in pot ready to cook
B. 1 lb. freshly made egg noodles (or ½ lb. dried egg noodles), cut 5 inches long
C. ¼ lb. Chinese cabbage, cut in ½ inch pieces, 1½ inches long
D. ¼ lb. snow pea pods
E. ¼ lb. bamboo shoots, sliced thin or shredded
F. ¼ cup imported black mushrooms (or white), sliced thin
G. ¼ cup water chestnuts, peeled or sliced thin
H. 2 cups sliced raw meat (pork, veal, beef or shrimp)
I. 2 teaspoons seasoning powder
J. 2 teaspoons soy sauce
K. a few drops sesame oil (optional)
L. salt and pepper to taste

PREPARATION

Put B in boiling water and boil 5 minutes. (Boil 10 minutes if dried egg noodles are used.) Rinse in cold water and drain. If dried black mushrooms are used, soak in warm water for 15 minutes, then slice.

COOKING

1. Bring A to boiling point.
2. Add B and boil 5 minutes.
3. Add C, D, E, F, G, H and boil 5 minutes.
4. Add I, J, K, L and stir thoroughly.

Serves 6.

6. CHOP SUEY SOUP (*Dep-Suey Tong*)

A. 8 cups super soup stock, in pot ready to cook
B. 1 cup meat, sliced or chopped (pork, veal, beef, ham or chicken)
C. 2 cups Chinese cabbage, cut in 1½ inch slices
D. 2 tablespoons water chestnuts, peeled and sliced
E. ¼ cup black or white mushrooms, sliced
F. 1 cup chicken liver and gizzard, sliced very thin
G. 2 teaspoons seasoning powder
H. 2 teaspoons soy sauce
I. salt and pepper to taste

PREPARATION

If you use imported black mushrooms, wash them well in cold water, then soak in warm water 15 minutes. Shred fine.

COOKING

1. Bring A to boiling point.
2. Add B and boil 5 minutes.
3. Add C, D, E, F and bring to a boiling point. Simmer 3 minutes.
4. Add G, H, I.

Serves 6.

7. SEAWEED SOUP (*Do Toy Tong*)

A. 8 cups super soup stock, in pot ready to cook
B. 1½ cups fresh pork (chicken, beef, veal, ham, may be substituted), sliced thin, or finely chopped
C. ¼ cup medium size dried shrimp (optional)
D. 2 cups dry imported native Chinese seaweed
E. 1 tablespoon seasoning powder
F. 2 teaspoons soy sauce
G. salt and pepper to taste
H. 2 tablespoons scallions, chopped fine

PREPARATION

Soak D in warm water 8 minutes. Rinse 5 or 6 times. Make sure all the sand is out. Clean and drain. Tear C into small pieces, soak in warm water for a few minutes.

COOKING

1. Bring A to boiling point.
2. Add B, C, bring to a boil and simmer 5 minutes.
3. Add D and boil 5 minutes.
4. Add E, F, G.
5. Sprinkle H on top of each serving.

Serves 6.

Note: 1 poached egg may be added to each bowl.

8. WATERCRESS SOUP (*Sai-Yong Toy Tong*)

A. 8 cups super soup stock, in pot ready to cook
B. 1 cup raw meat, sliced (beef, pork, veal, ham or chicken)
C. 6 slices fresh ginger (shredded very fine)
D. 2 bunches of watercress (about ½ lb. for each person)
E. 2 teaspoons seasoning powder
F. 2 teaspoons soy sauce
G. 6 drops sesame oil (optional)
H. salt and pepper to taste
I. ½ doz. eggs, each one poached separately

COOKING

1. Bring A to boiling point.
2. Add B, C; bring to a boil and simmer 5 minutes.
3. Add D and boil 3 minutes. Do not cover pot.
4. Add E, F, G, H. Stir well.
5. Float one egg (I) in each bowl of soup.

Serves 6.

9. TOMATO EGG SOUP (*Fan-Kar Don-Far Tong*)

A. 8 cups super soup stock, in pot ready to cook
B. 2 cups meat (pork, beef, veal, ham or chicken) chopped fine or sliced thin
C. 4 slices fresh ginger, shredded very fine
D. 6 cups fresh tomatoes
E. 2 teaspoons seasoning powder
F. 2 teaspoons soy sauce
G. salt and pepper to taste
H. 2 eggs, well beaten

PREPARATION

Put D in boiling water for 2 minutes; remove, peel and cut into 8 diagonal pieces.

COOKING

1. Bring A to boiling point.
2. Add B, C. Bring to boil and let simmer 5 minutes.
3. Add D and stir thoroughly. Boil 5 minutes.
4. Add E, F, G and stir thoroughly.
5. Add H slowly, and stir thoroughly.

Serves 6.

10. MACARONI CHOP SUEY SOUP
(*Tung-Som-Fon Dep-Sui Tong*)

A. 8 cups super soup stock, in pot ready to cook
B. 1½ cups raw meat (pork, chicken, veal, beef, ham, shrimp, dried shrimp or crabmeat may be used), chopped fine

c. 4 cups macaroni (American, Chinese or Italian)
d. 2 tablespoons water chestnuts, cut in thin slivers
e. ¼ cup mushrooms (black, white or fresh garden mushrooms), cut in thin slivers
f. 1½ cups vegetables, cut in thin slivers 1½ inches long
g. 2 teaspoons seasoning powder
h. 3 teaspoons soy sauce
i. 6 drops sesame oil
j. salt and pepper to taste
k. 2 tablespoons scallions, cut in thin slivers 1 inch long
l. 6 eggs, cooked 20 minutes and cut in halves

PREPARATION

Chop B very fine, form into balls. Add fish and more than one kind of meat, if desired. Soak C in cold water 3 minutes. Boil 5 minutes. Rinse in cold water.

COOKING

1. Bring A to boiling point.
2. Add B and boil 5 minutes.
3. Add C, D, E, F, and boil 2 minutes.
4. Add G, H, I, J, stirring thoroughly.
5. Serve by filling each bowl, adding K around the top and floating L in the middle.

Serves 6.

11. VERMICELLI EGG SOUP
(*Phen-Soo Don-Far Tong*)

a. 8 cups super soup stock, in pot ready to cook
b. 1½ cups meat (chicken, pork, beef, veal, ham, fresh shrimp, dried shrimp or duck), shredded fine
c. 4 cups vermicelli (about ¼ lb., dried)
d. 2 tablespoons water chestnuts, shredded fine
e. 2 eggs, beaten
f. 2 tablespoons scallions, cut in ⅟₁₆ inch pieces, shredded very fine
g. 2 teaspoons seasoning powder
h. 2 teaspoons soy sauce
i. salt and pepper to taste

PREPARATION

Soak C in cold water 30 minutes. Cut in 3 to 4 inch pieces with scissors.

COOKING

1. Bring A to boiling point.
2. Add B, C, D, bring to boil, then lower gas and simmer **15** minutes.
3. Add E slowly, stir thoroughly.
4. Add F, G, H, I and stir thoroughly.

Serves 6.

12. BEAN CURD STICK SOUP (*Foo-Jok Tong*)

A. 12 cups super soup stock, in pot ready to cook
B. 2 cups raw meat (chicken, pork, ham or veal—dried oysters may be added), cut in thin slivers
C. ½ lb. dried bean curd stick
D. 2 tablespoons black imported mushrooms, cut in thin slivers
E. ¼ cup Chinese red dates
F. ½ cup canned white nuts
G. ¼ cup water chestnuts, cut in thin slivers
H. 2 teaspoons seasoning powder
I. 1 teaspoon soy sauce
J. salt and pepper to taste

PREPARATION

Soak C and E, separately, in cold water 30 to 60 minutes.

COOKING

1. Bring A to a boiling point.
2. Add B, C, D, E, F, G, bring to boiling point, then lower the **gas** and let simmer 45 minutes.
3. Add H, I, J and stir thoroughly.

Serves 6.

13. MUSHROOM EGG SOUP
(*Dong-Koo Don-Far Tong*)

A. 8 cups super soup stock, in pot ready to cook
B. 2 cups raw meat, diced (chicken, turkey, pork, veal, beef or fresh shrimp)
C. 3 cups mushrooms (fresh mushrooms, black mushrooms or French white mushrooms), diced
D. 2 tablespoons water chestnuts, diced
E. 2 teaspoons seasoning powder
F. 2 teaspoons soy sauce
G. salt and pepper to taste
H. 2 eggs, beaten

COOKING

1. Bring A to boiling point.
2. Add B, C, D and boil 8 minutes.
3. Add E, F, G and stir thoroughly.
4. Add H slowly, stirring thoroughly.

Serves 6.

14. MUSHROOM BEAN CURD SOUP
(*Dong-Koo-Dow-Foo Tong*)

A. 9 cups super soup stock, in pot ready to cook
B. 1½ cups meat, diced in 1 inch pieces (chicken, pork, ham, veal or beef)
C. 4 cups bean curd, cut in 1 inch squares
D. ¼ cup mushrooms, diced
E. 2 tablespoons water chestnuts, diced
F. 1 cup Chinese okra or strip melon or pea pods, diced
G. 2 teaspoons seasoning powder
H. 2 teaspoons soy sauce
I. salt and pepper to taste
J. 6 drops sesame oil

COOKING

1. Bring A to boiling point.
2. Add B, C, D, E, bring to a boil, lower the gas and simmer one hour.
3. Add F and boil 2 minutes.
4. Add G, H, I, J and stir thoroughly.

Serves 6.

15. LO-HAN GOUR BEAN CURD SOUP
(*Lo-Han Gour Dow-Foo Tong*)

A. 9 cups super soup stock, in pot ready to cook
B. 4 cups bean curd cut in 1 inch squares
C. 2 cups meat, chopped fine (chicken, pork, veal, beef or ham)
D. 1 dried imported brown nut cut in 4 pieces
E. 2 tablespoons water chestnuts, chopped fine
F. 1 teaspoon seasoning powder
G. 6 drops sesame oil
H. salt and pepper to taste

COOKING

1. Bring A to boiling point.
2. Add B, C, D, E, bring to the boiling point, then lower gas and simmer for 1 hour.
3. Add F, G, H and stir thoroughly.

Serves 6.

16. CHICKEN AND CREAMED CORN SOUP
(*Guy-Yong Shok-Mi Tong*)

A. 5 cups super soup stock, in pot ready to cook
B. 2 cups chicken, chopped very fine (pork, lobster, shrimp or fresh crab may be substituted)
C. 2 cans #1½ cream style corn—beat with an eggbeater until creamy
D. 2 tablespoons cooked Virginia ham, chopped fine
E. 2 tablespoons water chestnuts, peeled and chopped fine
F. 2 teaspoons seasoning powder
G. salt and pepper to taste
H. 1 cup cream (milk may be used)
I. 2 eggs, well beaten

COOKING

1. Bring A to boiling point.
2. Add B and boil 5 minutes.
3. Add C, D and boil 5 minutes.
4. Add E, F, G and mix well.

5. Add H slowly, and stir thoroughly.
6. Add I slowly, and stir thoroughly just 1 minute.
Serves 6.

17. CHICKEN LETTUCE SOUP
(*Guy-Yong Sang-Toy Tong*)

A. 8 cups super soup stock, in pot ready to cook
B. 1 cup fresh chicken (pork, beef, veal or ham) sliced in thin slivers
C. 2 tablespoons water chestnuts, peeled and cut in thin slivers
D. ¼ cup imported black mushrooms (or fresh white mushrooms), cut in thin slivers
E. 4 heads lettuce, cut in small pieces
F. 2 teaspoons seasoning powder
G. 2 teaspoons soy sauce
H. salt and pepper to taste
I. 6 eggs, poached separately

COOKING

1. Bring A to boiling point.
2. Add B, C, D; bring to a boil and simmer 5 minutes.
3. Add E and boil 2 minutes.
4. Add F, G, H and stir thoroughly.
5. Float one egg (I) in each bowl of soup.
Serves 6.

18. DICED CUT CHICKEN PEA SOUP
(*Ching-Dow Guy-Lip Tong*)

A. 8 cups super soup stock, in pot ready to cook
B. 4 cups green peas (canned or fresh)
C. 1 cup raw chicken meat, diced (pork, beef, veal, ham or duck may be used)
D. ½ cup black imported or fresh mushrooms, diced
E. 2 tablespoons water chestnuts, peeled and diced
F. 2 teaspoons seasoning powder
G. 2 teaspoons soy sauce
H. salt and pepper to taste

COOKING

1. Bring A to boiling point.
2. Add B, C, D, E. Bring to a boil and simmer 5 minutes.
3. Add F, G, H and stir thoroughly.

Serves 6.

19. SUBGUM CHICKEN SOUP, I (*Subgum Guy Tong*)

A. 8 cups super soup stock, in pot ready to cook
B. ½ cup each tomatoes, Chinese cabbage, green peppers, onions, celery, water chestnuts, mushrooms and whole fresh peas
C. 1 cup raw chicken meat, diced (pork, veal, beef or ham)
D. 2 teaspoons seasoning powder
E. 2 teaspoons soy sauce
F. salt and pepper to taste

COOKING

1. Bring A to boiling point.
2. Add B, C; bring to a boil and simmer 8 minutes.
3. Add D, E, F, and stir thoroughly.

Serves 6.

Note: A dropped egg may be added to this recipe.

20. CHICKEN, HAM, WINTER MELON SOUP (*Won-Hoey Tung-Gar Guy-Yong Tong*)

A. 8 cups super soup stock, in pot ready to cook
B. 6 cups winter melon, cut in ½ inch cubes
C. 1 cup chicken meat, diced (pork, beef, veal, duck or dried shrimp)
D. 2 tablespoons cooked Virginia ham, diced
E. 2 tablespoons water chestnuts, peeled and diced

F. ¼ cup white mushrooms, diced
G. 2 teaspoons seasoning powder
H. 2 teaspoons soy sauce
I. salt and pepper to taste
J. 5 drops sesame oil (optional)

COOKING

1. Bring A to the boiling point.
2. Add B; bring to a boil, lower heat and let simmer for an hour.
3. Add C, D, E, F and cook for 10 minutes.
4. Add G, H, I, J and stir thoroughly.

Serves 6.

21. DRIED LILIES TRIPLE SHRED MEAT SOUP
(*Sam-Soo Gum-Cham Toy Tong*)

A. 8 cups super soup stock, in pot ready to cook
B. 1½ cups shredded fresh meats; use three kinds—choice of chicken, pork, beef, veal, ham, duck or liver
C. ¼ lb. dried lilies
D. 2 tablespoons water chestnuts, peeled, shredded
E. 2 teaspoons seasoning powder
F. 1 teaspoon soy sauce
G. salt and pepper to taste
H. ½ doz. eggs, poached individually

PREPARATION

Soak C in warm water for about 15 minutes, then rinse.

COOKING

1. Bring A to boiling point.
2. Add B, C, D and boil 8 minutes.
3. Add E, F, G and stir well.
4. Float one egg (H) in each bowl of soup.

Serves 6.

22. CHICKEN MUSTARD GREENS SOUP
(*Gai-Toy Guy Tong*)

A. 8 cups super soup stock, in pot ready to cook
B. 1½ cups fresh meat (chicken, duck, pork, veal, beef or ham), cut in thin slivers, or chopped
C. ¼ cup water chestnuts, peeled, sliced or chopped with B.
D. 6 thin slices of fresh ginger
E. 8 cups mustard greens (about 1 lb.), sliced in 1½ inch pieces, and rinsed
F. 2 teaspoons seasoning powder
G. 2 teaspoons soy sauce
H. salt and pepper to taste
I. 6 drops sesame oil (optional)
J. ½ doz. fresh eggs or salted preserved eggs, poached individually

COOKING

1. Bring A to boiling point.
2. Add B, C, D and boil 6 minutes.
3. Add E; boil 3 minutes without a cover.
4. Add F, G, H, I and stir thoroughly.
5. Float one egg (J) in each bowl of soup.

Serves 6.

23. BITTER MELON CHICKEN SOUP
(*Foo-Gar Guy Tong*)

A. 8 cups super soup stock, in pot ready to cook
B. 1½ cups fresh chicken meat, sliced very thin (pork, veal, beef, ham or dried shrimps may be substituted)
C. 2 tablespoons water chestnuts, peeled and sliced thin
D. ½ oz. salted spiced cabbage, soaked in water, rinsed and sliced thin
E. 4 cups bitter melon, cut in halves, seeds removed, and melon meat cut in thin slivers
F. 2 teaspoons seasoning powder
G. salt and pepper to taste
H. 2 teaspoons soy sauce
I. 6 eggs, poached separately

COOKING
1. Bring A to boiling point.
2. Add B, C, D and boil 5 minutes. If dried shrimp is used, boil 15 minutes.
3. Add E and boil 8 minutes.
4. Add F, G, H and stir thoroughly.
5. Float one egg (I) in each bowl of soup.

Serves 6.

24. HAIRY MELON CHICKEN SOUP
(*Dick-Gar Guy Tong*)

A. 8 cups super soup stock, in pot ready to cook
B. 1 medium-sized hairy melon, peeled (as you would peel a cucumber), diced in ¾ inch pieces
C. 1½ cups chicken meat, diced (pork, veal, beef, ham, fresh or dried shrimp)
D. 2 tablespoons water chestnuts, diced
E. 2 teaspoons seasoning powder
F. 1 teaspoon soy sauce
G. salt and pepper to taste

COOKING
1. Bring A to boiling point.
2. Add B, C, D and bring to boil again; lower heat one third and simmer 15 minutes.
3. Add E, F, G and stir thoroughly.

Serves 6.

25. CHICKEN WITH CHINESE HERBS SOUP
(*Yek Toy Guy Tong*)

A. 10 cups super soup stock, in pot ready to cook
B. 4 cups meat (chicken, pork, veal, mutton or duck), cut in
   ½ inch squares (pigs' feet may be used as substitute, in
   which case, cut them in half, then into 2 inch long pieces;
   this dish would then be called Pigs' Feet Chinese Herb
   Soup)
C. ½ cup sweet ginseng
D. ¼ cup red sweet cherries
E. ½ cup sweet root
F. ½ cup rice wine
G. ⅛ cup dragon's eye nut meat
H. 1 teaspoon seasoning powder
I. salt and pepper to taste

COOKING

1. Bring A to boiling point.
2. Add B; bring to a boil, lower heat three quarters and simmer 10
   minutes.
3. Add C, D, E, F, G and boil over low flame for 45 minutes.
4. Add H, I and stir thoroughly.

Serves 6.

Note: If pigs' feet or tails are used, boil them about ½ hour, then
add C, D, E, F, G and boil until tender.

26. LAMB WITH CHINESE HERBS SOUP
(*Yong-Yoke Yek-Toy Tong*)

Follow instructions in recipe No. 25, using lamb instead of chicken.

27. WHOLE WINTER MELON STUFFED WITH
VARIETIES (*Dong-Gar Chung*)

A. 1 winter melon about 6 to 8 lbs.
B. 2 cups chicken or duck meat, diced
C. 2 cups diced pork

D. ½ cup cooked Virginia ham, diced
E. 1 cup black imported mushrooms, diced
F. ½ cup white fresh mushrooms, diced
G. ¾ cup lotus seeds, dried or canned
H. ½ cup white nuts, dried or canned
I. ¾ cup water chestnuts, peeled, diced
J. ¾ cup bamboo shoots, diced
K. ¾ cup chestnuts
L. ¼ cup dried duck's gizzard, diced
M. 1 cup rice wine
N. 3 teaspoons seasoning powder
O. 2 teaspoons salt
P. 2 teaspoons soy sauce
Q. ¾ cup dried duck meat, diced

PREPARATION

Wash A and cut off about 3½ inches from the top. Save the top for a cover. Remove melon seeds and fibers. If H, K are dried, break them and soak in warm water 25 minutes. Soak L in water 2 hours and dice. Soak E in warm water 15 minutes.

COOKING

1. Use a bowl large enough to hold the melon.
2. Stuff melon with all the ingredients, then add some super soup stock until melon is full.
3. Cover melon with top which was cut off.
4. Fill a saucepan with about 5 inches of boiling water. (If a pressure cooker is used, about 2½ inches.)
5. Cook for 4 to 5 hours, depending on how old the melon is and how big. (If pressure cooker is used, cook for 1¾ hours, preferably by 18° steam.)

Serves 6.

How to serve: Take the top off, using a serving spoon. Pick all melon meat out. Mix well with all ingredients inside the melon, then serve in individual soup bowls.

28. CHICKEN GIBLET SOUP (*Guy-Foo Chee Tong*)

A. 8 cups super soup stock, in pot ready to cook
B. 2 sets chicken giblets, sliced
C. 1 cup Chinese cabbage, sliced
D. 2 tablespoons mushrooms (black or white), sliced
E. ⅛ cup water chestnuts, peeled and sliced
F. 1 teaspoon seasoning powder
G. 1 teaspoon soy sauce
H. salt and pepper to taste

COOKING

1. Bring A to boiling point.
2. Add B, C, D, E and cook 15 minutes.
3. Add F, G, H. Cook another 2 minutes.

Serves 6.

29. BOK-FAR FISH'S MAW CHICKEN SOUP
(*Bok-Far Gaw Guy Tong*)

A. 8 cups super soup stock, in pot ready to cook
B. 2 cups chicken meat, diced
C. ½ cup raw lean pork, diced
D. ½ cup rice wine
E. 1 cup sweet ginseng
F. 1 tablespoon dragon's eye nut meat
G. 4 cups fish's maw
H. 1 teaspoon seasoning powder
I. 1 teaspoon soy sauce
J. 1 teaspoon salt

PREPARATION

Soak G in warm water 3 hours, rinse in cold water 4 or 5 times, then dice-cut in small pieces.

COOKING

1. Bring A to boiling point.
2. Add B, C, D, E, F, G and cook 35 minutes.
3. Add H, I, J and cook another 15 minutes.

Serves 6.

30. DIAMOND BACK TERRAPIN CHICKEN SOUP
(*Yek-Toy Kwei Tong*)

A. 12 cups super soup stock
B. 2 diamond-back terrapins (from 5 to 6 inches)
C. 2 cups chicken meat
D. 1 cup pork
E. ¼ cup red dried berries
F. ½ cup sweet ginseng
G. 1 tablespoon dragon's eye nut meat
H. 1 cup rice wine
I. 3 slices fresh ginger
J. 2 teaspoons seasoning powder
K. 2 teaspoons soy sauce
L. salt and pepper to taste

PREPARATION

Pour A into soup pot, ready to cook. Put B in a deep pan of warm water and let them swim for a while, then turn on the gas and boil until they drown. (It takes about 15 minutes.) Cut B in half, then cut the meat in 1 inch cubes. Cut C, D in 1 inch pieces.

COOKING

1. Bring A to boiling point.
2. Put B, C, D in soup pot.
3. Add E, F, G.
4. Add H, I and bring to boiling point again; lower heat about two thirds and simmer for 2½ hours.
5. Add J, K, L.

Serves 6.

Note: Diamond-back terrapins are sold in New York's Chinatown.

31. WAI GAY CHICKEN SOUP (*Way Gay Guy Tong*)

A. 14 cups super soup stock
B. 4 cups chicken or 3 squabs (disjointed)
C. ¼ cup thick-sliced herb (wai shan)
D. ½ cup red berries
E. 1 cup rice wine
F. 6 slices fresh ginger
G. 2 teaspoons seasoning powder
H. 2 teaspoons soy sauce
I. salt and pepper to taste

PREPARATION

Pour A into soup pot, ready to cook. Cut B into 1 inch pieces.

COOKING

1. Bring A to boiling point.
2. Add B, then C, D, E, F and bring to boiling point again, lower heat two thirds and cook 2 hours.
3. Add G, H, I.

Serves 6.

32. BARLEY CHICKEN SOUP (*Ye Mei Guy Tong*)

A. 12 cups super soup stock
B. 3 cups boneless chicken
C. 1 cup barley (rice may be substituted)
D. 2 tablespoons water chestnuts
E. ½ cup white mushrooms
F. 2 teaspoons seasoning powder
G. salt and pepper to taste
H. 2 tablespoons cooked Virginia ham, chopped fine

PREPARATION

Pour A into soup pot, ready to cook. Chop B quite fine. Soak C in cold water 15 minutes. Dice D, E very fine.

COOKING

1. Bring A to boiling point.
2. Add B, C, D, E and bring to boiling point again, lower heat two thirds and let simmer 45 minutes.
3. Add F, G.
4. Sprinkle some ham (H) on each serving.

Serves 6.

33. CHICKEN BIRD'S NEST SOUP
(*Guy-Yong-Yen-Wor Tong*)

A. 8 cups super soup stock
B. ¼ lb. dried bird's nest, chopped fine (fish's maw may be substituted)

c. 2 cups chicken meat (or pork)
D. 2 tablespoons water chestnuts
E. 1½ cups milk or light cream
F. 3 egg whites, beaten
G. 3 tablespoons cornstarch
H. 3 teaspoons seasoning powder
I. salt and pepper to taste
J. ⅛ cup cooked Virginia ham, chopped very fine

PREPARATION

Pour A into soup pot, ready to cook. Soak B in cold water about 30 minutes. Drain. Put in about 4 cups of pure cold water and boil 30 minutes. Rinse in cold water. Clean out all black bits of feathers. Mix G in 1 cup cold water.

COOKING

1. Bring A to boiling point.
2. Add B, C, D and bring to boiling point again. Lower heat two thirds and simmer 30 minutes.
3. Add E and stir thoroughly.
4. Add F slowly; stir thoroughly.
5. Add G, H, I.
6. Sprinkle some ham (J) on each serving.

Serves 6.

Note: See Recipe No. 216 with regard to "bird's nest."

34. SUBGUM CHICKEN SOUP, II (*Subgum Guy Tong*)

A. 10 cups super soup stock, in pot ready to cook
B. 2 cups fresh chicken meat, diced
C. 1 cup fresh tomatoes, diced
D. 1 cup green peppers, diced
E. 2 cups celery, diced
F. ½ cup bamboo shoots, diced
G. 2 tablespoons water chestnuts, diced
H. ¼ cup mushrooms, diced (black or white)
I. 2 teaspoons seasoning powder
J. 2 teaspoons soy sauce
K. salt and pepper to taste

COOKING

1. Bring A to boiling point.
2. Add B and boil 15 minutes.
3. Add C, D, E, F, G, H and boil about 5 minutes.
4. Add I, J, K and stir well.

Serves 6.

35. FISH'S MAW CHICKEN SOUP
(*Kwi-Far Yu-Kow Tong*)

A. 12 cups super soup stock, in pot ready to cook
B. 2 cups chicken meat, diced
C. 6 cups fish's maw
D. ¼ cup water chestnuts, diced
E. 3 cups green vegetables (pea pods, mustard greens, Chinese cabbage, or green spinach) cut in 2 inch pieces
F. 2 teaspoons seasoning powder
G. 2 teaspoons soy sauce
H. salt and pepper to taste
I. 2 tablespoons cooked Virginia ham, chopped fine

PREPARATION

Soak C in hot water 1 hour; wash 5 or 6 times.

COOKING

1. Bring A to boiling point.
2. Add B, C, D and boil 30 minutes, then add E and boil 6 minutes.
3. Add F, G, H and stir thoroughly.
4. Sprinkle some ham (I) on each serving.

36. CHICKEN VERMICELLI SOUP
(*Fon-Soo-Guy Tong*)

A. 14 cups super soup stock, in pot ready to cook
B. 2 cups chicken meat, chopped fine (pork, beef, veal, turkey, ham, shrimp, or lobster may be substituted)
C. ¼ lb. vermicelli
D. ½ cup black or white mushrooms, shredded fine

E. 2 scallions (white part only) cut in ½ inch pieces
F. 2 teaspoons soy sauce
G. 2 teaspoons seasoning powder
H. ½ teaspoon pepper
I. salt to taste

PREPARATION

Soak C in cold water 30 minutes; drain and cut with scissors into 5 or 6 inch pieces.

COOKING

1. Bring A to boiling point.
2. Add B, C, D and boil 15 minutes.
3. Add E, F, G, H, I; stir well and bring to boiling point.

Serves 6.

37. SNOW WHITE FUNGUS CHICKEN SOUP
(*Guy-Yong Sut-Ye Tong*)

A. 10 cups super soup stock, in pot ready to cook
B. ¼ lb. snow white dry fungus
C. ¼ cup water chestnuts, shredded fine (or diced)
D. ¼ cup bamboo shoots, shredded fine (or diced)
E. 2 cups white chicken meat, cooked 10 minutes, then shredded (or diced)
F. ½ cup pork, shredded (cooked crabmeat or lobster may be used)
G. ½ lb. pea pods
H. 2 teaspoons soy sauce
I. 2 teaspoons seasoning powder
J. salt and pepper to taste

PREPARATION

Soak B in warm water about 30 minutes; rinse with cold water a few times.

COOKING

1. Bring A to boiling point.
2. Add B, C, D and boil about 20 minutes.
3. Add E, F, G and boil 5 minutes.
4. Add H, I, J.

Serves 6.

38. CHICKEN SHARK'S FIN SOUP
(*Guy Yong Yu Chee*)

A. 10 cups super soup stock
B. 1 lb. shark's fin (already cleaned)
C. 1 cup fresh water chestnuts, peeled, chopped fine
D. 2 cups bamboo shoots, chopped fine
E. 1 cup raw chicken white meat, chopped fine
F. 1 cup fresh crabmeat, chopped fine
G. 3 teaspoons seasoning powder
H. 1 teaspoon soy sauce
I. salt and pepper to taste; add a few drops sesame oil
J. whites of 4 eggs, beaten
K. 4 tablespoons cornstarch, mixed well in 8 tablespoons water
L. ¾ cup cooked Virginia ham, chopped fine

COOKING

1. Pour A into soup pot, ready to cook.
2. Add B, C, D and bring to a boil. Then lower heat two thirds and boil 60 minutes.
3. Add E and boil another 5 minutes.
4. Add F and boil 2 minutes more.
5. Add G, H, I and stir thoroughly.
6. Add J slowly, stir thoroughly.
7. Add K slowly, stir thoroughly.
8. Sprinkle some ham (L) on each serving.

Serves 6.

Note: Shark's Fin Soup is considered extremely rich in vitamins and one of the most nourishing of soups. Only the best restaurants serve genuine Shark's Fin Soup, since it is one of the most expensive of Chinese dishes. In China some restaurants feature Shark's Fin Soup at $10 to $100 a bowl, because it requires very careful preparation and skillful cooking.

Because it is so difficult to prepare, the author does not recommend that the novice in Chinese cookery try either this recipe or the one following until he is quite experienced in this culinary art.

Already cleaned shark's fin may be obtained in New York, Boston, San Francisco and Chicago Chinatowns; costs from $8.00 to $15.00 a pound and you must order it a week in advance.

39. SOM-SOO SHARK'S FIN SOUP
(*Som-Soo Wai Guy Chee*)

A. 10 cups super soup stock
B. 1 lb. shark's fin (already cleaned)
C. 1¾ cup bamboo shoots, sliced very thin, then shredded
D. 1 cup water chestnuts, sliced very thin, then shredded
E. 4 cups cooked chicken white meat, sliced very thin, then shredded
F. 2 cups pork, sliced very thin, then shredded
G. 1 cup Virginia ham, sliced very thin, then shredded
H. 2 teaspoons soy sauce
I. 2 teaspoons seasoning powder
J. salt and pepper to taste
K. whites of 4 eggs, beaten
L. 4 tablespoons cornstarch, mixed well with 8 tablespoons cold water
M. 12 drops of sesame oil

COOKING

1. Pour A into soup pot, ready to cook.
2. Add B, C, D and bring to a boil. Then lower heat two thirds and boil 1 hour.
3. Add E, F, G and boil 10 minutes.
4. Add H, I, J and stir thoroughly.
5. Add K slowly, and stir thoroughly.
6. Add L slowly, stirring constantly.
7. Pour 2 drops M in each serving.

Serves 6.

40. SNOW FROG MEAT CHICKEN SOUP
(*Guy-Yong Sheet-Gup Tong*)

A. 10 cups super soup stock, in pot ready to cook
B. 2 oz. dry snow frog meat
C. 4 cups cooked chicken white meat, chopped fine
D. 1 cup cooked Virginia ham, chopped fine
E. 2 tablespoons water chestnuts, peeled, chopped fine
F. 3 teaspoons seasoning powder
G. 1 teaspoon soy sauce
H. salt and pepper to taste

PREPARATION

Soak B in warm water 3 hours. Wash clean in cold water. Pick out the black pieces; use only those pieces which are cream colored and soft.

COOKING

1. Bring A to boiling point.
2. Add B, C, D, E and boil 5 minutes, then lower heat and simmer 30 minutes.
3. Add F, G and stir well.
4. Add H.

Serves 6.

41. BLACK MUSHROOM DUCK SOUP
(*Tung-Ko Op Tong*)

A. 12 cups super soup stock
B. 1 whole duck
C. ¼ cup dry black imported mushrooms
D. 1 doz. water chestnuts
E. 3 tablespoons soy sauce
F. 2 tablespoons sugar
G. 2 teaspoons seasoning powder
H. 2 teaspoons salt, dash of pepper and Chinese spices
I. 2 teaspoons rice wine

PREPARATION

Pour A into soup pot, ready to cook. Clean B, chop off head and feet, then cut it into 6 pieces. Wash C in cold water. Soak 15 minutes in warm water (two cupfuls), then drain the warm water off into soup pot. Mix E, F, G, H, I together. Use half of the seasoned mixture to soak C, and spread the other half thinly over B. Fry B in deep oil until brown.

COOKING

1. Bring A to boiling point.
2. Add B, C, D (as prepared above) and bring to boil again, lower the heat two thirds and simmer about 1½ hours.

Serves 6.

42. SWEET GINSENG SQUAB SOUP
(*Tong Som Bok-Opp Tong*)

A. 16 cups super soup stock
B. 6 squabs (about 6 lbs.) (add ½ cup pork, if desired)
C. 1 cup rice wine
D. 2 cups sweet ginseng
E. 1 tablespoon dragon's eye nut meat
F. 2 teaspoons seasoning powder
G. 1 teaspoon soy sauce
H. 3 slices fresh ginger
I. salt to taste

PREPARATION

Place A in soup pot, ready to cook. Cut B into about 8 to 10 pieces each.

COOKING

1. Bring A to boiling point.
2. Put B, C (and pork if used) in soup pot and bring to boiling point again; lower heat two thirds and boil 25 minutes.
3. Add D, E, F, G, H and boil 40 minutes.
4. Add I.

Serves 6.

43. SWEET GINSENG CHICKEN OR DUCK SOUP
(*Tong Som Guy or Opp Tong*)

Follow Recipe No. 42, using about 5 lbs. of duck, or chicken, instead of squabs.

44. LO-HAN GOUR WITH SIX KINDS OF HERBS
(*Lo-Han Gour Lok Mei Tong*)

A. 12 cups super soup stock, in pot ready to cook
B. 2 cups raw meat, chopped fine or sliced thin (chicken, pork, beef, veal or ham)
C. 2 packages of six kinds of herbs: luto seeds, almonds, sweet root, Chinese hundred blossoms, small ginseng, jade bamboo rinds (about ⅛ lb. each kind of herb)
D. 2 teaspoons seasoning powder
E. 1 teaspoon soy sauce
F. salt to taste (*do not use pepper!*)

PREPARATION

Soak the sweet root in bowl of water until ready to use.

COOKING

1. Bring A to boiling point.
2. Add B, C (except sweet root) and simmer slowly 1½ hours over low heat.
3. Add sweet root and boil 2 minutes.
4. Add D, E, F and stir thoroughly.

Serves 6.

Note: Six kinds of herbs may be purchased in any Chinese grocery store. Be sure to mention they are for soup. You need two packages for six persons.

45. SCALLOPS BEAN CURD SOUP
(*Kong-Yu Chew Dow Foo Tong*)

A. 9 cups super soup stock, in pot ready to cook
B. 3 cups bean curd, sliced in 1½ inch squares
C. 2 cups scallops, fresh or dried, sliced or diced
D. 2 tablespoons water chestnuts, sliced or diced
E. 2 tablespoons scallions, chopped fine
F. 2 teaspoons seasoning powder
G. 2 teaspoons soy sauce
H. 6 drops sesame oil
I. salt and pepper to taste

COOKING

1. Bring A to boiling point.
2. Add B, C, D; bring to boiling point again, then lower heat and simmer 1 hour.
3. Add E, F, G, H, I and stir thoroughly.

Serves 6.

Note: Scallions may be sprinkled on top of each serving.

46. BLACK MUSHROOM SWEET ROOT SOUP
(*Dong-Koo White-Shan Tong*)

A. 8 cups super soup stock, in pot ready to cook
B. 2 cups raw meat, sliced or chopped fine
C. 2 cups black imported mushrooms or French white mushrooms, cut in thin slivers
D. 2 tablespoons water chestnuts, sliced or chopped fine
E. ½ cup bamboo shoots, cut in thin slivers
F. 1 cup fresh or canned lotus seeds (diced celery may be substituted)
G. ¼ cup sweet root, soaked in cold water until ready to use
H. 2 teaspoons seasoning powder
I. 2 teaspoons soy sauce
J. 6 drops sesame oil
K. salt and pepper to taste

COOKING

1. Bring A to boiling point.
2. Add B, C, D, E, F and boil 18 minutes.
3. Add G and cook 2 minutes.
4. Add H, I, J, K and stir thoroughly.

Serves 6.

Note: Poached eggs may be used for garnishing.

47. BAMBOO PULP CRABMEAT SOUP
(*Hi-Wang Jok-Sang Tong*)

A. 10 cups super soup stock, in pot ready to cook
B. ¼ lb. bamboo pulp
C. 2 tablespoons water chestnuts, sliced very thin
D. ¼ cup bamboo shoots, cut same size as c
E. 2 cups fresh or canned crabmeat
F. 2 teaspoons soy sauce
G. 2 teaspoons seasoning powder
H. salt and pepper to taste
I. pea pods or green vegetables sprinkled on top of each serving (optional)

PREPARATION

Soak B in warm water about 30 minutes. Cut off old end, wash 5 or 6 times with cold water until all sand is out.

COOKING

1. Bring A to boiling point.
2. Add B, C, D and boil 25 minutes.
3. Add E and boil 5 minutes.
4. Add F, G, H, I and boil about 2 minutes.

Serves 6.

48. APPLE PIGS' FEET SOUP
(*Pan-Qur Gee-Gok Tong*)

A. 6 pigs' feet
B. 16 cups super soup stock
C. 6 eating apples
D. 1 teaspoon seasoning powder
E. 1 teaspoon soy sauce
F. salt and pepper to taste

PREPARATION

Place B in large soup pot, ready to cook. Cut A in halves and chop into 1½ inch pieces, crosswise. Cut C in halves, leaving skin on (or peel, if desired).

COOKING

1. Put A in pot filled with hot water. Boil 15 minutes. Rinse in cold water. Repeat this 3 times.
2. Bring B to boiling point.
3. Add A, C to B and bring to boil again. Lower heat two thirds and simmer 1½ hours, or until tender.
4. Add D, E, F.

Serves 6.

49. MIXED NUTS WITH GAME SOUP
(*Qor-Do Guy Tong*)

A. 16 cups super soup stock
B. ½ cup white nuts (canned)
C. ¼ cup chestnuts
D. 2 tablespoons water chestnuts
E. 1 doz. Chinese red dates
F. 2 tablespoons black mushrooms (cut large ones in half)
G. ¼ cup bamboo shoots (cut into 1 inch cubes)
H. 3 cups chicken (duck or squab may be substituted)
I. 2 teaspoons seasoning powder
J. 2 teaspoons soy sauce
K. salt and pepper to taste

PREPARATION

Place A in soup pot, ready to cook. Soak E, F in warm water 15 minutes. Cut D, E, F, G into ¼ inch pieces. Cut H into ½ inch pieces.

COOKING

1. Bring A to boiling point.
2. Add B, C, D, E, F, G, H. Bring to boiling point again. Lower heat one half. Simmer 1 hour.
3. Add I, J, K. Cook 5 more minutes.

Serves 6.

50. LUTO'S ROOT SOUP (*Ling-Gow Tong*)

A. 12 cups super soup stock, in pot ready to cook
B. 6 cups luto's roots (fresh or dried)
C. 6 slices fresh ginger, cut in very small thin slivers
D. 1 piece of dried tangerine skin
E. 2 cups meat cut in 1 inch pieces (chicken, pork, veal, beef, dried oysters, dried mark fish, duck or short ribs of beef) (Recommended: 1 cup duck and 1 cup pork, or 2 cups short ribs of beef; cut short ribs into 1½ inch pieces)
F. 2 teaspoons seasoning powder
G. 2 teaspoons soy sauce
H. salt and pepper to taste

PREPARATION

If using B *fresh,* peel off skin and cut in sections, then cut in halves, any size, and slice ¼ inch thick. If using B *dried,* soak in warm water—don't cut. Soak D in warm water 20 minutes, then clean off soft part of skin.

COOKING

1. Bring A to boiling point.
2. Add B, C, D and bring to a boil; lower heat two thirds and simmer for 1 hour.
3. Add E and boil 20 minutes.
4. Add F, G, H and stir thoroughly. Cook another 10 minutes.

Serves 6.

51. BEEF WITH CHINESE TURNIP SOUP
(*Gow-Bok Nan-Tong*)

A. 12 cups super soup stock, in pot ready to cook
B. 3 cups beef (short ribs or stew meat)
C. 2 teaspoons soy sauce
D. 4 teaspoons rice wine
E. 6 cups Chinese turnips, cut in 1½ inch squares
F. 2 tablespoons water chestnuts, cut in halves
G. 2 cups carrots, diced same size as turnips
H. 1 fresh leek (white part only) or ½ cup onions, chopped

I. 4 slices fresh ginger
J. 2 teaspoons seasoning powder
K. salt and pepper to taste

PREPARATION

Cut B in 1 inch square pieces; stir-fry 3 minutes, until brown, in 1 tablespoon oil. Add C, D and fry 2 minutes. Cover and cook 10 minutes more.

COOKING

1. Bring A to a boil; add B, prepared as above, and boil 10 minutes. Lower heat and let simmer 35 minutes.
2. Add E, F, G, H, I and bring to boiling point. Lower heat and simmer 20 minutes.
3. Add J, K; stir-fry thoroughly. Cook 5 minutes more.

Serves 6.

52. FISH BALL CABBAGE SOUP
(*Yu-Yen-Shou-Toy Tong*)

A. 8 cups super soup stock, in pot ready to cook
B. 2 cups fish cakes (See recipe No. 382)
C. 3 cups Chinese celery cabbage, sliced in 1½ inch pieces
D. ¼ cup black mushrooms, cut in thin slivers
E. 2 tablespoons water chestnuts, cut in thin slivers
F. 10 slices spiced cabbage, cut in thin slivers
G. 6 slices fresh ginger
H. 2 teaspoons seasoning powder
I. 2 teaspoons soy sauce
J. 6 drops sesame oil
K. salt and pepper to taste

COOKING

1. Bring A to boiling point.
2. Add B and boil 3 minutes.
3. Add C, D, E, F, G and boil 5 minutes.
4. Add H, I, J, K and stir thoroughly.

Serves 6.

53. ABALONE BLACK MUSHROOM SOUP
(*Bow-Yu Dong-Koo Tong*)

A. 8 cups super soup stock, in pot ready to cook
B. 3 cups abalone (canned preferred), diced or sliced
C. 3 cups meat (1 cup each pork, chicken, Virginia ham), diced or sliced
D. 1 cup black imported or white mushrooms, diced or sliced
E. 2 tablespoons water chestnuts, diced or sliced
F. 1 cup Chinese white cabbage, diced or sliced
   (*Note*: If you dice one of the above ingredients, dice them all.)
G. 2 teaspoons seasoning powder
H. 2 teaspoons soy sauce
I. salt and pepper to taste
J. 6 drops sesame oil

COOKING

1. Bring A to boiling point.
2. Add B, C, D, E and boil 10 minutes.
3. Add F and boil 2 minutes.
4. Add G, H, I, J and stir thoroughly.

Serves 6.

Note: A poached egg may be used as garnish.

54. ABALONE WITH BEAN CURD STICK SOUP
(*Foo-Jok-Bow-Yu Tong*)

A. 12 cups super soup stock, in pot ready to cook
B. 2 cups meat (chicken, pork, or veal), cut in 1 inch to 1½ inch squares
C. ½ lb. dried bean curd stick, cut in 2 inch long pieces
D. 2 tablespoons black imported mushrooms, cut in thin slivers
E. ½ cup Chinese red dates (soaked in cold water 1 hour)
F. 2 tablespoons water chestnuts, cut in thin slivers
G. 1 cup white nuts (canned preferred)
H. 2 cups abalone (canned preferred), cut in thin slivers
I. 2 teaspoons seasoning powder
J. 1 teaspoon soy sauce
K. salt and pepper to taste

COOKING

1. Bring A to boiling point.
2. Add B, C, D, E, F, G and bring to a boiling point.
3. Add H and boil 10 minutes, then lower heat and simmer for 1 hour.
4. Add I, J, K and stir thoroughly.

Serves 6.

WON-TON AND EGG ROLLS

Won-ton is one of the most popular dishes in China, and is usually eaten at luncheon or late supper. It is very similar to Italian ravioli and Jewish kreplach. Its skin, which is made of flour, eggs and salt, can be made at home or purchased in Chinatown or at any Chinese noodle factory by the pound. Each skin is about 6 or 8 inches square, and each pound contains about 18 or 20 skins. As with the home-made skins, they may be cut in quarters for won-tons or used whole for egg rolls.

The won-ton, or egg roll, skin is extremely versatile and, in Chinese cooking or adapted to American cooking, adds a delightful touch to any meal. Its uses are unlimited. For the explorer in culinary art, the use of the won-ton skins lends an element of surprise, and is a delight to the sight, smell and, above all, to the taste. This dinner table pleasure cannot be described, it must be experienced.

---

55. WON-TON (OR EGG ROLL) SKIN (*Won-Ton Pe*)

A. 2 cups flour
B. 1 egg, beaten
C. 1 teaspoon salt
D. ½ cup ice water

PREPARATION

Put A in large bowl. Add B and mix thoroughly. Add C and mix. Add D and mix until dough is formed. Knead until firm and smooth. Lay dough on a board or clean table and roll it until it is almost as thin as paper. Cut into 6 inch squares and stack them, making sure that each piece is well floured. Wrap in waxed paper and keep in refrigerator, no more than 2 weeks. The 6 inch squares may be used as egg roll skins; cut in half both ways, in 3 inch squares, 4 won-ton skins can be made out of each egg roll skin. (See recipe No. 62 for another method of preparing egg roll skin.)

[36]

56. WON-TON MEAT FILLING

A. 1 lb. lean raw pork, chopped very fine
B. 1 tablespoon fresh scallions, chopped very fine with A.
C. 2 eggs, beaten
D. ¾ teaspoon seasoning powder
E. ½ teaspoon salt and a dash of pepper

PREPARATION

Mix A, B together. Add C, D, E and mix thoroughly. (If mixture is not to be used immediately, keep in refrigerator.) To fill skin, proceed as follows. Using a small butter knife (wooden knife preferred), pick up about ½ teaspoon of meat (or fish) mixture and place on one corner of the won-ton skin. Roll almost to the opposite corner. Wet the left end with beaten egg, then bring right and left ends together and press firmly so that they stick together. The usual serving is 12 to 15 won-tons per person.

57. WON-TON SEAFOOD FILLING

A. ½ lb. filet of any kind of fish, chopped very fine
B. ½ lb. fresh shrimp (or dried shrimp), lobster or crabmeat, chopped very fine
C. 1 tablespoon fresh scallions, chopped very fine
D. 1 tablespoon cornstarch
E. 2 eggs, well beaten
F. ½ teaspoon salt and a dash of pepper

PREPARATION

Mix chopped ingredients, A, B, C, together. Add D, E, F and mix thoroughly. To fill skin, see No. 56, above.

58. WON-TON SOUP

A. 8 cups super soup stock, in pot ready to cook
B. 90 pieces won-ton, already prepared
C. 3 fresh scallions (white part only), chopped
D. 2 teaspoons seasoning powder
E. 2 teaspoons soy sauce
F. salt and pepper to taste
G. few drops sesame oil (optional)

PREPARATION

Put B in pot of boiling water, let simmer until they rise to surface and float. Remove won-tons, drain and then rinse them in cold water. Prepare soup bowls, putting 12 or 15 won-tons and some chopped scallions in each.

COOKING

1. Bring A to boiling point.
2. Add D, E, F and stir thoroughly.
3. Pour into each prepared bowl over won-ton, and serve immediately.

Serves 6.

59. CHICKEN WON-TON SOUP (*Guy Won-Ton Tong*)

A. 8 cups super soup stock, in pot ready to cook
B. 2 cups chicken meat, sliced thin or shredded
C. 90 pieces of won-ton, already prepared
D. 3 fresh scallions (white part only), chopped
E. 2 teaspoons seasoning powder
F. 2 teaspoons soy sauce
G. salt and pepper to taste

PREPARATION

See recipe No. 58, above.

COOKING

1. Bring A to boiling point.
2. Add B and boil 10 minutes.
3. Add E, F, G and stir thoroughly.
4. Pour into each prepared bowl, and serve immediately.

Serves 6.

Note: Roast duck or Chinese roast pork may be used, in which case this dish is called Chinese Roast Pork Won-Ton Soup or Roast Duck Won-Ton Soup. Roast beef, lamb, turkey or veal may also be used. If desired, each serving may be garnished with slices of hard-boiled egg.

60. WON-TON, Gam-Lo Style
(*Gam-Lo Won-Ton Tong*)

A. 8 cups super soup stock, in pot ready to cook
B. 90 pieces won-ton, already prepared
C. 6 eggs, hard-boiled, shelled and cut in halves
D. 6 pieces of chicken, any size (1 piece for each bowl)
E. 6 pieces of sliced ham, any size (1 piece for each bowl)
F. 6 pieces of roast duck, any size (1 piece for each bowl)
G. 3 fresh scallions (white part only), chopped
H. 2 teaspoons soy sauce
I. 2 teaspoons seasoning powder
J. salt and pepper to taste

PREPARATION

Put B in 10 cups of boiling water; boil until won-tons rise to surface; drain and rinse in cold water. Divide among 6 bowls. Place C
cut in half, in center of each bowl, then put one piece of each kind
of meat, D, E, F, around it. Divide G among the 6 bowls.

COOKING

1. Bring A to boiling point.
2. Add H, I, J and stir thoroughly.
3. Fill prepared bowls with soup, and serve immediately.

Serves 6.

Note: Gam-lo means "beautiful roast," so you may use any meat, and
as many kinds as desired.

61. FRIED WON-TON (*Jow Won-Ton*)

Prepare won-tons, as instructed in recipes No. 55 and No. 56. Put
about 3 inches of oil (or lard) in a large skillet, or deep pan. Heat
oil to boiling point. Fry won-tons until they float to surface, and
turn until both sides are brown.
Serve hot—plain, with duck sauce or with sweet and sour sauce.

Note: Fried won-tons are generally used for breakfast, served with
Congee, or late at night for a snack. The younger generation use
them at cocktail parties, bridge or mah-jong parties, or whenever
they entertain friends. They may also be used as appetizers.

The egg roll is a hot savory, usually served with tea or at a cocktail party or for a late evening snack. In this country, many restaurants serve it for an entree or appetizers. The author recommends it for any occasion.

62. EGG ROLLS (*Chun Guen*)

A. 2 cups flour
B. 1 cup water chestnut flour
C. 4 eggs, well beaten (save 2 tablespoons for folding)
D. 2 cups water
E. 4 tablespoons peanut oil
F. 1 cup roast pork, shredded
G. 1 cup shelled cooked fresh shrimps (or dried shrimps), chopped fine. (Fresh shrimp should be cooked 3 minutes; dried shrimp, 10 minutes.) Lobster or crabmeat may be substituted
H. 1½ cups celery, shredded fine
I. 1½ cups scallions, chopped fine
J. ½ cup peeled water chestnuts, chopped fine
K. 2 cups shredded bamboo shoots (canned) or 2 cups dried bamboo shoots
L. 3 teaspoons seasoning powder
M. 3 teaspoons soy sauce
N. 2 teaspoons sugar
O. salt and pepper to taste

PREPARATION FOR SKIN MIXTURE

Mix A and B together. Add C gradually and beat well. Add ½ teaspoon salt and beat 5 minutes. Add D; beat 5 minutes more. Grease well, and heat, a 6 or 7 inch frying pan. Lift the pan from the heat and pour into it 1½ tablespoons of the prepared mixture, turning the pan so that the mixture forms a very thin layer on the bottom. Cook on one side for about one minute over a low flame, or until mixture looks dry. Be careful not to burn. Remove from pan and place layer on large plate. Repeat until all the mixture is used. (See recipe No. 55 for other method of preparing skin.)

FILLING

1. Heat a large skillet.
2. Pour E into hot skillet.

3. Add about 1½ teaspoons salt.
4. Add F, G and stir-fry for 2 minutes.
5. Add H, I, J, K and mix well; stir-fry 5 minutes more.
6. Add L, M, N, O. Mix thoroughly and fry 2 minutes, stirring constantly.
7. Remove to large colander or bowl and mix again. Drain and let mixture cool.

FOLDING EGG ROLLS

Place about 3 tablespoons of filling mixture on center of skin, holding the ingredients together. Take the piece of skin nearest you and fold over the filling. Brush edges of skin with beaten egg. Fold both sides toward the center, then roll close and tight. The size should be about 1½ inches in diameter, 4 inches long. Repeat operation until filling is used up.

FRYING EGG ROLLS

Pour about 4 inches of oil (or lard) into deep skillet. Heat to about 350°; drop rolls into oil. Keep turning them, if necessary, until slightly brown; drain or dry with a towel. If they are not to be served immediately, cool and keep in refrigerator. They can be kept this way for a week. If they are to be used right away, fry until golden brown. Cut each roll into 3 or 4 pieces.

HOT SAVORIES (Shu-Mai or Dem-Som)

Shu-mai is usually served at breakfast or morning tea, luncheon and afternoon tea parties in Canton, China. Therefore, all high-class tea houses have many kinds of shu-mai and change the style every day. In general, they call it "dem-som" which means "have all your heart desires."

The author introduces only the few kinds of shu-mai which are most popular in the United States. These are easy for the housewife to make as a snack for a bridge party or similar occasion. Shu-mai will please your guests and make your party a great success.

---

63. FRESH SHRIMP SAVORY (*Har-Gow*)

A. 2 cups rice flour
B. 1 cup sago, crushed into flour
C. ½ teaspoon salt
D. 2 cups boiling water
E. 1½ cups cooked fresh shrimps, chopped
F. ½ cup cooked meat (pork, chicken, veal, turkey, ham)
G. 2 tablespoons water chestnuts, peeled, chopped fine
H. ¼ cup black mushrooms, soaked in warm water 15 minutes, chopped fine
I. 2 fresh scallions (white part only), chopped fine
J. 1½ cups Chinese white cabbage, chopped fine
K. 2 teaspoons seasoning powder
L. 1 cup shortening
M. salt and pepper to taste

PREPARATION AND COOKING

Sift A and B together in a large bowl. Add C and mix well. Bring D to boiling point, then pour into flour gradually, stirring constantly. Knead dough until firm. Cover dough with wet cloth until ready to use. (Makes enough skin for 2 to 3 dozen savories.) On a board, or clean table, cut dough into small pieces and roll into balls about 1¼ inches in diameter. Flatten each ball as thin as possible. Place E, F, G, H, I, J, K, L, M in a large bowl and mix together thoroughly. Put in refrigerator for an hour or more. When ready to use put about 1½ tablespoons of the filling in the center of the piece of dough. Gather up the sides of the dough and squeeze tightly together to seal. Repeat until filling is used up.

Put a small piece of wax paper on the bottom of each har-gow. Put savories in a colander. Use a very large pot with a rack in the bottom (if you have no rack to fit, invert 3 cups and set colander on these). Set colander on rack and put about 1½ inches of boiling water in pot. Steam for about 10 or 12 minutes. Serve savories immediately.

64. MEAT SAVORY WITH DOUGH SKIN
(*Yoke Shu-Mai*)

A. 2 cups raw meat, minced (pork, veal, lamb, chicken or turkey)
B. 1 cup fresh or dried shrimp, minced
C. 1½ cup Chinese white cabbage or American cabbage, chopped fine (these 3 ingredients may be put in a meat grinder and ground together)
D. 2 tablespoons water chestnuts, peeled, chopped fine
E. 3 fresh scallions (white part only), chopped fine
F. 2 teaspoons seasoning powder
G. 1 teaspoon soy sauce
H. salt and pepper to taste

PREPARATION

Make skin same as in recipe No. 55, only cut skin with a biscuit cutter about 3 inches in diameter. Mix all ingredients thoroughly. Place about 2 tablespoons of the mixture in center of a dough circle. Gather up the sides of the skin and press together to seal. Add more of the mixture, if necessary, to fill the skin. Place on a small square of wax paper, and put in a colander.

COOKING

Cook the same as in recipe No. 63, only steam 15 to 20 minutes. *Note:* Variations of this dish may be obtained by placing the mixture on fresh mushrooms or black mushrooms (Mushroom Shu-Mai); on pieces of green pepper (Green Pepper Shu-Mai); or on pieces of bean curd (Bean Curd Shu-Mai).

65. OYSTER BALLS (*Hosher Yuen*)

A. 2 doz. dried oysters
B. 3 cups filet of sole (halibut, haddock or cod)
C. 1½ cups fresh shrimp
D. 4 fresh scallions (white part only)
E. 2 cloves garlic
F. 2 cups meat (pork, chicken or turkey)
G. 2 teaspoons seasoning powder
H. 1 teaspoon pepper
I. 2 teaspoons sugar
J. 3 thin slices fresh ginger
K. salt to taste
L. 3 tablespoons cornstarch
M. 2 eggs, beaten
N. cracker meal

PREPARATION

Soak A in warm water 5 to 8 hours; clean out all the sand and stones. Put B, C, D, E, F, G, H, I, J through a meat chopper and grind twice. Add K to taste. Add L and mix well. Cover each oyster with the mixture and form into a ball. Repeat until all mixture is used up.

COOKING

1. Cook oyster balls in a double boiler 20 minutes. Drain and let cool. Save the juice.
2. When cold, dip the balls in M, then roll in N.
3. Fry in deep oil or lard, until golden brown.
   Serve hot with Duck Sauce, or use the juice to make brown gravy.

Serves 4.

Note: Chicken or turkey may be substituted for the dried oysters. Name of dish would change accordingly.

66. FRIED GLUTINOUS MEAT SAVORY
(*Hom Guy Leong*)

A. 2 cups glutinous rice flour
B. 1 medium-size boiled sweet potato, mashed
C. boiling water
D. dash salt
E. 2 tablespoons peanut oil
F. 1 teaspoon salt
G. 1 cup dried shrimp, chopped fine
H. ½ cup cooked meat (pork, veal, chicken or turkey), chopped fine
I. 2 cups sizchun salted cabbage, chopped
J. 2 cups celery, chopped fine
K. 2 tablespoons water chestnuts, peeled, chopped fine
L. ½ cup fresh scallions, chopped fine
M. 2 tablespoons soy sauce
N. 2 teaspoons seasoning powder
O. 2 teaspoons sugar

PREPARATION AND COOKING

Put A in a large bowl; pour boiling water into it, stirring constantly, until a thick paste is formed. Add B, D and mix. Knead to form a dough. Break dough into small pieces, roll into balls, and flatten each ball as thin as possible.

Pour E into a hot, deep skillet; keep over high heat until oil is at boiling point. Add F. Put in G and fry for 1 minute. Put in H and fry another minute. Lower heat. Add I, J, K, L, M, N, O and fry, stirring constantly, for about 5 minutes, until no juice is left. Place in a strainer to cool.

Put about a tablespoon of filling in the center of each piece of dough. Fold the skin over to one side (so that it looks like a half moon), double the edge and press together. Repeat until all the filling is used up.

Drop the prepared savories into boiling oil and fry until they float on the surface. When one side is brown, turn over. When both sides are nicely browned, they are ready to serve. They may be served hot or cold.

Note: Toast may be used instead of the skin; in which case the mixture could be used as a sandwich filling—and this would be called a Mandarin Sandwich.

67. HAIR SEAWEED FISH SHU-MAI
(*Fat-Toy Shu-Mai*)

A. 2 lbs. filet of pike or haddock, chopped fine
B. ½ lb. fresh shrimps, shelled, chopped fine
C. 4 tablespoons Virginia ham, chopped fine
D. 2 tablespoons fresh scallions (white part only), chopped fine
E. 4 cloves garlic, mashed
F. 1 tablespoon fresh leek (white part only), chopped fine
G. 3 teaspoons seasoning powder
H. 1 teaspoon sugar
I. 1½ teaspoon salt
J. ½ teaspoon pepper
K. ½ cup cornstarch
L. ½ lb. hair seaweed; soaked in warm water 30 minutes, rinsed with cold water 4 or 5 times
M. 3 cups soup stock

PREPARATION

Mix together A, B, C, D, ½ E, 2/3 G, H, 2/3 I, J, K. Stir until smooth paste is formed. Put L, M in soup pot; add remaining E, G, I. Cook 10 minutes; set aside until cool. Grease hands with peanut oil. Take 2 tablespoons of the first mixture and roll to form a ball. (This amount should make about 24 balls.) Take 2 tablespoons of the second mixture and wrap around each ball, leaving the top of the ball open.

COOKING

1. Put a rack in the bottom of a large pot; pour in about 2 inches of boiling water.
2. Place prepared balls on rack; cover, cook 20 minutes. Serve hot.

Serves 6.

Note: Fish Shu-Mai is one of the most popular hot savories in China. You may substitute for the seaweed any kind of vegetable or melon, and change the name of the dish accordingly.
The following vegetables or melons are suggested: green pepper, fresh or canned mushrooms, celery, cabbage, carrot, turnip (bamboo shoots may also be used); bitter melon, winter melon, Chinese okra, hairy melon.

After shu-mai is cooked, put on pieces of raw vegetable, such as cucumber, lettuce, tomato or water chestnut.

If desired, the following meats may be used, cut or sliced in pieces large enough to hold the ball (shu-mai): Chinese or American bacon, Chinese sausage, ham, chicken, turkey, beef, pork, veal, lamb.

RICE

In South and Southwest China, where rice is grown, rice is served at breakfast, lunch, dinner and supper. Inland and in Northwest China, rice is served only occasionally. This cookbook contains Cantonese recipes for the most part, so rice dishes are important. Rice should be included in all menus.

---

68. BOILED RICE

A. 1 cup long grained or patna rice
B. dash salt
C. 1½ cups cold water, for rice stored 6 months or more, or
1 cup cold water, if new rice is used (stored less than 6 months)

PREPARATION

Put A in plenty of cold water and rub thoroughly with hands; drain and rinse. Repeat until water appears clear; drain. Add B, C and let stand at least 30 minutes or longer.

COOKING

1. Have heat two thirds full; boil rice until no bubbles appear on surface. Lower heat and cook until you hear a "crackle" (this means the rice is beginning to form).
2. Turn heat low until rice forms a crust on the bottom, but does not burn. This takes about 15 minutes.
3. After the rice is served, save crust on bottom for fried rice. Keep in refrigerator. When ready to use it, soak first in cold water and it will separate easily.

Serves 2.

Note: One cup of raw rice equals 2 cups boiled rice.

69. STEAMED RICE IN DOUBLE BOILER

A. 1 cup rice
B. ¾ cup cold water
C. dash salt

PREPARATION

See No. 68, above.

COOKING

1. Put A and B in top of double boiler (water should always be ½ inch above rice).
2. Cover and let steam until all water disappears; this takes about 20 minutes.
3. Lower heat and cook for 20 minutes more.

Serves 2.

70. STEAMED RICE WITH MIXED MEAT
(*Yok-Yong Guy Chung Fon*)

A. 1 cup rice, prepared as in No. 69
B. 2 tablespoons chicken meat, diced
C. 2 tablespoons Virginia ham, diced
D. 2 tablespoons dried duck meat, diced
E. 2 tablespoons black mushrooms, soaked in cold water for 20 minutes, or in warm water for 15 minutes; drained and diced
F. 2 tablespoons Chinese white cabbage (white part only), diced
G. 2 tablespoons bamboo shoots, diced
H. 1 teaspooon seasoning powder
I. 2 teaspoons soy sauce
J. ½ teaspoon peanut oil
K. ½ teaspoon cornstarch
L. clove garlic, crushed
M. salt and pepper to taste
N. 2 eggs, poached separately
O. 1 teaspoon scallions, chopped fine

COOKING

1. While rice is cooking, mix together thoroughly all ingredients except N, O, and let stand about 10 minutes.
2. Put above mixture on top of rice, and steam another 20 minutes.
3. When ready to serve, put N on top of each serving and sprinkle O over all.

Serves 2.

71. STEAMED RICE WITH SEAFOOD
(*Hoy-Sen Fon*)

A. 1 cup rice, prepared as in No. 69
B. 1 cup fresh shrimp, lobster or crabmeat (frog's legs may be used)
C. a few pieces fresh ginger, shredded fine
D. 2 teaspoons soy sauce
E. 1 teaspoon seasoning powder
F. salt and pepper to taste
G. 1 teaspoon peanut oil (or drawn butter)
H. 1 teaspoon cornstarch
I. 1 teaspoon rice wine

COOKING

1. While rice is cooking, mix all other ingredients together.
2. Put mixture on top of rice and steam at least 40 minutes.

Serves 2.

72. STEAMED RICE WITH MIXED NUTS AND SALTED MEATS (*Hom-Yoke Fon*)

A. 1 cup rice, prepared as in No. 69
B. ½ cup mixed nuts, chopped (peanuts and chestnuts)
C. ½ cup salted meat, chopped (chicken, pork or ham)

COOKING

1. Put B, C in the middle of the rice in the double boiler, and steam over low heat about 2 hours.

Serves 2.

73. MANDARIN RICE (*Kon-Yon Fon*)

A. 2 cups rice, prepared as in No. 69
B. 2 teaspoons soy sauce
C. ½ teaspoon seasoning powder
D. 1 teaspoon rice wine
E. 1 teaspoon fresh ginger, crushed or shredded fine
F. ½ cup dried duck meat, shredded
G. ½ cup chicken meat, shredded
H. ½ cup Virginia ham (Smithfield), shredded

COOKING

1. While rice is cooking, mix thoroughly B, C, D, E, F, G, H and let stand about 15 minutes.
2. Put mixture on top of rice and steam 20 minutes more.

Serves 4.

74. STEAMED RICE, COUNTRY STYLE
(*Hong-Ton Fon*)

A. 2 cups long-grained rice, thoroughly washed
B. 4 cups mixed chopped green vegetables—carrots, turnips, spinach, tomatoes, peas, string beans, asparagus, Chinese cabbage
C. 2 cups sweet potatoes, cubed
D. salt and pepper to taste
E. 2 teaspoons seasoning powder

COOKING

1. Add 3 cups water or soup stock to A and cook in pan 20 minutes.
2. Add remaining ingredients, stir well and cook 5 minutes. Lower heat and cook 30 minutes.

Serves 4.

Note: If liquid evaporates too rapidly, add a little water or stock to keep mixture moist.

75. STEAMED RICE WITH CHINESE SAUSAGE
(*Lop-Ching Fon*)

A. 1 cup rice, prepared as in No. 69
B. 2 Chinese sausages, sliced or diced
C. 2 teaspoons soy sauce

COOKING

1. Steam A in double boiler 25 minutes.
2. Put B on top of rice and cook 15 minutes, lower heat and cook another 15 minutes.
3. Add C, mix well, and serve hot.

Serves 2.

76. STEAMED RICE WITH DRY-DUCK-and-MEAT CAKE (*Op Yoke Fon*)

A. 2 cups rice, prepared as in No. 69
B. 1 cup dry duck meat, minced or chopped fine
C. 1 cup pork or veal, minced or chopped fine
D. 2 tablespoons water chestnuts, minced
E. 1 teaspoon seasoning powder
F. 2 teaspoons soy sauce
G. salt and pepper to taste

COOKING

1. While rice is cooking, mix together all other ingredients to form a pancake.
2. Put meat cake on top of rice (in double boiler) and steam 25 minutes. Lower heat and steam 15 minutes more.

Serves 4.

77. FRIED RICE (*Chow Fan*)

A. 6 tablespoons peanut oil or lard
B. 1½ teaspoons salt
C. 2 eggs, well beaten
D. 2 cups bean sprouts (optional)
E. 1 cup onions, chopped fine

F. 2 teaspoons seasoning powder
G. 4 teaspoons light soy sauce
H. 10 cups cold cooked rice
I. ½ cup fresh scallions, chopped fine
J. 2 teaspoons heavy soy sauce
K. ½ teaspoon pepper

COOKING

1. Put A in hot skillet or cast-iron Dutch oven; add B.
2. Add C and stir-fry 1 minute, or until firm.
3. Add D, E, F, G and fry 2 minutes.
4. Add H, I, mix well and keep stirring 4 minutes.
5. Add J, K. Mix well.

Serves 6.

78. CHICKEN FRIED RICE (*Guy Chow Fan*)

A. 6 tablespoons peanut oil or lard
B. 1½ teaspoons salt
C. 2 eggs, well beaten
D. 2 cups cooked chicken meat, diced
E. 2 cups bean sprouts (optional)
F. 1 cup onions, chopped fine
G. 2 teaspoons seasoning powder
H. 4 teaspoons light soy sauce
I. 10 cups cold cooked rice
J. 1 cup fresh scallions, chopped fine
K. 2 teaspoons heavy soy sauce
L. ½ teaspoon pepper

COOKING

1. Put A in hot skillet or cast-iron Dutch oven.
2. Add B; stir well.
3. Add C and fry 1 minute, or until firm.
4. Add D, E, F, G, H, mix well and fry 2 minutes.
5. Add I, J, well mixed, fry and keep stirring for 4 minutes.
6. Add K. L. Mix well.

Serves 6.

Note: In place of chicken meat in this recipe, any other cold meat or fish (leftovers) may be used; the above dish would then be called by the name of the meat or fish used. Roast Pork Fried Rice, Chinese Roast Pork Fried Rice, Roast Beef Fried Rice, Boiled Ham Fried Rice, Roast Veal Fried Rice, Roast Lamb Fried Rice, Roast Turkey Fried Rice, Shrimp Fried Rice, Lobster Fried Rice, Crabmeat Fried Rice (the last three dishes may be made with either fresh or canned fish).

79. CHICKEN SUBGUM FRIED RICE
(*Subgum Guy Chow Fan*)

A. 5 tablespoons peanut oil or lard
B. 1½ teaspoons salt
C. 3 eggs, well beaten
D. 1 cup cooked chicken meat, chopped fine (or cooked pork, veal, ham, beef, turkey, lobster, crabmeat, shrimp, scallops)
E. ½ cup French or black mushrooms, chopped fine
F. ½ cup green peppers, chopped fine
G. ½ cup onion, chopped fine
H. ¼ cup canned pimientos
I. 2 teaspoons seasoning powder
J. 3 teaspoons light soy sauce
K. 2 teaspoons heavy soy sauce
L. ½ teaspoon pepper
M. 8 cups cold cooked rice
N. ¼ cup fresh scallions, chopped fine

COOKING

1. Put A in hot skillet or cast-iron Dutch oven.
2. Add B and stir well.
3. Add C and cook (like scrambled eggs) until firm, about 2 minutes.
4. Add D, E, F, G, H and stir-fry 2 minutes. Mix well, stirring constantly.
5. Add I, J, K, L. Mix well and fry 1 minute.
6. Add M, N. Mix thoroughly and fry, stirring constantly, for 4 minutes. Serve hot.

Serves 6.

Note: Any other cooked meat may be used instead of the chicken meat; the dish is called by the name of the meat used.

80. FRIED RICE WITH EIGHT VARIETIES
(*Butt-Bor Chow-Fan*)

A. 5 tablespoons peanut oil or lard
B. 1½ teaspoons salt
C. 3 eggs, well beaten
D. ¼ cup cooked chicken meat, chopped fine
E. ¼ cup cooked Virginia ham, chopped fine
F. ¼ cup cooked fresh or dried shrimp, chopped fine (if you use dried shrimp, soak in warm water 20 minutes and fry in oil or lard before you fry the eggs)
G. ¼ cup cooked lobster, chopped fine
H. ¼ cup French or black mushrooms, chopped fine
I. 1 cup bean sprouts or lettuce
J. ½ cup onions, chopped fine
K. 8 cups cold cooked rice
L. 2 teaspoons seasoning powder
M. 3 teaspoons light soy sauce
N. 2 teaspoons heavy soy sauce
O. ½ teaspoon pepper
P. ¼ cup fresh scallions, chopped fine

COOKING

1. Place A in hot skillet or cast-iron Dutch oven.
2. Add B and C and stir-fry (like scrambled eggs) until firm.
3. Add D, E, F, G and fry together 2 minutes.
4. Add H, I, J. Mix well, and fry 1 minute.
5. Add K. Mix well and fry 3 minutes, stirring constantly.
6. Add L, M, N, O, P. Mix well, fry 2 minutes, stirring thoroughly.

Serves 6.

81. FRIED RICE WITH LETTUCE AND OYSTER
SAUCE (*Sang-Toy Ho-You Chow-Fan*)

A. 3 tablespoons peanut oil or lard
B. 3 eggs, well beaten
C. 8 cups cold cooked rice
D. 4 cups lettuce, chopped fine
E. 5 tablespoons oyster sauce
F. 2 teaspoons seasoning powder
G. ½ teaspoon salt and pepper

COOKING

1. Put A in hot skillet or cast-iron Dutch oven.
2. Add B and scramble until firm.
3. Add C and fry 4 minutes, stirring constantly.
4. Add D, E, F, G. Mix well and fry 2 minutes.

Serves 6.

Note: If desired, you may add meat or seafood, such as chicken, pork, veal, ham, turkey, beef, shrimp, lobster, fish or scallops.

82. BOILED RICE WITH SHREDDED CHICKEN AND TOMATO SAUCE (*Guy Soo Fan*)

A. 2 cups boiled rice (freshly cooked)
B. 1 cup stewed tomatoes (canned) or
   2 medium fresh tomatoes, diced
C. ½ teaspoon seasoning powder
D. salt and pepper to taste
E. ¾ cup cooked chicken meat, shredded (boiled, roasted or barbecued)

COOKING

1. Put A on dinner plate.
2. Stew B 5 minutes.
3. Add C, D and cook 2 minutes more.
4. Pour mixture over A.
5. Put E on top of serving.

Serves 2.

83. BOILED RICE WITH DROPPED EGG AND OYSTER SAUCE (*Ho-You Don Fan*)

A. 2 cups fresh cooked boiled rice
B. 2 tablespoons oyster sauce
C. 2 eggs, poached separately

PREPARATION

Put A on dinner plate. Drop C over it. Pour B on top of each serving.

Serves 2.

84. FRIED RICE WITH EIGHT PRECIOUS INGREDIENTS (*Butt-Chen Chow-Fon*)

A. 3 tablespoons peanut oil
B. 2 cloves garlic, crushed
C. 3 eggs, beaten
D. 10 cups warm boiled rice
E. 1½ teaspoons salt
F. 4 tablespoons cooked chicken or turkey meat, chopped
G. 4 tablespoons cooked dried duck meat, chopped
H. 4 tablespoons cooked Chinese pork sausages, chopped
I. 4 tablespoons cooked Virginia ham, chopped
J. 4 tablespoons cooked Chinese or American bacon, chopped
K. 4 tablespoons cooked dried shrimps, soaked in warm water 30 minutes, chopped
L. 4 tablespoons fresh cooked lobster meat, chopped
M. 4 tablespoons fresh cooked or canned crabmeat, chopped
N. 2 tablespoons light soy sauce
O. 1 teaspoon heavy soy sauce
P. 1 tablespoon seasoning powder
Q. 1 teaspoon sugar
R. ½ cup soup stock
S. 1 cup scallions (white part only), chopped fine
T. 1 cup lettuce, chopped very fine
U. 1 teaspoon pepper

PREPARATION

Mix N, O, P, Q, R together well, stir up before using.

COOKING

1. Put A in a hot large skillet. Add B; add C and scramble until firm.
2. Add D and E; stir-fry 5 minutes.
3. Add F, G, H, I, J, K, L, M; fry, stirring thoroughly, 2 minutes.
4. Add egg mixture and stir-fry 3 minutes.
5. Add S, T, U and stir-fry 2 minutes more.

Serves 10.

Note: This dish is for parties, banquets or for families of at least ten people.

85. RICE-GRUEL or CONGEE (*Joke-Suey*)

A. 1 cup rice, washed, soaked in water 5 hours or more
B. 2 or 3 lbs. pork neck bones
C. 1 gallon water and salt and pepper to taste

COOKING

1. Put A, B, C in a large pot; bring to boil, lower heat and simmer 2 hours. Remove bones, then beat with wire or rotary beater until thick and creamy.

Serves 6.

Note: Serve with shredded preserved sweet pickles and ginger. If served for breakfast, serve with doughnuts, cereals or crackers.
Sliced meat, chicken, fish or shrimps may be added shredded. If these are used, add a pinch of seasoning powder, chopped scallions and soy sauce.

If you have any Congee left, it may be kept in refrigerator. When you want to serve it, just heat it up; if it is too heavy, add soup stock or water.

BARBECUED PORK AND SPARE RIBS

86. CHINESE BARBECUED PORK (*Char-Shu*)

A. 2 lbs. pork chops, cut ¾ inch thick with the ribs and fat on (pork shoulder or butt may be used, cut in strips about 1½ inches wide and 4 to 6 inches long)
B. 1½ teaspoons salt
C. 1 tablespoon sugar
D. 4 tablespoons soy sauce
E. 2 cloves garlic, crushed
F. 2 tablespoons honey
G. 1 tablespoon rice wine or 2 tablespoons sherry wine
H. 2 tablespoons Chinese vegetable sauce (apple or pineapple sauce may be substituted)

PREPARATION

Sprinkle or rub B and C on A, and let stand 2 hours or more. Dry with clean towel. Mix thoroughly D, E, F, G, H. Soak A, as prepared above, in mixture about 30 minutes. Remove pork, place in broiler or roast in 400° oven for 10 minutes. Lower heat to 250° and roast 20 minutes (on a rack). Turn off oven, let some of the heat out, and keep pork in oven until ready to serve.

Serves 4.

87. BARBECUED SPARE RIBS (*Shu Pe-Good*)

A. 2 lbs. fresh pork spare ribs, hack each rib from top to bottom—do not sever
B. 1½ teaspoons heavy soy sauce
C. 5 tablespoons light soy sauce
D. 1 tablespoon sugar
E. 1 tablespoon honey
F. 2 tablespoons Chinese vegetable sauce (apple or pineapple sauce may be substituted)
G. 2 cloves garlic, crushed very fine
H. 2 teaspoons salt

[59]

PREPARATION

Mix B, C, D, E, F, G, H together well. (One teaspoon rice wine may be added to mixture, if desired.) In a large bowl, soak A in mixture, 1 to 2 hours or more.

BARBECUING

1. Place A on broiler and broil until both sides are brown, or roast in moderate oven.
2. Hack each rib off—if too long, cut in two—then serve hot or cold with duck sauce and hot mustard.

STIR-FRY PORK

The basis of the chow yoke (stir-fry pork) dishes is mixed vegetables. Even the well-known (in America) chop suey is of this family. In chow yoke, you can use whatever vegetables you happen to have on hand and whatever meat is available. It is one of the most versatile of the basic Chinese dishes. In the preparation of chow yoke of any kind, the sequence, quantity and timing in blending of the ingredients are extremely important.

Grace the table with a chow yoke to accompany an American meat dish, or with a Chinese meat course. The ingredients used are very good for the digestion. The more you make these dishes, the better they will be, and you will find that a good chow yoke will round out a perfect meal to everyone's delight.

---

88. STIR-FRY PORK WITH ONIONS
(*Ton-How Chow Gee Yoke*)

A. 2 tablespoons peanut oil or lard
B. ½ teaspoon salt
C. ¾ lb. fresh raw pork (tenderloin, butts or boned shoulder), sliced thin
D. 1 teaspoon rice wine or 2 tablespoons sherry wine
E. 1 clove garlic, crushed
F. 1 teaspoon light soy sauce
G. 1 medium-size onion, sliced thin
H. 2 fresh scallions (white part only), cut about 1 inch long
I. ½ cup soup stock
J. 1 teaspoon heavy soy sauce
K. 1 teaspoon cornstarch
L. 1 teaspoon seasoning powder
M. ½ teaspoon sugar
N. ¼ cup water
O. dash of pepper

PREPARATION

Mix D, E, F together. Mix together J, K, L, M, N, O. Stir thoroughly when ready to use.

COOKING

1. Put A in a large frying pan or skillet.
2. Place over high heat until smoking.
3. Put B in A.
4. Add C; stir-fry until meat is brown.
5. Add D, E, F preparation and stir 1 minute.
6. Add G, H; stir-fry another minute.
7. Pour I in pan with all ingredients. Cover pan and bring to a boil.
8. Add J, K, L, M, N, O mixture. Stir thoroughly as you put this in. Cook until gravy thickens.

Serves 2.

89. STIR-FRY ASSORTED VEGETABLES WITH PORK (*Gar-Toy Chow Gee-Yoke*)

A. ½ lb. fresh raw pork (tenderloin, butts, boned shoulder or side pork)
B. 2 lbs. assorted vegetables, such as celery, green peppers, tomatoes, onions, bean sprouts, asparagus, turnips, beets, carrots, spinach, broccoli, cabbage, Chinese cabbage, mustard greens, fungus, mushrooms, luto's root, dried turnips, dried golden lilies, bamboo shoots, water chestnuts, golden shoots, Yock Leong shoots, bean sticks, scallions, string beans, peas, Chinese pea pods, cucumbers. You may use as many kinds as you wish. There is no limit.

Use same method and ingredients as in recipe No. 88. You may slice or shred the vegetables, as you desire.

90. STIR-FRY PEA PODS, DRIED TURNIPS WITH PORK (*Shet-Dow Toy-Pan Chow Gee Yoke*)

A. 1 tablespoon peanut oil
B. 1 teaspoon salt
C. 2 cloves garlic, crushed

D. ½ lb. fresh raw pork (tenderloin, butts, boned shoulder or side pork)
E. 1 teaspoon rice wine
F. 2 teaspoons light soy sauce
G. 1 teaspoon sugar
H. 1 cup pea pods, cut in two if you wish
I. 1 cup dried Chinese turnips
J. ½ medium sized onion, sliced
K. ¼ cup black or white mushrooms, sliced
L. ½ cup canned bamboo shoots, sliced into thin pieces no larger than pea pods
M. ¼ cup fungus
N. ¼ cup dried golden lilies
O. 1 cup soup stock
P. ½ cup water
Q. 1 tablespoon cornstarch
R. 1 teaspoon seasoning powder

PREPARATION

Soak I, M, N in cold water for 25 minutes. If black mushrooms are used, soak them in warm water 15 minutes—soak these three ingredients in separate bowls, then squeeze dry. Mix P, Q, R together. Mix together E, F, G. You may add 1 tablespoon water.

COOKING

1. Put A in a large frying pan or skillet. Heat until oil smokes, then add B and C. Fry 2 seconds.
2. Add D. Stir-fry until pork is brown. Add E, F, G preparation. Stir 1 minute.
3. Add H, I, J, K, L, M, N. Stir-fry constantly, thoroughly, about 3 minutes.
4. Add O. Cover and cook 5 minutes.
5. Add P, Q, R preparation. Stir-fry until gravy thickens.

Serves 2 or 3.

91. STIR-FRY PORK WITH MUSHROOMS
(*Moo-Koo Chow Gee-Yoke*)

A. 1 tablespoon peanut oil or lard
B. 1 teaspoon salt
C. 1 lb. fresh raw pork (pork loin, tenderloin or lean fresh ham), sliced
D. 1 cup fresh or canned mushrooms, sliced
E. ¼ cup water chestnuts, peeled and sliced
F. 2 teaspoons light soy sauce
G. ½ teaspoon sugar
H. 1 teaspoon rice wine
I. ¼ cup fresh scallions, chopped
J. 1 tablespoon Chinese preserved sweet pickles, shredded
K. 1 teaspoon Chinese preserved sweet ginger, shredded
L. 1½ cups soup stock
M. ½ cup water
N. 1½ tablespoons cornstarch
O. 1 teaspoon heavy soy sauce
P. 1 teaspoon seasoning powder

PREPARATION

Mix together well M, N, O, P. Stir well when ready to use. Mix together F, G, H in another cup. You may add 1 tablespoon water.

COOKING

1. Put A in a large frying pan or skillet. Heat over high flame until smoking, then add B.
2. Add C. Stir-fry until pork is brown.
3. Add D, E. Stir-fry 2 minutes. Add F, G, H preparation. Stir-fry another minute.
4. Add I, J, K. Stir-fry 1 minute.
5. Add L. Cover and cook 2 minutes, then add M, N, O, P preparation. Stir constantly until gravy thickens. Serve with boiled rice.

Serves 2 or 3.

92. STIR-FRY PORK WITH BLACK MUSHROOMS
(*Dung-Koo Chow Gee-Yoke*)

Use same method and ingredients as in recipe No. 91. Black mushrooms must be soaked in warm water about 10 to 15 minutes before slicing. Save the water for cooking.

93. STIR-FRY CHINESE CABBAGE WITH PORK
(*Bok-Toy Chow Gee-Yoke*)

A. 1 tablespoon peanut oil or lard
B. 1 teaspoon salt
C. 1 clove garlic, crushed
D. ½ lb. fresh raw pork (tenderloin, butts, boned shoulder or side pork), cut in thin slivers
E. 2 teaspoons light soy sauce
F. ½ teaspoon fresh ginger, shredded fine
G. 1 teaspoon rice wine
H. 1½ lbs. Chinese green cabbage or celery cabbage. Wash and slice about 1 to 1½ inches long, or cut across in thin slices
I. 1 cup fresh or canned mushrooms, sliced
J. ¾ cup soup stock
K. ¼ cup water
L. 1 tablespoon cornstarch
M. 1 teaspoon heavy soy sauce
N. 1 teaspoon seasoning powder
O. ½ teaspoon sugar

PREPARATION

Mix together K, L, M, N, O. Stir well when ready to use. Mix together E, F, G. You may add 1 tablespoon water.

COOKING

1. Put A in a large frying pan or skillet. Heat over high flame until oil smokes. Add B and C. Fry 30 seconds.
2. Add D to pan. Stir and fry until pork is brown, then add E, F, G preparation. Stir and fry 30 seconds.
3. Add H, I. Stir-fry constantly for 2 minutes.
4. Add J. Cover, and cook 3 minutes.
5. Add K, L, M, N, O preparation. Stir-fry until gravy thickens.

Serves 2 or 3.

94. STIR-FRY CELERY WITH PORK
(*Hong-Kan Chow Gee-Yoke*)

Use same method and ingredients as in recipe No. 93. Add onions, bean sprouts or any of your favorite vegetables to it (1 cup each).

95. STIR-FRY PORK WITH CURRY
(*Kur-Li Chow Gee-Yoke*)

A. 1 tablespoon peanut oil
B. ½ teaspoon salt
C. 1 lb. fresh raw pork, sliced ½ inch thick and about 1 to
   1½ inches long
D. 1 onion, sliced
E. 1 green pepper, sliced
F. 1 tablespoon curry powder
G. 1 tablespoon cornstarch
H. dash Chinese spices
I. 1 teaspoon lemon juice
J. 2 cups soup stock
K. 1 teaspoon seasoning powder

COOKING

1. Put A in a large frying pan or skillet. Heat until oil almost
   smokes. Add B.
2. Add C. Stir-fry for 2 minutes.
3. Add D, E. Stir-fry for 3 minutes, then lower the heat.
4. Add F. Stir-fry for 5 minutes.
5. Mix together well G, H, I, J, K. Add gradually. Stir until boiling, and simmer for 25 minutes, or until gravy thickens.
   Serve with cooked rice.

Serves 4.

96. STIR-FRY PORK CHOP WITH ASSORTED
VEGETABLES (*Chow Pork Chop Kew*)

A. 1 tablespoon peanut oil or lard
B. clove garlic
C. 1 teaspoon salt
D. 1 lb. pork chops sliced into 4 pieces. Pan-fry, broil or roast
   in Chinese style (see recipe No. 86), then cut into 1 inch
   squares
E. 2 cups Chinese cabbage, sliced 1 inch to 1½ inches thick
F. ¼ cup bamboo shoots, sliced thin and cut from 1 inch to
   1½ inches long
G. 2 tablespoons water chestnuts, peeled and sliced thin
H. ¼ cup black or white mushrooms, sliced

I. 1 cup pea pods, each pod cut in 2 pieces. You may substitute other vegetables, such as asparagus, green peppers, tomatoes, onions, broccoli, etc.
J. 1 teaspoon light soy sauce
K. 1 teaspoon sugar
L. 1 teaspoon rice wine
M. ½ cup water
N. 1 tablespoon cornstarch
O. 1 teaspoon seasoning powder
P. 1 teaspoon heavy soy sauce
Q. 2 teaspoons tomato catsup
R. dash pepper
S. 1 cup soup stock

PREPARATION

Mix together well M, N, O, P, Q, R. Stir thoroughly before you use in cooking. Mix J, K, L. Add another tablespoon water.

COOKING

1. Put A in a large frying pan or skillet. Heat oil over high flame until almost smoking. Add B and C. Stir ½ minute.
2. Add D. Stir and fry thoroughly 1 minute.
3. Add E, F, G, H, I. Stir and fry for 3 minutes.
4. Add J, K, L preparation. Stir another minute and add S. Cover and cook 3 minutes.
5. Add M, N, O, P, Q, R preparation. Stir thoroughly and constantly until gravy thickens.

Serve with cooked rice or Potato Saute, recipe No. 410.

Serves 4.

96A. STIR-FRY PORK WITH BEAN CURD
(*Dow-Foo Chee Gee-Yoke*)

A. 1 tablespoon peanut oil or lard
B. ½ teaspoon salt
C. clove garlic, crushed
D. 1 qt. bean curd, cut in 1 inch squares
E. ½ lb. fresh raw pork (tenderloin, butts, boned shoulder or side pork), cut in thin slivers.
F. 1 teaspoon light soy sauce
G. 1 teaspoon sugar
H. 1 teaspoon rice wine
I. ½ teaspoon pepper
J. 2 fresh scallions (white part only), cut 1 inch long, crosswise, shredded
K. 1 cup thinly sliced onions
L. ¼ cup black or white mushrooms, sliced
M. ½ cup water
N. 1 tablespoon cornstarch
O. 1 teaspoon seasoning powder
P. 1 teaspoon heavy soy sauce
Q. 1 tablespoon oyster sauce
R. 1 cup soup stock

PREPARATION

Mix together M, N, O, P, Q. Stir well when ready to use. Mix F, G, H, I.

COOKING

1. Put A in large frying pan or skillet. Heat over a high flame until almost smoking. Add B, C. Stir about ½ minute.
2. Fry D until light brown on both sides. Remove from pan and put aside.
3. Fry E. Stir-fry until brown. Add F, G, H, I preparation.
4. Add J, K, L and put D back in skillet. Add R. Cover and cook for 5 minutes.
5. Add M, N, O, P, Q preparation. Stir-fry until gravy thickens.

97. PICKLED MUSTARD GREENS WITH PORK
(*Hom-Toy Chow Gee-Yoke*)

A. 1 lb. pickled mustard greens, sliced thin, washed clean and squeezed dry
B. 1 tablespoon peanut oil or lard
C. ½ lb. fresh raw pork (tenderloin, butts or side pork), sliced thin
D. 1 teaspoon fresh ginger, sliced very fine
E. 1 teaspoon rice wine
F. 1 teaspoon light soy sauce
G. 3 tablespoons vinegar
H. 3 tablespoons sugar
I. 1 teaspoon cornstarch
J. ½ teaspoon curry powder (optional)
K. ½ cup soup stock

PREPARATION

Mix D, E, F together. Mix G, H together. Mix I, J with 2 tablespoons water.

COOKING

1. Put A in a very hot skillet; stir-fry 4 to 5 minutes or until dry. Put aside until ready to use.
2. Put B in hot skillet; add C; stir-fry until pork is light brown. Add D, E, F preparation, stir-fry 1 minute.
3. Put A back in skillet; add K. Stir thoroughly with pork for 2 minutes. Add G, H preparation. Stir well 1 minute.
4. Add I, J preparation, stirring constantly 2 minutes.
   Serve with boiled rice or potatoes.

Serves 2.

98. STIR-FRY BITTER MELON WITH PORK
(*Foo-Gar Chow Gee-Yoke*)

A. 1 tablespoon peanut oil or lard
B. ¼ teaspoon salt
C. 2 cloves garlic
D. 1 tablespoon preserved black beans, crushed
E. ½ lb. fresh raw pork (tenderloin, butts, boned shoulder or side pork), cut in thin slices
F. 2 lbs. bitter melon (canned or fresh), cut in halves (seeds removed), and then cut in thin slices
G. 2 teaspoons light soy sauce
H. dash pepper
I. ½ teaspoon sugar
J. 1 teaspoon rice wine
K. 1 cup soup stock
L. 1 tablespoon cornstarch
M. 1 teaspoon seasoning powder

PREPARATION

Boil F about 3 minutes. Rinse in cold water and drain. (Canned melon does not require boiling.) Mix together G, H, I, J. Add 1 tablespoon water. Stir well when ready to use. Mash C, D together in a separate bowl. Mix together L, M in a bowl with ½ cup water. Stir well when ready to use.

COOKING

1. Put A in a large frying pan or skillet. Heat over high flame until almost smoking, then add B.
2. Add C, D preparation to the oil; fry ½ minute.
3. Add E. Stir-fry until pork is brown.
4. Add F. Stir-fry 2 minutes.
5. Add G, H, I, J preparation. Stir thoroughly.
6. Add K. Cover and cook 5 minutes.
7. Add L, M preparation and stir-fry until gravy thickens.

Serves 4.

99. STIR-FRY MUSTARD GREENS WITH PORK
(*Kai-Toy Chow Gee-Yoke*)

Use same method and ingredients as for recipe No. 98, except use 1 lb. mustard greens instead of melon, and do *not* boil the greens. Use your own judgment as to what size to cut them.

Serves 2 or 3.

100. STIR-FRY CAULIFLOWER WITH PORK
(*Yer Toy Far Chow Gee-Yoke*)

A. 1 tablespoon peanut oil or lard
B. 1 teaspoon salt
C. 1 clove garlic, crushed
D. ½ lb. fresh raw pork (tenderloin, butt, boned shoulder or side pork), cut in thin slivers
E. 1 tablespoon light soy sauce
F. 1 teaspoon sugar
G. 1 teaspoon rice wine
H. 2 lbs. cauliflower, cut about ¼ inch thick, and about 1½ to 2 inches long
I. 1½ tablespoons Chinese preserved sweet pickle, shredded fine
J. ½ tablespoon preserved sweet ginger, shredded fine
K. 1 cup soup stock
L. ½ cup water
M. 1 tablespoon cornstarch
N. ½ teaspoon heavy soy sauce
O. 1 teaspoon seasoning powder
P. dash pepper

PREPARATION

Mix together L, M, N, O, P. Stir well when ready to use. Mix well E, F, G. Add 1 tablespoon water. Put H in boiling water. Boil about 3 minutes, then drain.

COOKING

1. Put A in a large frying pan or skillet. Heat over high flame until almost smoking.
2. Add B, then C. Fry for a few seconds.
3. Add D. Stir-fry about 3 minutes, until pork is brown.
4. Add E, F, G preparation. Stir-fry 1 minute.
5. Add H, then add I, J. Stir-fry 2 minutes.
6. Add K. Cover and cook 3 minutes. Add L, M, N, O, P preparation. Stir constantly until gravy thickens.

Note: If sweet pickle and ginger are not used, you may use preserved black beans.

101. STIR-FRY GREEN BEANS WITH PORK
(*Dow-Doi Chow Gee-Yoke*)

Use same method and ingredients as in recipe No. 100, using beans in place of cauliflower. Cut green beans about 1 to 2 inches long, boil 4 minutes and drain.

102. STIR-FRY ASPARAGUS WITH PORK
(*Le-Shon Chow Gee-Yoke*)

Use same method and ingredients as in recipe No. 100, using asparagus in place of cauliflower. Cut asparagus about the same size as string beans—1 to 2 inches long.

103. STIR-FRY PEA PODS WITH PORK
(*Shet-Dow Chow Gee-Yoke*)

Use same method and ingredients as in recipe No. 100, using pea pods in place of cauliflower. Cut pea pods in two pieces, if you desire.

104. STIR-FRY PORK WITH PINEAPPLE
(*Bo-Lo Chow Gee-Yoke*)

A. 1 tablespoon peanut oil or lard
B. ½ teaspoon salt
C. 1 lb. lean pork (pork chop or tenderloin), sliced thin
D. ¼ cup fresh green peppers, sliced
E. 1 cup canned sliced pineapple
F. ¼ cup water chestnuts, peeled and sliced
G. ¼ cup mixed sweet pickles, sliced the same size as pineapple
H. 1 cup soup stock
I. 2 tablespoons cornstarch, dissolved
J. 1 tablespoon sugar
K. 2 teaspoons light soy sauce
L. 1 teaspoon seasoning powder
M. ½ cup water

PREPARATION

Mix together I, J, K, L, M. Put aside in a small bowl; stir thoroughly when ready to use.

COOKING

1. Put A in a large frying pan or skillet. Heat over high flame until it almost burns.
2. Add B.
3. Add C. Stir-fry until pork is brown.
4. Add D. Stir-fry with pork about 2 minutes.
5. Add E, F, G. Stir-fry another minute.
6. Add H. Cook until boiling.
7. Add prepared mixture. Stir-fry until gravy thickens.

Serves 2 or 3.

105. STIR-FRY PORK WITH BROCCOLI
(*Kai-Lun Chow Gee-Yoke*)

A. 1 tablespoon peanut oil
B. ½ teaspoon salt
C. 1 clove garlic
D. ½ lb. fresh raw pork (tenderloin, butt or boned shoulder), sliced thin
E. 2 tablespoons light soy sauce
F. ½ teaspoon shredded fresh ginger
G. 2 teaspoons sugar
H. 1 teaspoon rice wine
I. 5 cups broccoli (tender parts only), cleaned and sliced about 1¼ inches long
J. ½ cup celery, sliced thin
K. ½ cup onion, sliced thin
L. 2 tablespoons French mushrooms or Chinese black mushrooms, sliced thin
M. 1 cup soup stock
N. ½ cup water
O. 1½ tablespoons cornstarch
P. 1 teaspoon heavy soy sauce
Q. dash pepper
R. 1 teaspoon seasoning powder

PREPARATION

Mix E, F, G, H in small bowl. Add 1 tablespoon water. Put aside until ready to use. Mix in another cup N, O, P, Q, R. Stir well when ready to use. Drop I in boiling water. Boil about 3 minutes. Do not cover. Drain.

COOKING

1. Put A in a large frying pan or skillet and heat over high flame until oil almost burns.
2. Add B, C, then add D. Stir-fry about 4 to 5 minutes, until brown.
3. Add E, F, G, H preparation and stir 1 minute.
4. Add I, J, K, L. Stir thoroughly and constantly for 2 minutes.
5. Add M. Cover and cook 2 minutes.
6. Add N, O, P, Q, R preparation. Stir thoroughly until gravy thickens.

Serves 2 or 3.

106. STIR-FRY CABBAGE WITH PORK
(*Yer-Toy Chow Gee-Yoke*)

A. 2 tablespoons peanut oil or lard
B. 1 teaspoon salt
C. 1 clove garlic
D. ½ lb. fresh raw pork (tenderloin, butts, boned shoulder, or side pork), sliced thin, or shredded
E. ¼ cup Chinese preserved pickles and ginger, shredded. Proportion: two thirds pickle to one third ginger
F. 2 teaspoons light soy sauce
G. 1 teaspoon seasoning powder
H. 1 teaspoon sugar
I. 1 teaspoon rice wine
J. 2 lbs. American cabbage, shredded as for sauerkraut
K. 1½ cups soup stock

PREPARATION

Mix together well F, G, H, I. Add 1 tablespoon water. Stir well before using.

COOKING

1. Put A in a large frying pan or skillet. Heat over high flame until smoking.
2. Add B and C. Fry for a few seconds.
3. Add D, E. Stir-fry until pork is brown, then add prepared mixture. Stir-fry another minute.
4. Add J. Fry, stirring constantly, for 3 or 4 minutes.
5. Add K. Cover, and cook for 3 minutes.

Serves 2.

107. STIR-FRY PORK WITH GREEN PEPPERS AND TOMATOES (*Lard-Dew Fan-Ghar Chow Gee-Yoke*)

A. 1 tablespoon peanut oil or lard
B. 1 clove garlic, crushed
C. ½ teaspoon salt
D. ½ lb. fresh raw pork (tenderloin, butt, boned shoulder), cut in thin slivers
E. 2 teaspoons light soy sauce
F. ½ teaspoon finely shredded fresh ginger
G. 1 teaspoon rice wine
H. 3 medium-size fresh tomatoes, sliced into 8 pieces each, diagonal
I. 3 medium-size green peppers, clean out seeds and slice into 10 to 14 pieces each
J. 2 tablespoons fresh or canned mushrooms, sliced
K. ½ medium size onion, sliced
L. ¾ cup soup stock
M. ½ cup water
N. 1 tablespoon cornstarch
O. dash pepper
P. 1 teaspoon seasoning powder
Q. 1 teaspoon sugar

PREPARATION

Put I in boiling water for about 2 minutes. Rinse in cold water, and drain. Mix together M, N, O, P, Q. Stir well when ready to use. Mix together E, F, G.

COOKING

1. Put A in a large frying pan or skillet. Heat until oil smokes.
2. Add B. Fry for 1 minute.
3. Add C; then add D. Stir-fry about 4 or 5 minutes, until brown.
4. Add E, F, G preparation. Cook 1 minute.
5. Add H, I, J, K. Stir-fry 2 minutes.
6. Add L. Cover, and cook 2 minutes.
7. Add M, N, O, P, Q preparation. Stir-fry thoroughly until gravy thickens.

Serves 2.

108. STIR-FRY PORK WITH OYSTER SAUCE
(*Chow Ho-You Gee-Yoke*)

A. 1 tablespoon peanut oil or lard
B. ½ teaspoon salt
C. 1 clove garlic
D. 1 lb. fresh raw pork (tenderloin or butt), cut in thin slivers
E. 1 teaspoon light soy sauce
F. 1 teaspoon rice wine
G. 1 cup soup stock
H. 2 tablespoons oyster sauce (imported)
I. 1 teaspon heavy soy sauce
J. 1 teaspoon sugar
K. 1 tablespoon cornstarch
L. 1 tablespoon sweet vegetable sauce
M. 1 teaspoon seasoning powder
N. 1 cup fresh scallions, cut into 1 inch long pieces, then split

PREPARATION

Mix H, I, J, K, L, M together with ½ cup water; stir up thoroughly before using. Mix E, F together.

COOKING

1. Put A in a hot skillet, use high flame. Add B and C.
2. Add D. Stir-fry until pork is light brown.
3. Add E, F preparation, and stir for 1 minute.
4. Add G. Cover, and cook 2 minutes.
5. Add H, I, J, K, L, M preparation; stir-fry until gravy thickens; add N.

Serve with rice or toast.

Serves 2.

109. STIR-FRY PORK WITH BEAN SPROUTS AND OYSTER SAUCE (*Hooyu Gar-Toy Chow Gee-Yoke*)

A. 2 tablespoons peanut oil or lard
B. pinch salt
C. ½ lb. fresh raw pork (tenderloin, butt, boned shoulder or side pork), cut in thin slices
D. 1 clove garlic, crushed
E. 1 teaspoon rice wine
F. ¾ lb. bean sprouts, washed and drained
G. 2 tablespoons Chinese preserved sweet pickles and ginger, shredded; proportion: one third ginger to two thirds pickles
H. 2 fresh scallions (white part only), cut 1 inch long
I. 1 cup soup stock
J. 3 tablespoons oyster sauce
K. 1 tablespoon cornstarch
L. 1 teaspoon seasoning powder
M. ½ teaspoon sugar
N. dash pepper
O. ½ cup water

PREPARATION

Mix together well J, K, L, M, N, O. Stir well before using.

COOKING

1. Put A in large frying pan or skillet over high heat, until oil smokes.
2. Add B, then add C. Stir-fry until pork browns.
3. Add D. Cook together with pork about 1 minute.
4. Add E.
5. Add F, G, H. Stir constantly about 2 minutes.
6. Add I. Cover, and boil about 2 minutes.
7. Add prepared mixture. Stir well until gravy thickens.

Serves 2.

110. VERMICELLI WITH PORK
(*Gee-Yoke Chow Fon-Soo*)

A. 1 tablespoon peanut oil or lard
B. 1 teaspoon salt

c. ½ lb. fresh raw pork (tenderloin, butts, boned shoulder), cut in thin slivers

D. 1 cup black mushrooms, soaked in warm water, shredded fine

E. 1½ cups Chinese cabbage, shredded fine (broccoli may be substituted)

F. 1 cup celery, shredded fine

G. ½ lb. vermicelli, soaked in warm water 30 minutes, cut into desired length and drained

H. 3 cups soup stock

I. 2 fresh scallions (white part only), chopped about ½ inch long

J. ½ cup water

K. 1 teaspoon fresh ginger, shredded very fine

L. 1 teaspoon rice wine

M. ½ teaspoon heavy soy sauce

N. 2 teaspoons light soy sauce

O. ¼ teaspoon pepper

P. 1 teaspoon seasoning powder

PREPARATION

Mix together well J, K, L, M, N, O, P. Stir well when ready to use.

COOKING

1. Put A in a large frying pan or skillet over a high flame until oil smokes. Add B.
2. Add C. Stir-fry until pork is golden brown.
3. Add D, E, F. Stir-fry 2 minutes.
4. Add G. Stir-fry thoroughly 1 minute.
5. Add H. Cover, and cook over a medium flame about 5 minutes. Add more soup stock if necessary.
6. Add I.
7. Add prepared mixture. Stir thoroughly.

Serves 4.

111. STIR-FRY LUTO'S ROOTS WITH PORK
(*Long Gow Chow Gee-Yoke*)

A. 1 tablespoon peanut oil
B. 1 teaspoon salt
C. 1 clove garlic
D. 1 cup fresh raw pork (tenderloin, butts, boned shoulder or side pork), cut in thin slices
E. 2 cups luto's roots, cleaned and sliced very thin
F. 1 teaspoon rice wine
G. 1 teaspoon light soy sauce
H. dash pepper
I. 1 medium-size onion, sliced
J. 1½ cups celery, sliced thin
K. ½ cup bamboo shoots, sliced thin, same size as celery
L. 1 cup Chinese cabbage, sliced thin
M. 2 fresh scallions (white part only), cut about 1½ inches long
N. 1 cup soup stock
O. ½ cup water
P. 1 teaspoon heavy soy sauce
Q. 1 tablespoon cornstarch
R. 1 teaspoon seasoning powder

PREPARATION

Mix together well O, P, Q, R. Stir well when ready to use. Mix well F, G, H. You may add 1 tablespoon water.

COOKING

1. Put A in a large frying pan or skillet, over high heat, until oil smokes. Add B and C.
2. Add D. Stir-fry until light brown.
3. Add E. Stir-fry 2 minutes.
4. Add F, G, H preparation. Stir-fry 1 minute.
5. Add I, J, K, L, M. Stir-fry constantly 2 minutes.
6. Add N. Cover, and cook 5 minutes.
7. Add O, P, Q, R preparation. Stir-fry until gravy thickens.

Serves 3.

112. STIR-FRY PORK WITH THREE KINDS OF BAMBOO SHOOTS (*Sam Shoon Chow Gee-Yoke*)

A. 1 tablespoon peanut oil or lard
B. 1 teaspoon salt
C. 1 clove garlic
D. 1½ cup fresh raw pork (tenderloin, boned shoulder, butts, or side pork), cut in thin slivers
E. 1 teaspoon rice wine
F. 2 teaspoons light soy sauce
G. dash fresh ginger, shredded fine
H. 1 cup celery, sliced
I. ½ cup onions, sliced
J. ½ cup pea pods or broccoli (if you use broccoli, slice thin)
K. ½ cup black mushrooms, soaked in warm water 30 minutes, sliced
L. 2 tablespoons water chestnuts, peeled, sliced
M. ½ cup bamboo shoots, sliced
N. ½ cup dehydrated golden bamboo shoots, soaked in warm water 24 hours, sliced thin
O. ½ cup dehydrated jade bamboo shoots, soaked in warm water 24 hours, sliced thin
P. 1 cup soup stock
Q. ½ cup water
R. 1 tablespoon cornstarch
S. 1 teaspoon seasoning powder
T. ½ teaspoon heavy soy sauce
U. 1 teaspoon sugar

PREPARATION

Mix together E, F, G. Add 1 tablespoon water. Mix well Q, R, S, T, U. Stir well before using.

COOKING

1. Put A in a large frying pan or skillet. Heat oil until it is smoking. Add B, then C.
2. Add D. Stir-fry until pork is golden brown. Add E, F, G preparation. Stir-fry ½ minute.
3. Add H, I, J, K, L, M, N, O. Stir and fry thoroughly for 3 minutes.
4. Add P. Cover and cook from 8 to 10 minutes.
5. Add Q, R, S, T, U preparation. Stir-fry until gravy thickens and is smooth.

Serves 3 or 4.

113. STIR-FRY PORK WITH CHINESE TURNIPS
(*Lo-Bok Gee-Yoke*)

A. 1 tablespoon peanut oil or lard
B. ½ teaspoon salt
C. 1 clove garlic, minced
D. 1 cup fresh raw pork (tenderloin or butts), cut in thin slivers
E. 2 teaspoons light soy sauce
F. 1 teaspoon rice wine
G. ½ teaspoon fresh ginger, shredded very fine
H. 4 cups Chinese turnips, peeled and shredded fine
I. ½ cup leek or scallions, chopped fine
J. 1 cup soup stock
K. ½ cup water
L. 1 teaspoon heavy soy sauce
M. 1 teaspoon sugar
N. 1 teaspoon seasoning powder
O. 1 tablespoon cornstarch

PREPARATION

Mix K, L, M, N, O. Stir up well before using. Mix E, F, G and add 1 tablespoon water.

COOKING

1. Put A in a large skillet over a high flame until oil is almost smoking. Add B and C.
2. Add D. Stir-fry until pork is light brown.
3. Add E, F, G preparation. Stir for ½ minute.
4. Add H and I. Stir well until all ingredients are thoroughly mixed.
5. Add J. Cover and cook 10 minutes, or until vegetables are tender.
6. Add K, L, M, N, O preparation. Stir frequently until gravy thickens. Serve with cooked rice.

114. DEEP-FRY BEAN CURD WITH THREE KINDS OF SHREDDED MEATS (*Sam-Soo Hung Shu Dow-Foo*)

A. 1 tablespoon peanut oil or lard
B. 1 teaspoon salt
C. 1 clove garlic
D. ½ cup canned bamboo shoots, shredded fine

E. ½ cup black mushrooms, soaked in warm water for 15 minutes, shredded fine
F. ½ cup celery, cut about 1 inch to 2 inches long, shredded fine
G. 1 teaspoon light soy sauce
H. 1 teaspoon rice wine
I. 1 teaspoon sugar
J. ½ cup soup stock
K. ½ cup water
L. 1 tablespoon cornstarch
M. 1 teaspoon heavy soy sauce
N. 1 teaspoon seasoning powder
O. 1 tablespoon oyster sauce
P. dash pepper
Q. 6 cakes bean curds, cut into 1 inch squares and fried in deep fat until light brown
R. 1½ cups roast pork or Chinese roast pork, shredded fine
S. ½ cup cooked Virginia ham, shredded fine
T. ½ cup cooked chicken or turkey meat, shredded fine

PREPARATION

Mix well K, L, M, N, O, P. Stir thoroughly before using. Mix G, H, I. Add 1 tablespoon water.

COOKING

1. Put A in a large frying pan or skillet. Heat the oil until almost smoking, then add B, C. Stir ½ minute.
2. Add D, E, F. Stir and fry 3 minutes.
3. Add G, H, I preparation. Stir and fry 1 minute.
4. Add J. Cook until boiling.
5. Add K, L, M, N, O, P preparation. Stir and fry until gravy thickens. Turn off heat.
6. Put Q in casserole. Pour the cooked mixture over bean curd.
7. Sprinkle R, S, T on top.

Serves 4.

115. DEEP-FRY BEAN CURD WITH CHINESE ROAST PORK (*Char-Shu Hung Shu Dow-Foo*)

Use the same method and main ingredients as in recipe No. 114 (for Chinese Roast Pork see recipe No. 86). Deep-fry bean curd means fry bean curds in deep oil until golden brown. In this recipe, use only the roast pork; do not use the other meats noted in recipe above.

116. DEEP-FRY PORK WITH ASSORTED VEGETABLES (*Hung Shu Yoke, Gar-Toy*)

A. 2 tablespoons light soy sauce
B. dash pepper
C. 1 teaspoon sugar
D. 1 teaspoon rice wine
E. 1 lb. fresh raw pork (pork loin, tenderloin or lean fresh ham), diced into 1 inch squares
F. ½ cup water
G. 1 teaspoon seasoning powder
H. 1 tablespoon cornstarch
I. 1 teaspoon heavy soy sauce
J. 2 eggs, beaten
K. ¾ cup flour
L. 1 tablespoon peanut oil
M. ½ teaspoon salt
N. 1 clove garlic
O. 1 cup pea pods
P. 1 cup Chinese cabbage, sliced thin
Q. ½ cup onion, sliced
R. 1 cup celery, sliced thin
S. 2 tablespoons water chestnuts, peeled and sliced
T. ¼ cup bamboo shoots, cut same size as half a pea pod
U. 1 cup soup stock

PREPARATION

Mix A, B, C, D together; add 1 tablespoon water. Add E to this mixture. Let pork soak 10 minutes or more. Mix F, G, H, I. Stir thoroughly before using. Mix J, K and add a dash of salt. Stir well until a smooth batter is formed. Drop E into batter until coated on all sides. Take the pork out with fork or chop sticks, piece by piece; drop into deep hot oil and fry until golden brown.

COOKING

1. Put L in a large frying pan or skillet; heat the oil until it almost smokes. Add M and N.
2. Add O, P, Q, R, S, T. Stir-fry 2 minutes.
3. Add prepared E. Stir-fry 1 minute, or until all is well mixed.
4. Add U. Cover and cook 3 minutes.
5. Add F, G, H, I preparation. Fry, stirring constantly, until gravy thickens.
   Serve with cooked rice.

Serves 4.

117. DEEP-FRY PORK MEAT BALL WITH LETTUCE AND SWEET VEGETABLE SAUCE (*Jow Yoke-Yon*)

A. 1 lb. fresh raw pork (tenderloin or butt), chopped fine
B. 1 cup fresh lean Virginia ham, chopped fine
C. 3 heads fresh scallions (green and white), chopped fine
D. 1 cup black mushrooms (soaked in warm water for 15 minutes), chopped fine
E. ¼ cup peeled fresh water chestnuts, chopped fine
F. 1 teaspoon seasoning powder
G. 1 teaspoon light soy sauce
H. 1 teaspoon sugar
I. 1 teaspoon salt
J. ½ teaspoon pepper
K. ½ teaspoon curry powder
L. 1 teaspoon rice wine
M. ½ cup cornstarch
N. 2 eggs, beaten
O. 1 qt. peanut oil
P. 1 head Iceberg lettuce, sliced
Q. 2 tablespoons vegetable sauce

PREPARATION

Chop A, B, C, D, E very fine. Add F, G, H, I, J, K, L. Mix well. Add M, N. Stir until mixture has a pastelike quality. Roll into balls as large as water chestnuts (about 1 inch in diameter).

COOKING

1. Pour O into a deep skillet. Heat to boiling point.
2. Pick up balls with chopsticks, or fork, one by one. Fry in deep oil until golden brown. Serve with P and Q.

Serves 2.

118. BRAISED PORK WITH CHINESE RED CHEES` `
(*Nam-Yu Gee-Yoke*)

- A. 1 teaspoon peanut oil
- B. 2 cloves garlic, crushed
- C. ¼ teaspoon salt
- D. 1 lb. fresh raw pork, cut into 1 inch cubes
- E. 1 teaspoon light soy sauce
- F. 1 teaspoon rice wine or 1 tablespoon sherry wine
- G. 1 teaspoon sugar
- H. 1 teaspoon seasoning powder
- I. 2 tablespoons Chinese red cheese
- J. 2 cups soup stock

PREPARATION

Mix E, F, G, H together. Stir well before using.

COOKING

1. Put A into a hot skillet, over high flame. Add B, C.
2. Add D and stir-fry until pork is light brown.
3. Add prepared mixture and stir-fry 1 minute. Add I. Stir thoroughly.
4. Add J. Cover. Lower flame, braise until pork is tender.
   Serve with boiled rice.

Serves 2 or 3.

119. BRAISED PORK WITH CHINESE TURNIPS AND RED CHEESE (*Nam-Yu Gee-Yoke Lo-Bok*)

Use same method and ingredients as in recipe No. 118, adding 2 lbs. of Chinese turnips. Peel turnips and cut them into 1½ inch cubes. Add turnips after pork is half done.

120. STEAMED PORK WITH CHINESE WHITE CHEESE (*Foo-Yu Jan Gee-Yoke*)

A. 1 lb. fresh raw pork (boned pork chop, tenderloin or butts), cut in thin slivers
B. 1 tablespoon white cheese

COOKING

1. Place A in deep dish.
2. Mix B with A thoroughly.
3. Place a rack on bottom of a large pot and put plate on rack. Pour in 1½ inches boiling water; cover, steam 25 minutes, or until pork is done.
   Serve with boiled rice or potatoes.

Serves 2 or 3.

121. STEAMED PORK WITH SHRIMP SAUCE (*Hom-Har Jan Gee-Yoke*)

A. 1 lb. fresh raw pork (boned pork chop or butt), cut in thin slivers
B. 1 tablespoon shrimp sauce
c. 1 teaspoon ginger, shredded very fine

COOKING

Use the same method as in recipe No. 120. When cooked, add 1 teaspoon cooked peanut oil. Serve with boiled rice.

Serves 2 or 3.

122. CHINESE PORK CHOPS (*Gee-Par*)

A. ½ lb. (2) pork chops boned, fried or broiled
B. 1 clove garlic, crushed, or 1 teaspoon garlic powder
c. 2 tablespoons oyster sauce

COOKING

1. Before broiling or frying chops, sprinkle garlic over meat.
2. After chops are done, add oyster sauce.
   Serve with boiled rice or potatoes.

Serves 1.

123. STEAMED PORK WITH SALTED CABBAGE
(*Chung-Toy Jan Gee-Yoke*)

A. 1 lb. fresh raw pork (boned pork chops), sliced in thin slivers
B. ½ cup salted cabbage, chopped fine
C. 2 tablespoons water chestnuts, peeled, chopped fine
D. 1 teaspoon peanut oil
E. 1 teaspoon cornstarch
F. 1 teaspoon seasoning powder
G. 2 teaspoons light soy sauce

COOKING

1. Mix all ingredients in a deep dish.
2. Cook same way as in recipe No. 122 for about 30 minutes, or until done.
   Serve with boiled rice.

Note: Salted Chinese cabbage is produced in different parts of China; each kind has a unique taste and its own aromatic condiment, such as: Chung Toy, produced in Canton; Moy Toy, produced in Waichow; Char Toy, produced in Szechwan; Tung Toy, also produced in Canton.
They are all good for steamed pork; also good in soups.

124. STEAMED MINCED PORK WITH WATER
CHESTNUTS (*Mar-Tai Gee-Yoke Beng*)

A. 1 lb. fresh raw pork (chops, tenderloin or butts), chopped very fine
B. 10 fresh peeled water chestnuts, chopped
C. 1 teaspoon seasoning powder
D. 1 tablespoon light soy sauce
E. 1 teaspoon salt
F. ½ teaspoon peanut oil
G. few drops of sesame seed oil (optional)

PREPARATION

Slice A into thin slices, then chop. Add B. Continue to chop until very fine. Add C, D, E, F, G. Mix thoroughly. Put in deep platter, shaping mixture to form a thin pancake.

COOKING

1. Use a large pot containing 3 inches of boiling water, with a rack on bottom.
2. Place platter on rack. Cover and steam 25 minutes, or until pork is done.
   Serve with boiled rice or boiled potatoes.

Serves 2.

125. STEAMED MINCED PORK WITH HAM
(*For Hui Jan Gee-Yoke Beng*)

Use same method and ingredients as in recipe No. 124. Add Virginia ham, chopped fine, before forming pancake.

126. STEAMED MINCED PORK WITH SALTED EGGS (*Hom-Don Jan Gee-Yoke Beng*)

Use same method and ingredients as in recipe No. 124. Add 2 salt-treated eggs. Put sliced egg yolks on top of pancake, then steam for 45 minutes or more.

Note: Mix egg whites with pork.

127. STEAMED MINCED PORK WITH SALTED FISH
(*Hom-Yu Jan Gee-Yoke Beng*)

Use same method and ingredients as in recipe No. 124. Add chopped salted fish to mixed ingredients or slice fish and drop on top of cake before steaming.

128. STEAMED MINCED PORK WITH DRIED DUCK'S MEAT (*Lip Op Yoke Gee-Yoke Beng*)

Use same method and ingredients as in recipe No. 124. Grind duck meat and mix with all other ingredients.

129. STEAMED MINCED PORK WITH CHINESE PORK SAUSAGES (*Lip-Ching Jan Gee-Yoke Beng*)

Use same method and ingredients as in recipe No. 124. Use sausage, either chopped together with ingredients or sliced and placed on top of cake before steaming.

130. STUFFED GREEN PEPPERS WITH PORK
(*Yen Ting-Dew*)

A. 1 lb. fresh raw pork (tenderloin or butts)
B. 1½ cups fresh filet of sole or haddock
C. 1 cup fresh or canned crabmeat
D. ¼ cup black mushrooms, soaked in warm water 15 minutes
E. ¼ cup water chestnuts, peeled and chopped
F. 1 teaspoon seasoning powder
G. 1 teaspoon light soy sauce
H. dash pepper
I. 2 fresh scallions (white part only), ground
J. 1 teaspoon salt
K. 10 large fresh green peppers, tops cut off and seeds removed

PREPARATION

Grind together A, B, C, D, E. Add F, G, H, I, J and mix thoroughly. Stuff prepared ingredients into K.

COOKING

1. Place the stuffed green peppers in a colander. Steam 35 minutes in a covered pot with 1½ inches of boiling water, or bake in a moderate oven (350° F.) for 30 minutes.

Serves 5.

131. STUFFED MUSHROOMS WITH PORK
(*Yen Moo-Koo*)

Use same method and ingredients as in recipe No. 130. Use black mushrooms instead of peppers: 25 medium-size black mushrooms; soak mushrooms 30 minutes in warm water.

132. STUFFED HAIRY MELON WITH PORK
(*Yen Dick-Kar*)

Use same method and ingredients as in recipe No. 130. Use hairy melon instead of peppers: 1 large melon, peeled, cut into sections about 1 inch thick and seeds removed.

133. STUFFED BITTER MELON WITH PORK
(*Yen Foo-Kar*)

Use same method and ingredients as in recipe No. 130. Use bitter melon instead of peppers: 2 large melons, cut into sections about 1 inch thick, or halved. Remove seeds.

134. STEAMED PORK WITH FIVE KINDS OF SPICES AND POTATOES (*Eng Hong Gee-Yoke*)

A. 1 teaspoon 5 kinds of spices
B. 2 tablespoons light soy sauce
C. 1 teaspoon heavy soy sauce
D. 1 teaspoon sugar
E. 1 teaspoon sweet vegetable sauce
F. 1 teaspoon seasoning powder
G. 1½ teaspoons salt
H. 2 lbs. fresh raw pork (pork chops or butts), cut into 1 inch cubes
I. 4 lbs. raw potatoes, peeled and cut into 1½ inch cubes

PREPARATION

Mix A, B, C, D, E, F, G together. Marinate H in this preparation from 10 to 24 hours. Turn occasionally so that the mixture will soak into the meat.

COOKING

1. Put I in a pan or large casserole (a double boiler would be best). Add pork on top. Steam 1 hour, or until pork is tender.

Note: Five kinds of spices may be obtained in any Chinese supply house.

135. BRAISED PORK WITH JADE BAMBOO SHOOTS
(*Yock-Leong Shoon Min Gee-Yoke*)

A. 1 tablespoon peanut oil or lard
B. ½ teaspoon salt
C. 2 cloves garlic, crushed
D. 1 lb. fresh raw pork (butts or shoulder), cut into 1 inch cubes
E. 1 tablespoon light soy sauce
F. 1 teaspoon sugar
G. 1 teaspoon seasoning powder
H. 1 teaspoon rice wine
I. 1 teaspoon curry powder
J. 1 teaspoon hot sauce
K. dash pepper
L. ¼ cup water
M. ¼ cup grated Chinese red cheese (if you do not care for cheese you may substitute oyster sauce)
N. ¼ lb. jade bamboo shoots (weigh dry). Soak in warm water 24 hours; change water several times if necessary. Cut into thin slivers
O. 3 cups soup stock
P. ½ cup onion, sliced

PREPARATION

Mix together E, F, G, H, I, J, K, L. Stir well when ready to use.

COOKING

1. Put A in a large frying pan or skillet. Heat over high flame until oil smokes. Add B and then C.
2. Add D. Stir-fry until golden brown.
3. Add prepared mixture. Stir and fry 3 minutes so pork will absorb all the ingredients.
4. Add M.
5. Add N and stir thoroughly.
6. Add O. Lower heat. Cover, and let simmer about 30 minutes.
7. Add P. Mix well and simmer another 15 minutes. Add more soup stock if necessary.

Serves 4.

136. BRAISED PORK WITH BEAN STICKS
(*Foo-Jok Min Gee-Yoke*)

A. 1 tablespoon peanut oil
B. 1 clove garlic
C. 1 teaspoon salt
D. 1 lb. fresh raw pork (butt or shoulder), cut into 1 inch cubes
E. 1 tablespoon light soy sauce
F. 1 tablespoon rice wine
G. ½ teaspoon fresh ginger, shredded fine
H. 1 teaspoon sugar
I. 1 teaspoon seasoning powder
J. ½ lb. dried second bean sticks, soaked in cold water 25 minutes
K. 1 cup bamboo shoots, cut diagonally
L. 1 cup black mushrooms, cut into 2 or 4 pieces each
M. 10 Chinese red dates, soaked in water 25 minutes
N. 1 cup white nuts or chestnut meats. Cook about 1 hour, separate and save liquid, for soup stock
O. 12 water chestnuts, peeled, and cut into 3 or 4 pieces each
P. 3 cups soup stock

PREPARATION

Mix E, F, G, H, I together.

COOKING

1. Put A in a large frying pan or skillet. Heat oil until it smokes. Add B, C.
2. Add D. Stir-fry until pork is light brown.
3. Add prepared mixture. Stir-fry 1 minute.
4. Add J, K, L, M, N, O. Stir-fry thoroughly for 2 minutes.
5. Add P. Cover and cook to boiling point. Lower flame and simmer 45 to 60 minutes.

Serve with rice.

Serves 4.

137. PORK WITH POTATOES (*See-Doy Chee-Yoke*)

A. 1 tablespoon peanut oil or lard
B. ½ teaspoon salt
C. dash fresh ginger, sliced very fine
D. 2 tablespoons salted black beans, crushed
E. 2 cloves garlic, crushed
F. 1 teaspoon light soy sauce
G. 1 teaspoon heavy soy sauce
H. 1 teaspoon rice wine or 2 tablespoons sherry wine
I. dash pepper
J. ½ lb. fresh raw pork, ground fine
K. 3 lbs. potatoes, peeled, sliced or cubed
L. 4 cups soup stock

PREPARATION

Put C, D, E in a bowl. Mash together. Add F, G, H, I. Mix well.

COOKING

1. Put A in a large skillet. Heat over high flame until almost smoking. Add B.
2. Add prepared mixture. Stir-fry ½ minute.
3. Add J. Stir 2 minutes.
4. Add K. Stir-fry until all ingredients are well mixed.
5. Add L. Cover and cook until boiling, then lower flame. Let simmer 25 to 35 minutes or until potatoes are tender and soup stock thickens.

Serve with boiled rice.

Serves 4.

138. PORK SAUTE WITH CHESTNUTS AND MUSHROOMS (*Lut-Do Gee*)

A. 1 tablespoon peanut oil
B. 1 teaspoon salt
C. 1 lb. fresh raw pork (tenderloin or butts), cut into 1 inch cubes
D. 2 teaspoons light soy sauce
E. 3 cups soup stock
F. 1 cup chestnuts, shelled

G. 1 cup black mushrooms, soaked in warm water 15 minutes. Cut large ones in two.

H. 1 cup water chestnuts, peeled, cut in halves

I. 1 cup white nuts, shelled (optional, any kind of nut may be substituted)

COOKING

1. Put A in hot skillet. Add B. Cook over high flame.
2. Add C. Stir-fry until pork is light brown. Add D. Stir-fry 1 minute.
3. Add E.
4. Add F, G, H, I. Mix them well. Cover over low flame, and let simmer for 1 hour, or until pork and chestnuts are tender.

Serve with boiled rice.

Serves 2 or 3.

139. DICED CUT ROAST PORK WITH VEGETABLES AND ALMONDS (*Char-Shu Din*)

A. 1 tablespoon peanut oil

B. 1 teaspoon salt

C. 1 clove garlic, crushed

D. 2 cups barbecued or roast pork, diced

E. 1 cup celery (tender part only), diced

F. 1 cup bamboo shoots, diced

G. 1 cup mushrooms, diced

H. 2 tablespoons scallions (white part only), diced

I. 1 cup onion, diced

J. 2 cups Chinese cabbage (white part only), diced

K. 4 tablespoons water chestnuts, peeled, diced

L. 1 tablespoon light soy sauce

M. 1 tablespoon rice wine or 4 tablespoons sherry wine

N. ½ teaspoon fresh ginger, chopped very fine

O. ½ cup soup stock

P. 2 tablespoons roast almonds (if large-size almonds, crush)

Q. 1 tablespoon cornstarch

R. 1 teaspoon heavy soy sauce

S. 1 teaspoon sugar

T. 1 teaspoon seasoning powder

PREPARATION

Mix L, M, N together with 1 tablespoon water. Stir well before using. Mix Q, R, S, T together with ½ cup water. Stir up well before using.

COOKING

1. Put A in a large skillet over high flame until oil is smoking. Add B and C.
2. Add D. Stir-fry ½ minute.
3. Add E, F, G, H, I, J, K. Stir-fry thoroughly 4 minutes.
4. Add L, M, N preparation. Stir thoroughly 2 minutes.
5. Add O. Cover, cook 3 minutes.
6. Add P.
7. Add Q, R, S, T preparation. Stir-fry thoroughly until gravy thickens and is smooth.

Serves 2 or 3.

Note: Roast lamb, beef, turkey, chicken, duck, veal, shrimps, lobster or crabmeat is also good in this recipe.

140. DICED CUT PORK WITH FRESH PEAS
(*Ching Dow Chee-Yoke Din*)

Use same method and ingredients as in recipe No. 139. Add 1 cup fresh or frozen peas (*never* use canned peas) to vegetables.

141. DICED CUT CHINESE ROAST PORK WITH ASPARAGUS (*Char-Shu Le-Shon Din*)

Use same method and ingredients as in recipe No. 139. Use Chinese roast pork instead of fresh pork, and add 1 cup diced cut asparagus to vegetables.

142. DICED CUT PORK WITH STRING BEANS
(*Dow Doy Din*)

Use same method and ingredients as in recipe No. 139. Add 1½ cups fresh string beans, diced, to vegetables.

143. DICED CUT PORK WITH PEA PODS
(*Shet-Dow Gee-Yoke Din*)

Use same method and ingredients as in recipe No. 139. Add 1½ cups diced pea pods to vegetables.

144. DICED CUT PORK WITH BROCCOLI
(*Kai-Leang Chee-Yoke Din*)

Use same method and ingredients as in recipe No. 139. Add 2 cups diced cut broccoli to vegetables.

145. PAPER WRAPPED PORK (*Ge Bow Chee-Yoke*)

A. 1 lb. fresh raw pork (tenderloin or chops), cut in ¾ inch cubes
B. 6 fresh scallions (white part only), cut 1 inch long, then split in halves
C. ¼ cup light-dark soy sauce
D. 2 teaspoons heavy soy sauce
E. 1 teaspoon fresh ginger, crushed
F. 1 teaspoon seasoning powder
G. 1 teaspoon sugar
H. 1 teaspoon garlic powder
I. 2 teaspoons vegetable sauce
J. 1 teaspoon rice wine

PREPARATION AND COOKING

Mix together C, D, E, F, G, H, I, J. Put A in this mixture. Let soak about 30 minutes. Stir and turn pork occasionally. Cut pieces of wax paper about 6 inches square. Remove pieces of pork from mixture with a fork, one by one. Wrap up each piece of pork with 1 piece of B. Or put 7 or 8 pieces of pork and 7 or 8 pieces of scallion in a wax paper bag and seal tightly. French fry pork (in bag) in deep hot oil or lard for 10 minutes. Serve hot with sliced tomato and lettuce as garnish.

Serves 2.

146. SWEET AND SOUR PORK
(*Tiem-Shoon Gee-Yoke*)

A. ½ teaspoon seasoning powder
B. 1 teaspoon light soy sauce
C. 1 teaspoon rice wine or 2 tablespoons sherry wine
D. ½ teaspoon fresh ginger, crushed
E. 1½ lbs. fresh raw pork, cut in 1 inch cubes
F. 3 eggs, beaten
G. ½ cup all purpose flour
H. 2 tablespoons cornstarch
I. 1 tablespoon cornstarch
J. 1 teaspoon heavy soy sauce
K. 1 cup water
L. 1 cup sugar
M. 1 cup vinegar
N. 1 cup sweet pickle (plain or mixed), cut in 1 inch cubes or diagonally
O. 2 large green peppers, cut diagonally into 8 to 10 pieces each
P. 1 large tomato, cut in wedges 8 to 10 pieces each
Q. 1 cup canned sliced pineapple, cut in cubes
R. ½ cup preserved sweet ginger, sliced thin (optional)

PREPARATION

Mix A, B, C, D together. Soak E in this mixture 10 minutes or more. Beat F, G, H together until smooth paste is formed. Remove pork and dip in batter, then fry in deep hot peanut oil until golden brown. Mix I, J together, and add ½ cup water. Stir up well before using.

COOKING

1. Pour K into hot skillet; add L, M and cook until sugar is dissolved.
2. Add N, O, P, Q, R and cook 2 minutes.
3. Add I, J preparation and stir-fry 2 minutes.
4. Add fried pork. Stir-fry until gravy thickens and is smooth.

Serves 2 or 3.

147. LICHEE SWEET AND SOUR PORK
(*Lichee Tiem Shoon Gee-Yoke*)

Use same method and ingredients as in recipe No. 146. Add one can of preserved lichee. If desired, green peppers and tomatoes may be omitted.

148. MINCED PORK WITH WATER CHESTNUTS
(*Mar-Hi Gee-Yoke Soong*)

A. 1 tablespoon peanut oil or lard
B. ½ teaspoon salt
C. ½ clove garlic, minced
D. 1 lb. fresh raw pork (butt or tenderloin), minced
E. ¼ lb. fresh peeled water chestnuts, chopped fine
F. 1 tablespoon fresh white leek, chopped fine
G. ½ cup soup stock
H. 1 tablespoon light soy sauce
I. 1 teaspoon heavy soy sauce
J. 1 teaspoon seasoning powder
K. ½ teaspoon sugar
L. 1 teaspoon rice wine
M. ½ teaspoon Chinese chili sauce
N. 1 teaspoon cornstarch mixed in ½ cup water
O. few drops sesame seed oil
P. dash pepper

PREPARATION

Mix well together H, I, J, K, L, M, N, O, P. Stir well before using.

COOKING

1. Put A in large skillet. Heat until oil is almost smoking. Add B and C.
2. Add D, E, F. Stir-fry until pork is golden brown. Add G. Cover, and cook 3 minutes.
3. Add prepared mixture. Stir-fry 2 minutes.
   Serve with boiled rice, toast or French rolls.

Serves 2 or 3.

149. MINCED PORK WITH FRESH GREEN PEAS
(*Cheng-Dow Gee-Yoke Soong*)

Use same method and ingredients as in recipe No. 148. In step 2 add 1 cup fresh green peas. Cook 7 minutes instead of 3, then add prepared mixture.

150. MINCED PORK WITH STRING BEANS
(*Dow-Doy Gee-Yoke Soong*)

Use same method and ingredients as in recipe No. 148. In step 2 add 1 cup fresh green beans. Cut into ¼ inch pieces, as big as peas. Cook 7 minutes, then add prepared mixture.

Note: Other variations of recipe No. 148 may be obtained by adding broccoli, green peppers, asparagus or pea pods.

151. PORK SPARE RIBS WITH BLACK BEAN SAUCE
(*Dow-Shee Pai-Good*)

A. 1 teaspoon peanut oil
B. ½ teaspoon salt
C. 2 lbs. fresh pork spare ribs, cut in 1 inch lengths
D. 2 tablespoons salt black beans, washed and crushed
E. 2 cloves of garlic, crushed
F. 2 tablespoons fresh leek (white part only), chopped fine
G. 1 teaspoon light soy sauce
H. 1 teaspoon rice wine or 2 tablespoons sherry wine
I. ½ cup soup stock
J. 2 teaspoons seasoning powder
K. 1 teaspoon sugar
L. 1 tablespoon cornstarch
M. ½ cup water
N. 2 teaspoons heavy soy sauce
O. 1 fresh scallion (white part only), cut in 1 inch lengths

PREPARATION

Mix D, E, F, G, H together well; add 1 tablespoon water. Mix J, K, L, M, N together. Stir up before using.

COOKING

1. Put A in hot skillet; add B.
2. Add C. Stir-fry until pieces are golden brown; drain off excess fat and lower heat.
3. Add D, E, F, G, H preparation and stir-fry 2 minutes, stirring frequently until mixed well.
4. Add I. Cover and cook 2 minutes.
5. Add J, K, L, M, N preparation. Stir constantly until gravy thickens and is smooth.
6. Add O on top of each serving.

Serves 2 or 3.

Note: Brown bean sauce may be used instead of black bean sauce.

STIR-FRY BEEF

152. STIR-FRY BEEF WITH GRAVY
(*Chow Gow-Yoke*)

BASIC RECIPE

A. 1 tablespoon peanut oil
B. ¼ teaspoon salt
C. 1 clove garlic
D. 1 cup onion, sliced thin
E. ½ lb. flank or sirloin steak, sliced very thin (about ⅛ inch)
F. 1 fresh scallion (white part only), cut in ½ inch pieces
G. 1 teaspoon seasoning powder
H. 1 teaspoon light soy sauce
I. ½ teaspoon sugar
J. dash of pepper
K. 1 teaspoon rice wine or 2 tablespoons sherry wine
L. ½ teaspoon fresh ginger, shredded very fine
M. a few drops of sesame seed oil
N. ¼ cup soup stock
O. 1 tablespoon cornstarch
P. ½ teaspoon heavy soy sauce

PREPARATION

Mix together G, H, I, J, K, L, M. Add 1 tablespoon water. Stir well before using. Mix together O, P with 4 tablespoons water. Stir well before using.

COOKING

1. Put A in hot skillet; add B and C.
2. Add D. Stir-fry 1 minute.
3. Add E. Stir-fry 1 minute.
4. Add F and stir-fry for about ½ minute.
5. Add G, H, I, J, K, L, M preparation and stir-fry 1 minute more.
6. Add N. Cook 1 minute or until boiling. Do *not* cover.

7. Add O, P preparation. Stir constantly until gravy thickens and is smooth.
Serve with boiled rice or potatoes.
Serves 2.

153. STIR-FRY BEEF WITH OYSTER SAUCE
(*Hoo-Yu Gow-Yoke*)

Use basic recipe No. 152. Add 2 tablespoons oyster sauce to G, H, I, J, K, L, M preparation.

154. STIR-FRY BEEF WITH MUSHROOMS
(*Moo-Koo Chow Gow-Yoke*)

Use basic recipe No. 152. Add ½ cup sliced white or black mushrooms same time as onions.

155. STIR-FRY BEEF WITH GREEN PEPPER
(*Pepper Steak or Lard-Dew Gow*)

Use basic recipe No. 152. Add 2 cups green peppers. Cut peppers in half, clean out seeds, slice (or cut diagonally) and place pepper in boiling water for 3 minutes. Rinse in cold water and drain. Add same time as onions.

156. STIR-FRY BEEF WITH TOMATOES
(*Fan-Gar Chow Gow-Yoke*)

Use basic recipe No. 152. Add 2 cups tomatoes, cut diagonally. Add same time as onions.

157. STIR-FRY BEEF WITH BEAN SPROUTS
(*Kar-Toy Chow Gow-Yoke*)

Use basic recipe No. 152. Add 4 cups bean sprouts (at same time as onions) and 1 full teaspoon of heavy soy sauce.

158. STIR-FRY BEEF WITH CHINESE CABBAGE
(Bok-Toy Chow Gow-Yoke)

Use basic recipe No. 152, substituting 2 cups Chinese cabbage for onions.

159. STIR-FRY BEEF WITH MUSTARD GREENS
(Guy-Toy Chow Gow-Yoke)

Use basic recipe No. 152, substituting 2 cups mustard greens for onions.

160. STIR-FRY BEEF WITH TOMATOES AND GREEN PEPPERS *(Fan-Kor Lard-Dew Chow Gow-Yoke)*

Use basic recipe No. 152. Add 1 cup tomatoes and 1 cup of green peppers, all cut diagonally. Add same time as onions.

161. STIR-FRY BEEF WITH PEA POD (SNOW PEA)
(Sheet-Dow Chow Gow-Yoke)

Use basic recipe No. 152. Add 1½ cups pea pods same time as onions.

162. STIR-FRY BEEF WITH FRESH PEAS OR FROZEN PEAS *(Ching-Dow Chow Gow-Yoke)*

Use basic recipe No. 152. Add 1 cup fresh or frozen peas same time as onions. Dice beef and onions.

163. STIR-FRY BEEF WITH PICKLED MUSTARD GREENS *(Hom-Toy Chow Gow-Yoke)*

Use basic recipe No. 152. Add 2 cups pickled mustard greens. Wash, squeeze dry and dice-cut about ½ inch square. Add same time as onions; also add 2 tablespoons sugar and 1 tablespoon vinegar.

164. STIR-FRY BEEF WITH CELERY
(*Hong-Kin Chow Gow-Yoke*)

Use basic recipe No. 152. Add 2 cups celery, cut diagonally, same time as onions.

165. STIR-FRY BEEF WITH ASSORTED VEGETABLES (*Kar-Toy Chow Gow-Yoke*)

Use basic recipe No. 152. Add 1 cup each of 3 more vegetables, such as bean sprouts, pea pods, tomatoes, green peppers, Chinese cabbage, American cabbage, celery, string beans, broccoli, cauliflower, asparagus, luto's roots, mustard greens, etc. Cook a few extra minutes, or until vegetables are tender, then add 1 teaspoon sugar and 1 teaspoon heavy soy sauce.

166. STIR-FRY BEEF WITH BROCCOLI
(*Guy-Liang Chow Gow-Yoke*)

Use basic recipe No. 152. Add 2 cups broccoli, cut 1 inch long; split the heavier pieces in half. Cook 3 minutes and drain. Add same time as onions, then add 2 teaspoons sugar.

167. STIR-FRY BEEF WITH CAULIFLOWER
(*Yer-Toy Far Chow Gow-Yoke*)

Use basic recipe No. 152. Add 2 cups cauliflower, cut diagonally and boil for 3 minutes, same time as onions. Use 1 teaspoon heavy soy sauce also.

168. STIR-FRY BEEF WITH ASPARAGUS
(*Le-Shoon Chow Gow-Yoke*)

Use basic recipe No. 152. Add 2 cups asparagus tips, cleaned and cut about 1 inch long. Boil 3 minutes. Add same time as onions, then add 1 teaspoon heavy soy sauce.

169. STIR-FRY BEEF WITH STRING BEANS
(*Dow-Doy Chow Gow-Yoke*)

Use basic recipe No. 152. Add 2 cups fresh string beans, cut 1 to 1½ inches long. Boil 3 minutes in salted water and drain. Add same time as onions.

170. STIR-FRY BEEF WITH BITTER MELON
(*Foo-Kur Chow Gow Yoke*)

Use basic recipe No. 152. Add 2 cups bitter melon. Remove all pulp and seeds, and cut in thin slivers; boil for 3 minutes and drain. Add same time as onions. Add 1 teaspoon black beans, mashed, same time as garlic.

171. STIR-FRY BEEF WITH LUTO'S ROOTS
(*Ling-Gow Chow Gow-Yoke*)

Use basic recipe No. 152. Add 2 cups of luto's roots, sliced very thin, same time as onions.

172. STIR-FRY BEEF WITH NEW GINGERS
(*Do-Kan Chow Gow-Yoke*)

Use basic recipe No. 152. Add ½ cup fresh new gingers, sliced very thin, same time as onions.

173. STIR-FRY BEEF WITH PRESERVED SWEET PICKLE AND GINGERS
(*Char-Qur Kan Chow Gow-Yoke*)

Use basic recipe No. 152. Add 2 tablespoons sweet preserved pickles and 1 tablespoon ginger same time as onions.

174. STIR-FRY BEEF WITH CHINESE TURNIPS
(*Lo-Bok Chee Gow-Yoke*)

Use basic recipe No. 152. Add 3 cups Chinese turnips, sliced the size of dominoes, about ½ inch thick, boiled for 5 to 6 minutes. Add same time as onions.

175. STIR-FRY BEEF WITH SALTED CHINESE CABBAGE (*Chung-Toy Chow Gow-Yoke*)

Use basic recipe No. 152. Add ¼ cup salted Chinese cabbage, chopped fine, same time as onions.

176. SAUTÉ BEEF WITH POTATOES
(*Gow-Yoke Gee Shee-Doy*)

A. 1 teaspoon peanut oil
B. 1 teaspoon salt
C. 1 clove garlic
D. ½ lb. beef (stew meat), ground
E. ½ teaspoon fresh ginger, shredded very fine
F. 1 tablespoon black beans, crushed
G. 2 teaspoons light soy sauce
H. 1 teaspoon rice wine
I. 3 lbs. potatoes, cut into 1 inch cubes
J. 3 cups soup stock
K. 1 teaspoon seasoning powder
L. 1 teaspoon heavy soy sauce
M. ½ cup water

PREPARATION

Mix E, F, G, H together, and add 1 tablespoon water. Stir well before using. Mix K, L, M. Stir well before using.

COOKING

1. Put A in large hot skillet and add B and C.
2. Add D. Stir-fry 2 minutes.
3. Add E, F, G, H preparation. Stir-fry 1 minute.
4. Add I. Stir-fry thoroughly for 3 minutes.
5. Add J, and cover. Lower heat and simmer for 25 minutes. Add water if necessary.
6. Add K, L, M preparation and stir well.
   Serve with boiled rice.

Serves 2.

177. BEEF WITH CURRY (*Currie Gow-Yoke*)

A. 1 teaspoon peanut oil
B. ½ teaspoon salt
C. 1 cup onions, cut diagonally
D. 1 lb. potatoes, cut into 1½ inch cubes
E. 1 lb. stew beef, cut into 1 inch cubes
F. 2 tablespoons curry powder
G. ½ teaspoon fresh ginger, shredded very fine
H. 1 teaspoon sugar
I. 1 teaspoon rice wine
J. 3 cups soup stock
K. 1 teaspoon cornstarch
L. 1 teaspoon seasoning powder

PREPARATION

Mix together G, H, I and add 1 tablespoon water. Stir well before using. Mix K, L with ¼ cup water.

COOKING

1. Put A in large hot skillet and add B.
2. Add C, D, E. Stir-fry 3 minutes.
3. Add F. Stir-fry thoroughly about 3 or 4 minutes.

4. Add G, H, I preparation. Stir-fry 2 minutes.
5. Add J. Cover and lower heat. Simmer 25 minutes, or until beef is tender.
6. Add K, L preparation and stir until gravy thickens and is smooth.

Serve with boiled rice.

Serves 2.

178. VERMICELLI WITH BEEF (*Fon-Soo Gow Yoke*)

A. 1 tablespoon peanut oil
B. ½ teaspoon salt
C. ¼ lb. dried Chinese vermicelli (or long rice), soaked in cold water for 30 minutes, drained and cut in 3 or 4 inch long pieces
D. 3 cups soup stock
E. 1 teaspoon seasoning powder
F. 1 teaspoon sugar
G. 1 teaspoon light soy sauce
H. ½ teaspoon heavy soy sauce
I. 1 teaspoon rice wine
J. ½ teaspoon pepper
K. ½ lb. beef, shredded very fine
L. 2 eggs, scrambled
M. 1 fresh scallion (white part only), chopped fine

PREPARATION

Mix together E, F, G, H, I, J with K and let stand until meat is well marinated.

COOKING

1. Put A in hot large skillet and add B.
2. Add C. Stir-fry 1 minute.
3. Add D. Cover, cook over low heat 15 minutes.
4. Add prepared mixture and stir well. Cook another 2 minutes.
5. Add L and M. Mix well.

Serves 3.

179. BEAN CURD WITH BEEF
(*Hon-Shu Dow-Foo Gow*)

A. 1 tablespoon peanut oil
B. 1 teaspoon salt
C. 1 clove garlic, crushed
D. 1 cup beef, ground or chopped fine
E. 1 teaspoon light soy sauce
F. 1 teaspoon rice wine or 2 tablespoons sherry wine
G. dash of pepper
H. few drops of sesame seed oil
I. 3 cups bean curd, cut into 1 inch squares
J. ½ cup celery or bamboo shoots, shredded very fine
K. ½ cup black mushrooms, shredded very fine (soak in warm water 15 minutes before shredding)
L. 1 teaspoon seasoning powder
M. 1 teaspoon sugar
N. 1 teaspoon heavy soy sauce
O. 1 teaspoon cornstarch
P. 2 fresh scallions (white part only), chopped fine

PREPARATION

Fry I in deep oil until light brown. Mix L, M, N, O together with ½ cup cold water; stir well before using. Mix E, F, G, H together, and add 1 tablespoon water.

COOKING

1. Put A in large hot skillet. Add B and C.
2. Add D. Stir-fry 2 minutes.
3. Add E, F, G, H preparation and stir thoroughly.
4. Add prepared bean curd and mix well.
5. Add J, K and stir-fry 2 minutes.
6. Add L, M, N, O preparation and stir-fry until gravy is smooth.
7. Sprinkle P on top of each serving.

Serves 2.

180. STEAK WITH ASSORTED VEGETABLES
(*Steak Kew*)

A. 1 tablespoon peanut oil
B. 1 teaspoon salt
C. 1 clove garlic, crushed
D. ½ cup Chinese pea pods, sliced
E. ¼ cup onions, sliced or cut diagonally
F. ¼ cup celery, sliced same size as onions
G. ¼ cup Chinese celery cabbage, cut same size as onions
H. ¼ cup black or white mushrooms, sliced
I. ¼ cup bamboo shoots, sliced
J. 2 tablespoons water chestnuts, peeled and sliced
K. 1½ lbs. sirloin steak, broiled or fried, sliced into small
   pieces (do not broil steak until all ingredients are ready;
   steak should be rare)
L. 1 teaspoon light soy sauce
M. 1 teaspoon rice wine
N. 1 teaspoon sugar
O. a few drops sesame oil
P. 1 cup soup stock
Q. 1 teaspoon seasoning powder
R. 1 tablespoon tomato catsup or Chinese sweet vegetable
   sauce
S. 1 teaspoon heavy soy sauce
T. 1 tablespoon cornstarch
U. dash of pepper
V. ½ teaspoon prepared mustard

PREPARATION

Mix L, M, N, O together and add 1 tablespoon water. Stir well
before using. Mix together Q, R, S, T, U, V and add ½ cup water.
Stir well before using.

COOKING

1. Put A in large hot skillet and add B and C.
2. Add D, E, F, G, H, I, J. Stir-fry 3 minutes.
3. Add K. Stir to mix thoroughly with all vegetables.
4. Add L, M, N, O preparation. Stir-fry thoroughly about 1 minute.
5. Add P. Cover and cook 2 minutes.
6. Add Q, R, S, T, U, V preparation. Mix thoroughly, stirring constantly until gravy thickens and is smooth.
   Serve with boiled rice or bread.

Serves 2 or 3.

181. CHINESE STEAK WITH MUSHROOMS AND OYSTER SAUCE (*Tong-Yan Yoke-Par*)

A. 1½ lbs. sirloin steak
B. ½ teaspoon garlic powder
C. 1½ cups soup stock
D. 1 teaspoon light soy sauce
E. 2 tablespoons oyster sauce
F. 1 teaspoon seasoning powder
G. 1 teaspoon Chinese sweet vegetable sauce (catsup may be substituted)
H. 1 teaspoon prepared mustard
I. 1 tablespoon cornstarch
J. ½ cup black or white mushrooms, diced
K. 1 teaspoon salt

PREPARATION

Mix D, E, F, G, H, I together and add ½ cup water. Stir well before using.

COOKING

1. Broil A. When one side is golden brown, sprinkle B on it, then turn and sprinkle B on other side. Broil until medium well done. Slice into small pieces (any size you desire).
2. Pour C into hot skillet. When soup is boiling, add prepared mixture and J, K. Stir until thick, then pour over the steak.

Serves 2.

182. BRAISED BEEF NORTHERN STYLE (*Hon-Shu Koo-Law Gow-Yoke*)

A. 2 lbs. beef, cut in 1 inch cubes
B. 1 tablespoon heavy soy sauce
C. 2 tablespoons light soy sauce
D. 1 tablespoon Chinese hot sauce
E. 1 tablespoon honey
F. 1 teaspoon curry powder
G. dash of pepper
H. 1 teaspoon garlic powder
I. dash of Chinese spice

J. 1 tablespoon rice wine
K. 1 teaspoon Chinese vegetable sweet sauce
L. 3 cups soup stock

PREPARATION

Mix all ingredients together except A and L. Put A in this mixture, and keep in refrigerator from 1 to 3 days. Stir every few hours, so that the meat will be soaked thoroughly with the mixture.

COOKING

1. Pour 1 cup L into deep skillet or pot. Add steak. Cook over low heat about 30 minutes. Add remaining L gradually and continue cooking until meat is tender. Garnish with vegetables in season and fried mushrooms.
Serve with boiled rice or mashed potatoes.

Serves 4.

183. PAPER-WRAPPED STEAK (*Ge Bow Yoke-Par*)

A. 1½ lbs. sirloin or tenderloin steak, sliced in domino shape, about 1½ inches long and 1 inch thick
B. 1 bunch fresh scallions (white part only) cut 1½ inch long and split in half
C. 4 tablespoons light soy sauce
D. 1 teaspoon heavy soy sauce
E. 1 teaspoon sugar
F. 2 teaspoons seasoning powder
G. 2 teaspoons Chinese sweet vegetable sauce
H. 1 teaspoon salt
I. 1 teaspoon prepared mustard
J. ½ teaspoon garlic powder
K. dash of pepper
L. few drops of sesame seed oil
M. 1 teaspoon rice wine

PREPARATION

Mix C, D, E, F, G, H, I, J, K, L, M together. Put A in mixture and let soak for 30 to 60 minutes. Place each piece of A with one piece B in the middle of a piece of wax paper (6 inches square). Fold the side in front of you. Fold left-hand side, then right-hand side. Roll upper part and tuck between both sides of the paper. Repeat operation until all pieces of steak are wrapped.

COOKING

1. Fry the wrapped-up steak in deep hot oil for 7 to 10 minutes. Drain and serve on hot plate with potatoes or boiled rice.

Serves 3.

CHOW MEIN

184. EGG NOODLES

A. 5 cups flour
B. 4 large, or 6 small, eggs
C. 1 teaspoon salt
D. 2 tablespoons egg powder

PREPARATION

Mix A, B, C, D together; knead until firm. Use a large heavy rolling pin. Roll dough on a floured table until very flat; fold over a couple times and roll again and again, until almost paper thin. During the final rolling stage, dust dough with dry flour each time you roll. Fold dough up and shred. If the noodles are not to be used immediately, let dry for future use.

Note: Fresh egg noodles may be ordered or bought at any Chinatown noodle factory or supply house.

185. FRIED EGG NOODLES

SOFT-FRY

Make noodles as instructed in recipe No. 184. Add 2 tablespoons peanut oil to 5 cups of noodles, and mix thoroughly. Put noodles in bamboo-tier or colander on rack in a large pot or deep fry pan, with 2 or 3 inches boiling water in bottom of pot. Cover. Steam 15 minutes. Let cool.

Put 3 tablespoons peanut oil in a hot skillet; fry noodles until light brown on both sides (inside of noodle must be soft). It takes about 6 to 8 minutes, on low flame, to fry soft noodles.

Serves 3 or 4.

Note: Always use soft-fry noodles in Chow Mein, Cantonese Style.

Soak freshly made egg noodles in hot deep oil (about 85°) for 2 minutes. Remove noodles (do *not* drain) and let them absorb excess fat for about 4 or 5 minutes.

Heat oil to about 350° and replace noodles in it. Fry, and keep turning noodles until all are golden brown.

If desired, make the soft-fry noodles, and instead of frying them in the 3 tablespoons oil, do as instructed above, fry in deep oil until crisp and brown.

Note: Crisp-fry noodles may be purchased in any Chinatown noodle factory or you may buy canned crisp noodles in any grocery store.

186. SOFT EGG NOODLE CHOW MEIN, CANTONESE STYLE (*Kwong-Tung Chow Mein*)

A. 1 tablespoon peanut oil
B. 1 teaspoon salt
C. 1 clove garlic, crushed
D. 1 cup raw lean pork, shredded fine
E. 1 cup bamboo shoots, shredded fine
F. 1 cup celery (tender part only), shredded fine
G. 1 cup Chinese cabbage (white part only), shredded fine
H. 4 tablespoons pea pods, shredded fine
I. 4 tablespoons black mushrooms, soak in warm water 30 minutes
J. 4 tablespoons water chestnuts, peeled, shredded fine
K. 1 tablespoon light soy sauce
L. 1 teaspoon rice wine or 2 tablespoons sherry wine
M. 1 teaspoon fresh ginger, shredded very fine
N. 10 drops sesame seed oil
O. 2 cups soup stock
P. ½ cup water
Q. 1½ tablespoons cornstarch
R. 1 teaspoon heavy soy sauce
S. 1 teaspoon sugar
T. 1½ teaspoons seasoning powder
U. 4 cups soft cooked egg noodles
V. 2 tablespoons Chinese roast pork, shredded very fine

PREPARATION

Mix K, L, M, N together well; add 1 tablespoon water. Stir up before using. Mix P, Q, R, S, T. Stir up before using.

COOKING

1. Put A in hot skillet; add B and C.
2. Add D; stir-fry 2 minutes.
3. Add E, F, G, H, I, J; stir-fry thoroughly 3 minutes.
4. Add K, L, M, N preparation; stir constantly 2 minutes.
5. Add O. Cover and cook 4 minutes; stir again thoroughly 1 minute.
6. Add P, Q, R, S, T preparation gradually; stir constantly 2 minutes.
7. Put U in a deep platter; pour mixture over noodles; garnish with V on each serving.

Serves 2 or 3.

Note: Chicken, turkey, beef, veal, lamb, lobster, shrimp, crabmeat, or duck may be substituted for pork; the name of the dish would change accordingly, such as Soft-Fry Noodle Chicken Chow Mein, Cantonese Style or Kwong-Tung Guy Chow Mein, etc.

187. PORK CHOW MEIN (*Gee-Yok Chow Mein*)

Follow same method and ingredients as in recipe No. 186. Use crisp-fry noodles instead of soft-fry noodles. Chicken, turkey, beef, veal, lamb, duck, lobster, shrimp or crabmeat may be substituted for pork.

Note: For Chicago Chow Mein, add ½ teaspoon heavy soy sauce and ½ cup white mushrooms.

188. PORK SUBGUM CHOW MEIN
(*Gee-Yoke Subgum Chow Mein*)

A. 1 tablespoon peanut oil
B. 1 teaspoon salt
C. 1 clove garlic, crushed
D. 1 cup fresh raw pork, diced
E. 2 teaspoons light soy sauce
F. dash pepper
G. few drops sesame oil
H. 1 teaspoon rice wine
I. 1 cup celery, diced
J. 1 cup bamboo shoots, diced
K. 1 cup black or white mushrooms, diced
L. 1 cup fresh green peppers, diced
M. 1 cup onions, diced
N. ¼ cup water chestnuts, peeled
O. 4 cups soup stock
P. 1 cup fresh tomatoes, diced
Q. 2½ tablespoons cornstarch
R. 2 teaspoons seasoning powder
S. 1 teaspoon heavy soy sauce
T. 1 teaspoon sugar
U. 2 tablespoons boiled Virginia ham, chopped very **fine**
V. 2 tablespoons roasted almonds, crushed
W. 2 hard-boiled eggs, diced
X. 4 to 5 cups noodles (crisp or soft-fried)

PREPARATION

Mix E, F, G, H together. Add 2 tablespoons water. Stir well before using. Use ½ cup water to mix Q, R, S, T together. Stir well before using.

COOKING

1. Place A in large, hot skillet, then add B and C.
2. Add D and stir-fry 2 minutes.
3. Add E, F, G, H preparation, and stir-fry 1 minute.
4. Add I, J, K, L, M, N and stir-fry thoroughly for 2 minutes. Add O, cover, and cook 3 minutes. Add P and mix well. Add Q, R, S, T preparation, stir thoroughly until gravy thickens and is smooth.

Serves 2 or 3.

SERVING, FAMILY STYLE

Place the chow mein gravy in a large bowl in the center of the dining table; use a smaller dish for the ham, almonds and eggs. Use a large deep dish for the noodles. Put some of the noodles on each plate, and pour some chow mein gravy and vegetables over them. Then put some egg, almonds and ham on top of each serving. *Note:* This is the basic subgum chow mein recipe. You may substitute for the pork: chicken, turkey, beef, veal, lamb, lobster, shrimp or crabmeat. If beef, lobster, shrimp or crabmeat is used, less cooking time is required. When different kinds of meat or seafood are used the name of the dish changes accordingly. Other variations of this dish may be obtained by using walnuts, pineapple, more almonds or more mushrooms.

CHOP SUEY

189. PORK CHOP SUEY (*Gee Dep Suey*)

BASIC RECIPE

A. 1 tablespoon peanut oil
B. 1 teaspoon salt
C. 1 clove garlic, crushed
D. 1 cup raw lean pork, cut in thin slivers
E. 1 cup Chinese cabbage (white part only), sliced thin
F. 1 cup celery (tender part only), sliced thin
G. 3 cups bean sprouts
H. 1 cup onion, sliced thin
I. 1 teaspoon light soy sauce
J. 1 teaspoon rice wine or 2 tablespoons sherry wine
K. a few drops of sesame oil
L. ½ cup soup stock
M. 1 tablespoon cornstarch
N. 1 teaspoon seasoning powder
O. 1 teaspoon sugar
P. 1 teaspoon heavy soy sauce
Q. dash of pepper

PREPARATION

Mix I, J, K together; add 1 tablespoon water. Stir up well before using. Mix M, N, O, P, Q together with ½ cup water. Stir up well before using.

COOKING

1. Put A in hot skillet, add B, C.
2. Add D. Stir-fry 2 minutes.
3. Add E, F, G, H. Stir-fry 2 minutes.
4. Add I, J, K preparation. Stir thoroughly 1 minute.

5. Add L. Cover and cook 3 minutes.
6. Add M, N, O, P, Q preparation. Stir thoroughly until gravy thickens and is smooth.

Serves 2.

Note: One cup beef, veal, lamb, shrimp, crabmeat or lobster may be used instead of pork.

190. MUSHROOM CHOP SUEY (*Moo-Koo Dep Suey*)

Follow basic recipe No. 189. Add ¼ cup sliced white mushrooms to vegetables.

191. TOMATO CHOP SUEY (*Fan-Ghar Dep Suey*)

Follow basic recipe No. 189. Add 1 or 2 medium tomatoes, cut into 6 or 7 pieces, to vegetables.

192. GREEN PEPPER CHOP SUEY
(*Lard-Dew Dep Suey*)

Follow basic recipe No. 189. Add 1 large sliced green pepper to vegetables.

193. PINEAPPLE CHOP SUEY (*Boo-Loo Dep Suey*)

Follow basic recipe No. 189. Add 1 cup sliced pineapple to vegetables.

194. VEGETABLE CHOP SUEY (*Qur-Toy Dep Suey*)

Follow basic recipe No. 189. Add ¼ cup sliced water chestnuts, ¼ cup sliced bamboo shoots, ¼ cup sliced mushrooms, and 1 cup of one or more kinds of the following vegetables: green pepper, tomatoes, broccoli, asparagus, cauliflower, mustard greens, string beans or pea pods. Add same time as other vegetables.

195. CHICAGO CHOP SUEY (*Che-Ka-Go Dep Suey*)

Follow basic recipe No. 189. Add ¼ cup white mushrooms, ¼ cup black mushrooms, ¼ cup bamboo shoots, ¼ cup water chestnuts to other vegetables. Add 1 teaspoon extra heavy soy sauce to corn-starch mixture.

196. FINE CUT CHOP SUEY (*You-Sai Dep Suey*)

Follow basic recipe No. 189. Add vegetables listed in recipe No. 194, shredding very fine, instead of slicing them. To these add ¼ cup white mushrooms, ¼ cup bamboo shoots and ¼ cup water chestnuts, cut very fine.

197. SUBGUM PORK CHOP SUEY
(*Subgum Gee Dep Suey*)

A. 1 tablespoon peanut oil
B. 1 teaspoon salt
C. 1 clove garlic, crushed
D. 1 cup raw lean pork, diced
E. 1 cup celery, cut fine
F. 1 cup onion, cut fine
G. 1 cup Chinese cabbage (white part only), cut fine
H. 1 cup bamboo shoots, cut fine
I. 1 cup white mushrooms, cut fine
J. ½ cup water chestnuts, peeled and cut fine
K. ½ cup green peppers, cut fine
L. ½ cup tomatoes, cut larger
M. ½ cup pea pods (broccoli, string beans, asparagus, carrots or peas may be substituted) cut fine
N. 2 tablespoons water
O. 1 teaspoon light soy sauce
P. 1 teaspoon rice wine or 2 tablespoons sherry wine
Q. dash of pepper
R. a few drops sesame seed oil
S. ½ cup soup stock
T. 1 tablespoon cornstarch
U. 1 teaspoon seasoning powder
V. 1 teaspoon sugar
W. 1 teaspoon heavy soy sauce

PREPARATION

Mix N, O, P, Q, R. Stir up well before using. Mix T, U, V, W and add ½ cup water. Stir up well before using.

COOKING

1. Put A in hot skillet, add B, C.
2. Add D. Stir-fry 2½ minutes.
3. Add E, F, G, H, I, J, K, L, M. Stir-fry thoroughly 3 minutes.
4. Add N, O, P, Q, R preparation. Stir thoroughly 1 minute.
5. Add S. Cover and cook 3 minutes.
6. Add T, U, V, W preparation. Stir-fry until gravy thickens and is smooth.

Note: One cup chicken, duck, beef, veal, lamb, lobster, shrimp, crabmeat or scallops may be used instead of pork.

198. CHICKEN CHOP SUEY (*Guy Dep Suey*)

A. 1 tablespoon peanut oil or lard
B. ½ teaspoon salt
C. 1 clove garlic, mashed
D. 1 cup chicken meat, cut in thin slivers
E. ½ cup lean raw pork, cut in thin slivers
F. 1 teaspoon light soy sauce
G. 1 teaspoon rice wine
H. ½ teaspoon fresh ginger root, shredded very fine
I. 1 cup celery, sliced thin
J. 1 cup bamboo shoots, sliced thin
K. 1 cup mushrooms, sliced thin
L. ¼ cup fresh or canned water chestnuts, sliced
M. 1 cup fresh Chinese cabbage (white part preferred), sliced thin
N. 1 cup soup stock
O. 1 tablespoon cornstarch
P. 1 teaspoon heavy soy sauce
Q. 1 teaspoon seasoning powder
R. dash of pepper
S. 1 teaspoon sugar

PREPARATION

Mix F, G, H together. Add 1 tablespoon water. Stir up well before using. Mix O, P, Q, R, S together. Add ½ cup water. Stir up well before using.

COOKING

1. Put A in very hot skillet. Add B and C.
2. Add D and E. Stir-fry 2 minutes, or until light brown.
3. Add F, G, H preparation. Stir-fry thoroughly 1 minute.
4. Add I, J, K, L, M. Stir-fry 3 minutes.
5. Add N. Cover and cook 2 minutes.
6. Add O, P, Q, R, S. Stir-fry until gravy thickens and is smooth. Serve with boiled rice.

Serves 2.

199. CHICKEN GIBLET CHOP SUEY
(*Guy-Foo Chee Dep Suey*)

Use same method and ingredients as in recipe No. 198. Eliminate chicken meat. Use one or more sets of chicken giblets, sliced very thin.

Note: One cup of pea pods, broccoli, asparagus, celery or cabbage may be added to any kind of chop suey. Other variations may be obtained by substituting for the chicken: turkey, duck, beef, veal, lamb, fish, lobster, shrimp or crabmeat. One cup of walnuts, almonds, pineapple or fungus may also be added.

CHICKEN

---

200. STIR-FRY BALL CHICKEN WITH ASSORTED VEGETABLES (*Chow Guy Kew*)

A. 1 tablespoon peanut oil
B. 1 teaspoon salt
C. 1 clove garlic, mashed
D. 1 lb. chicken white meat, sliced very thin, about 2½ to 3 inches square (the thinner it is sliced, the easier it will form into balls)
E. ¼ lb. lean fresh pork, sliced very thin (optional)
F. 1 teaspoon light soy sauce
G. 1 teaspoon rice wine
H. 1 teaspoon fresh ginger, shredded very fine
I. 1 cup pea pods, cut in halves crosswise
J. 1 cup bamboo shoots, sliced thin
K. ½ cup black or white mushrooms, sliced thin
L. 1 cup Chinese cabbage, sliced about same size as pea pods
M. 1 cup celery, sliced thin
N. ¼ cup fresh or canned water chestnuts, peeled and sliced thin
O. ½ cup onions, sliced
P. 1 green scallion, split in half, in 1 inch long pieces
Q. 1 cup soup stock
R. 1 teaspoon heavy soy sauce
S. 1 tablespoon cornstarch
T. 1 teaspoon seasoning powder
U. 1 teaspoon sugar
V. dash pepper

PREPARATION

Mix F, G, H. Add 1 tablespoon water. Stir well before using. Mix R, S, T, U, V. Add ½ cup water. Stir well before using.

COOKING

1. Put A in hot skillet over high heat.
2. Add B and C.
3. Add D, E. Stir-fry 3 minutes, or until meat rolls up like a ball. Add F, G, H preparation and stir-fry thoroughly about 1 minute.
4. Add I, J, K, L, M, N, O. Stir-fry thoroughly 3 minutes.
5. Add P.
6. Add Q. Cover and cook 5 minutes.
7. Add R, S, T, U, V preparation, and cook until gravy thickens and is smooth.

   Serve with rice.

Serves 2 or 3.

201. STIR-FRY BALL CHICKEN WITH STRAW OR GRASS MUSHROOMS (*Tao-Koo Guy Kew*)

Use same method and ingredients as in recipe No. 200, using straw mushrooms instead of black or white mushrooms. Clean straw mushrooms by soaking them in 1 pint of hot water about 15 minutes. Rinse again and again until all the sand is gone, then drain with cheese cloth. Save the water for soup stock when cooking.

202. STIR-FRY BALL CHICKEN WITH PINEAPPLE (*Boo-Loo Guy Kew*)

Use same method and ingredients as in recipe No. 200. Add 1 cup canned sliced pineapple to vegetables.

203. STIR-FRY BALL CHICKEN WITH LICHEE (*Lichee Guy Kew*)

Use same method and ingredients as in recipe No. 200. Add 1 cup canned lichee to vegetables.

204. STIR-FRY BONELESS CHICKEN IN BATTER WITH ASSORTED VEGETABLES (*Wat Guy Kew*)

A. 1 lb. chicken meat, cut into 1 inch cubes
B. 3 teaspoons rice wine
C. 2 teaspoons sugar
D. ½ teaspoon fresh ginger, shredded very fine
E. few drops of sesame seed oil
F. 3 teaspoons light soy sauce
G. 2 eggs, beaten
H. ¾ cup flour
I. 1 tablespoon peanut oil
J. ¾ teaspoon salt
K. 1 clove garlic, mashed
L. 1 cup fresh Chinese pea pods
M. 1 cup Chinese cabbage, sliced about 1 inch long
N. 1 cup bamboo shoots, sliced same size as cabbage
O. 2 tablespoons fresh water chestnuts, peeled and sliced
P. ¼ cup black or white mushrooms, sliced
Q. 1 cup soup stock
R. 1 teaspoon heavy soy sauce
S. 1 tablespoon cornstarch
T. 1½ teaspoons seasoning powder
U. dash of pepper

PREPARATION

Mix B, C, D, E, F together; divide into 2 equal parts. Mix G, H; add a pinch salt and ½ teaspoon T. Mix R, S, remaining T, U; add ½ cup water. Stir well before using. Soak A in half the B, C, D, E, F preparation for 30 minutes or longer.

COOKING

1. Beat G, H preparation. Have hot deep fat ready. Dip pieces of chicken in batter and fry in hot oil until golden brown.
2. Put I in very hot skillet. Add J and K.
3. Add L, M, N, O, P. Stir-fry 2 minutes. Add other half of B, C, D, E, F preparation and stir thoroughly.
4. Add Q. Cover and cook 5 minutes.
5. Add R, S, T, U preparation. Stir-fry until gravy thickens and is smooth. Remove from skillet and put in bowl or deep plate.
6. Put prepared chicken on top of mixture, and garnish with parsley.

205. FRIED BONELESS CHICKEN IN BATTER, KIM MON STYLE (*Kim Mon Guy*)

A. 1 fresh-killed chicken, 5 to 6 lbs.; split breast, remove intestines, clean and dice giblet and heart
B. 2 tablespoons light soy sauce
C. 2 tablespoons rice wine
D. 1 teaspoon fresh ginger root, crushed
E. 2 teaspoons sugar
F. 2 teaspoons seasoning powder
G. ½ teaspoon sesame seed oil
H. 1 teaspoon garlic powder
I. 2 eggs, beaten
J. ½ cup water chestnut flour
K. ½ cup all purpose flour
L. 1 tablespoon cornstarch
M. ½ teaspoon heavy soy sauce
N. dash of pepper
O. 1 head lettuce
P. 1 tablespoon peanut oil or lard
Q. ½ teaspoon salt
R. 1 clove garlic, crushed
S. 1 cup Chinese black mushrooms, soaked in warm water 15 minutes and then shredded
T. 1 cup bamboo shoots, shredded
U. 1 cup pea pods, shredded
V. ½ cup water chestnuts, peeled and sliced
W. 1 cup celery, shredded about same size as mushrooms and bamboo shoots
X. ¾ cup soup stock
Y. ½ cup chopped parsley

PREPARATION

Bone A. Cut meat into pieces about 1 inch by 2 inches. Mix B, C, D, E, F, G, H. Stir well; then divide into 2 equal parts. Soak A in half of mixture 30 minutes or more. Remove ginger. Mix I, J, K, and beat to a smooth paste (add a pinch of salt, pepper and seasoning powder). Mix L, M, N; add ½ cup water. Stir up well before using.

COOKING

1. Use a fork or chop stick; pick chicken pieces up one by one and dip in I, J, K preparation. Fry in deep fat until golden brown. Place in deep plate lined with O.

2. Put P in very hot skillet; add Q and R.
3. Add S, T, U, V, W and diced giblets. Stir-fry 2 minutes.
4. Add second half of B, C, D, E, F, G, H mixture; stir thoroughly about 1 minute.
5. Add X. Cover and cook 2 minutes.
6. Add L, M, N preparation. Stir until gravy thickens and is smooth. Pour over chicken; garnish with Y.

Serves 4.

206. FRIED BONELESS CHICKEN WITH MIXED NUTS IN BATTER (*Ng Yen Soo Guy*)

A. 1 fresh-killed chicken, 4 to 5 lbs., washed and cleaned, skinned and boned; cut chicken into 4 parts (save giblets and heart for another dish)
B. 2 tablespoons light soy sauce
C. 1 teaspoon sugar
D. 1 tablespoon rice wine
E. 1 teaspoon fresh ginger
F. 1 teaspoon sweet vegetable sauce
G. 1 teaspoon heavy soy sauce
H. ¾ teaspoon salt
I. 1 teaspoon garlic powder
J. few drops sesame seed oil
K. 3 eggs, beaten
L. ½ cup water chestnut flour
M. ½ cup all purpose flour
N. 1 cup mixed nuts, roasted, crushed almost powderlike
O. 1 head lettuce
P. 1 cup chopped parsley
Q. 1 piece of lemon
R. sliced tomatoes

PREPARATION AND COOKING

Mix B, C, D, E, F, G, H, I, J. Beat up K, L, M, then add N; mix together thoroughly. Soak A in B, C, D, E, F, G, H, I, J preparation for 30 minutes or more. Remove and dip chicken in batter mixture, and fry in deep fat until golden brown. Line a deep plate with O. Put chicken in plate and garnish with P, Q, R.

Serves 4.

207. SWEET AND SOUR CHICKEN
(*Tiem-Shoon Guy Kew*)

A. 1 lb. chicken meat, cut in 1 inch cubes
B. 1 teaspoon light soy sauce
C. 1 teaspoon seasoning powder
D. ¼ teaspoon salt
E. ½ cup flour
F. 2 eggs, well beaten
G. ½ cup vinegar
H. ½ cup sugar
I. 2 cups mixed sweet pickles, sliced or cut into cubes
J. 1 tablespoon cornstarch

PREPARATION

Mix B, C, D together. Let A soak in this preparation for 10 to 15 minutes. Mix E, F together to form a smooth paste. Add ½ cup water to J. Stir well before using.

COOKING

1. Remove chicken from B, C, D and dip in batter E, F. Fry in deep fat or peanut oil until golden brown, and put aside.
2. Put G in hot skillet. Add ½ cup water.
3. Add H, and cook until sugar dissolves.
4. Add fried chicken meat and I and mix thoroughly.
5. Add cornstarch preparation, and stir thoroughly until gravy thickens and is smooth.

   Serve hot with rice.

Serves 2.

208. CHICKEN SAUTE WITH OYSTER SAUCE
(*Hoo-Yu Guy Lok*)

A. 2 tablespoons peanut oil
B. 1 teaspoon salt
C. 2 cloves garlic, mashed
D. 1 to 2½ lbs. spring chicken or broiler, cut through the bone into small pieces about 1 by 1½ inches
E. 2 tablespoons oyster sauce
F. 2 teaspoons light soy sauce

G. 1 teaspoon rice wine
H. 1 teaspoon fresh ginger, shredded very fine
I. 1 cup soup stock
J. 2 green scallions, split and cut into pieces about 1 inch long
K. 1 teaspoon sugar
L. 1 tablespoon cornstarch
M. 1 teaspoon heavy soy sauce
N. 1 teaspoon seasoning powder

PREPARATION

Mix E, F, G, H. Add 1 tablespoon water. Stir well before using. Mix K, L, M, N, and add 4 tablespoons water. Stir well before using.

COOKING

1. Put A in very hot skillet over high heat. Add B and C.
2. Add D and stir-fry 5 minutes or until golden brown.
3. Add E, F, G, H preparation, and stir-fry thoroughly about 2 minutes.
4. Add I. Cover, lower heat and cook until tender. Add more soup stock if necessary.
5. Add J and K, L, M, N preparation. Stir-fry until gravy thickens and is smooth.
   Serve with boiled rice.

Serves 2 or 3.

209. TOMATO CATSUP CHICKEN SAUTE
(*Fon-Kar Guy Lok*)

Use same method and ingredients as in recipe No. 208. Add 2 tablespoons tomato catsup to oyster sauce preparation.

210. CURRY CHICKEN SAUTE (*Kar-Le Guy Lok*)

Use same method and ingredients as in recipe No. 208. Add 2 tablespoons curry powder to oyster sauce preparation.

211. CHICKEN SAUTE WITH BLACK BEAN SAUCE
(*Dow-Shee Guy Lok*)

Use same method and ingredients as in recipe No. 208. Add 1 tablespoon mashed black beans to oyster sauce preparation.

212. CHICKEN SAUTE WITH THREE KINDS OF MUSHROOMS (*Sam-Koo Guy Lok*)

Use same method and ingredients as in recipe No. 208. Add the following same time as soup stock: ¼ cup sliced white mushrooms, ¼ cup sliced black mushrooms (soaked in water 15 minutes before slicing) and ¼ cup straw mushrooms. The straw mushrooms should be washed first with cold water, then put in bowl of warm water; rinse until all sand is gone, then drain with cheese cloth. Save the warm water for soup stock.

213. BOILED BONELESS CHICKEN, YOKE LING STYLE (*Yoke Ling Guy*)

A. 1 chicken, 5 to 6 lbs.
B. 3 or 4 stalks broccoli (clean and use tender part only)
C. 1½ cups milk or cream
D. 2 tablespoons butter
E. 1 teaspoon seasoning powder
F. ½ teaspoon rice wine
G. 1 teaspoon sugar
H. ½ teaspoon salt
I. 1 tablespoon cornstarch

COOKING

1. Boil A in pressure cooker 15° about 20 minutes.
2. Boil B (uncovered) 3 minutes and drain.
3. Heat C; add D, E, F, G, H.
4. Mix I with ¼ cup water, and add to milk mixture, stirring until smooth.
5. Bone and slice A and spread on dinner plate, garnish all around with broccoli.

6. Pour cornstarch mixture over chicken and serve immediately.
Serves 4.

Note: This makes an excellent main dish for a formal dinner or party. If you have no pressure cooker, use a large pot and cook chicken 45 minutes.

214. BONELESS CHICKEN GARNISHED WITH 100 FLOWERS (*Bok Far Guy*)

Use same method and ingredients as in recipe No. 213. Garnish with cooked cauliflower, broccoli, asparagus tips, raw carrots, cucumbers and tomatoes cut in flower-like shapes and placed around the chicken. Several kinds of real flowers, such as white roses, yellow or white chrysanthemums and white lilies, may also be used.

215. BONELESS CHICKEN WITH CREAM SAUCE (*Ni Lo Guy*)

Use same method and ingredients as in recipe No. 213. Dice the chicken meat and garnish with lettuce. Sprinkle with finely cut or chopped Virginia ham and cooked fresh peas.

216. FRIED BONELESS CHICKEN WITH STRIPS OF BACON (*Wor Hep Guy*)

A. 2 lbs. chicken meat, cut in 1 inch cubes
B. 1 teaspoon salt
C. 1 tablespoon light soy sauce
D. 1 teaspoon seasoning powder
E. 1 teaspoon rice wine
F. 1 tablespoon sweet vegetable sauce
G. few drops of sesame oil
H. ¾ cup all purpose flour
I. 2 eggs, beaten
J. 1 lb. sliced bacon

PREPARATION AND COOKING

Mix B, C, D, E, F, G together in a bowl. Soak A in this preparation for 15 minutes or more; turn chicken frequently. Blend H, I together to form a smooth paste. Wrap A, piece by piece, in strips of J. Dip bacon-wrapped chicken in batter mixture. Fry in deep oil until golden brown. Garnish with sliced tomatoes.

Serves 3 or 4.

217. PAPER-WRAPPED CHICKEN (*Gee Bow Guy*)

A. 1½ lbs. chicken meat, cut into 1 inch cubes
B. 4 tablespoons light soy sauce
C. 1 teaspoon heavy soy sauce
D. 1 teaspoon sugar
E. 1 teaspoon seasoning powder
F. 2 teaspoons Chinese sweet vegetable sauce
G. ½ teaspoon salt
H. dash pepper
I. ½ teaspoon prepared mustard or curry powder
J. ½ teaspoon garlic powder
K. few drops sesame seed oil
L. 1 teaspoon rice wine
M. 1 doz. fresh scallions (white part only), split in halves and cut into pieces about 1 to 1½ inches long

PREPARATION AND COOKING

Blend together B, C, D, E, F, G, H, I, J, K, L. Soak A in this preparation for 30 minutes to 1 hour, or more. Cut wax paper into 4 inch squares. Place a piece of chicken and piece of scallion in middle of piece of wax paper. Fold the side nearest you. Fold left-hand side, then right-hand side. Roll upper part toward you, and tuck between both sides of paper. Fry wrapped chicken in deep hot peanut oil about 10 minutes. Drain and serve in hot plate.

Serves 3.

218. FRIED CHICKEN, CHINESE STYLE (*Jow Guy*)

A. 1 chicken, 4 to 6 lbs., cleaned and dried
B. ½ cup light soy sauce

c. 1 tablespoon brown bean sauce
D. 1 teaspoon sugar
E. 1 teaspoon rice wine
F. 1 teaspoon fresh ginger, shredded very fine
G. 1 clove garlic, crushed
H. dash pepper
I. 1 teaspoon salt

PREPARATION

Mix B, C, D, E, F, G, H, I. Cut A in half. Put prepared mixture on both halves, inside and out, and let soak an hour or more.

COOKING

1. Steam prepared A in double boiler about 30 minutes, or until tender. Cool.
2. Fry chicken in deep peanut oil until golden brown, cut each half into 3 pieces.
   Serve with fried potatoes or boiled rice.

Serves 4.

219. FRIED BONELESS CHICKEN, CHINESE STYLE
(*Char Doo Guy*)

Use the same method and ingredients as in recipe No. 218. Cook chicken until tender; remove bones carefully. Roll pieces of chicken in a batter made of 2 eggs, well beaten; ¾ cup cornstarch or flour (to form a paste); and a pinch of salt and seasoning powder. Fry chicken in deep oil until golden brown.

220. ROAST CHICKEN, CHINESE STYLE
(*Kook Chun Guy*)

A. 1 chicken, 4 to 6 lbs., cleaned and dried
B. 1 teaspoon seasoning powder
c. 1 teaspoon heavy soy sauce
D. 1 teaspoon dried tangerine peel, chopped
E. 1 teaspoon sweet vegetable sauce or brown bean sauce
F. 2 cups soup stock

PREPARATION AND COOKING

Mix B, C, D, E, F. Tie chicken's neck with a string, then put the mixture into the chicken, and truss. Brush the skin with light soy sauce. Roast in oven at 450° for 10 minutes, then at 300° for 25 minutes.

221. BOILED CHICKEN WITH SOY SAUCE
(*Bok You Guy*)

A. 1 spring chicken, about 3 to 4 lbs., cleaned and dried
B. 1 qt. light soy sauce
C. 1 tablespoon peanut oil
D. 1 teaspoon sesame seed oil

PREPARATION AND COOKING

Put A in B and let soak overnight. Brush thoroughly with C, D. Put chicken in double boiler and steam 25 minutes, or until tender; or roast in oven until tender.

Serves 3.

222. ROAST CHICKEN WITH FIVE KINDS OF SAUCES (*Eng Ding Guy*)

A. 1 fresh-killed chicken, 3 to 5 lbs., cleaned and dried
B. 3 tablespoons light soy sauce
C. 1 teaspoon heavy soy sauce
D. ½ cup brown bean sauce, mashed very fine
E. 1 tablespoon sweet vegetable sauce
F. 1 teaspoon Chinese hot sauce
G. 1 tablespoon duck sauce
H. 1 teaspoon garlic powder
I. dash pepper
J. 1 teaspoon fresh ginger, shredded very fine
K. 1 tablespoon rice wine
L. 1 tablespoon sugar or honey
M. ½ teaspoon salt
N. 1 teaspoon dried tangerine peel, soaked in warm water 10 to 35 minutes, cleaned, shredded very fine
O. 1½ cups soup stock or water

PREPARATION AND COOKING

Mix B, C, D, E, F, G, H, I, J, K, L, M, N and blend well. Rub some of the prepared mixture on the chicken's skin. Add water or soup stock to the remainder and fill inside of chicken. Truss chicken so that the mixture cannot leak out. Roast in moderate oven 350° for 30 minutes, or until tender. Use juice in chicken as sauce when serving.

Serves 3.

223. FRIED BONELESS CHICKEN, SWEET SAUCE
(*Wor Shu Guy*)

A. ½ of 5-lb. chicken, cooked in double boiler 30 minutes
B. 1 egg, beaten
C. ½ cup flour
D. ½ teaspoon salt
E. 1 teaspoon cornstarch
F. 1 teaspoon heavy soy sauce
G. 1 tablespoon light soy sauce
H. 1 tablespoon sugar or honey
I. 1 teaspoon seasoning powder
J. ¼ cup mixed nuts (almonds, walnuts, pecans, peanuts), cracked into small pieces

PREPARATION

Remove all bones from A (disjoint or use whole). Mix B, C, D together. Add ½ cup water to E. Mix F, G, H, I. Add 1 tablespoon water; stir well before using.

COOKING

1. Put about ½ inch of oil in a pan and heat. Roll A in B, C, D preparation and fry in hot oil until golden brown all over.
2. Put cornstarch mixture in another pan and cook until smooth and thick. Add F, G, H, I preparation. Mix well.
3. Place fried chicken on an oval-shaped plate, and pour sauce over it. Add J and serve.

Serves 2.

224. FRIED CHICKEN WITH DRIED LILIES
(*Gum Toy Wat Guy*)

A. 2 tablespoons peanut oil
B. 1 teaspoon salt
C. 1 clove garlic, mashed
D. half spring chicken
E. 1 tablespoon light soy sauce
F. 2 teaspoons rice wine
G. 1 teaspoon fresh ginger, shredded very fine
H. 1 teaspoon seasoning powder
I. dash of pepper
J. ½ cup pork (use pork butt), shredded fine
K. 1 oz. dried lilies, soaked in warm water 10 to 15 minutes, and squeezed dry
L. ½ cup black mushrooms, soaked in warm water 5 minutes and sliced
M. ½ doz. dried red dates, soaked in warm water 15 minutes, stones removed, sliced
N. ¾ cup soup stock

PREPARATION

Mix E, F, G, H, I together with 1 tablespoon water; stir up well before using. Put J in prepared mixture.

COOKING

1. Put A in hot skillet. Add B and C.
2. Drop D in hot oil and fry, over moderate heat, skin side down until brown. Turn over and fry the other side 2 to 3 minutes.
3. Add prepared pork and cook 2 minutes.
4. Add K, L, M.
5. Add N. Cover and cook 10 minutes, or until tender.
   Serve with boiled rice.

Serves 1.

225. CHICKEN STUFFED WITH GLUTINOUS RICE
(*Noo-Mei Guy*)

A. 1 spring chicken, about 4 to 5 lbs., cleaned
B. 2 cups glutinous rice, washed, soaked in water 10 hours or more

c. ¼ cup Virginia ham, chopped very fine
d. ½ cup white or black mushrooms, chopped very fine (black mushrooms must be soaked in warm water 15 minutes)
e. 1 cup Chinese sausage (about 1 pair), chopped very fine
f. ¼ cup chestnuts, peeled, cooked until tender, chopped very fine
g. ¼ cup walnut meats, roasted, chopped very fine
h. 1 teaspoon seasoning powder
i. 1 teaspoon rice wine
j. 1 teaspoon sugar
k. 2 tablespoons scallions, chopped very fine
l. 2 teaspoons salt (garlic salt is best)
m. 1 tablespoon light soy sauce
n. 2 tablespoons Chinese parsley, chopped

PREPARATION

Open up A. Cut through the breast. Flatten chicken. Clean the giblets. Mix B, C, D, E, F, G, H, I, J, K. Add 1 teaspoon salt. Mix together in a large bowl. Add ½ cup water. Remove some of white breast meat from chicken and chop up with giblets. Add to mixture.

COOKING

1. Put prepared mixture in a bowl on a rack in a large pot with about 3 inches boiling water. Cover. Steam 50 minutes. Add water if necessary, and lower heat.
2. Mix L, M together. Brush all over chicken.
3. Put chicken on top of mixture. Cover. Steam another 45 minutes. Turn off heat but cover to keep rice hot.
4. Take chicken out; bone when cool.
5. Fry chicken in deep oil, about 400°, until skin is crisp and golden brown. Then chop up to any size you wish. Put on top of rice. Garnish with N.

Serves 4.

Note: This is an excellent cold-weather dish for a large party or banquet.

226. CHICKEN STUFFED WITH BIRD'S NEST
(*Yen-Wor Chun Guy*)

A. 1 spring chicken, about 3½ to 4½ lbs. (wash, clean, slit back, remove all intestines, save giblets for other dishes)
B. ¼ lb. bird's nest (soak in cold water for 30 minutes, then drain. Put in about 4 or 5 cups pure cold water and boil 30 minutes. Rinse in cold water. Clean out all black bits of feathers)
C. ½ cup raw Virginia ham, chopped very fine
D. ¼ cup water chestnuts, peeled and chopped very fine
E. 1 teaspoon seasoning powder
F. 1 tablespoon rose or rice wine
G. 1 teaspoon salt
H. 5 cups super soup stock

PREPARATION AND COOKING

Mix B, C, D, E, F, G. Stuff prepared mixture inside A. Put chicken in a large bowl or pot. Add H. Place bowl on rack in large pot containing 4 inches boiling water. Cover and steam over low heat 2 to 3 hours, until chicken is tender. Add more boiling water to pot, if necessary.

Serves 4.

Note: Birds' Nests are found on the Malayan Archipelago in the Pacific Ocean. A certain kind of swallow catches fish during the summer and stores the best part in its nest for its young to eat during the winter. The bird also digests a certain kind of marine plant which is transformed into a gelatinous matter with which it makes its nest. In the fall the natives of the island collect the nests and sell them to Chinese merchants, who bring them back to the mainland. It has been found that the nests contain rich vitamins and nourishment, so that in China swallow birds' nests are considered one of the most nutritious and delicious foods. They are, of course, very expensive, so that besides being a delicacy it is a rare dish.

227. DICED CUT CHICKEN MEAT WITH ALMONDS
(*Hon-Yen Guy Din*)

BASIC RECIPE

A. 1 tablespoon peanut oil
B. ½ teaspoon salt
C. 1 clove garlic, mashed
D. 1½ cups white chicken meat, diced
E. ½ cup raw lean pork, diced
F. 1 teaspoon light soy sauce
G. 1 teaspoon fresh ginger root, shredded very fine
H. 1 teaspoon rice wine
I. 1 cup bamboo shoots, diced
J. 1 cup mushrooms (French or Chinese black mushrooms), diced
K. 1 cup Chinese cabbage (white part only), diced
L. 1 cup celery, diced
M. 1 cup onion, diced
N. 1 cup soup stock
O. 1 tablespoon cornstarch
P. 1 teaspoon seasoning powder
Q. 1 teaspoon heavy soy sauce
R. 1 teaspoon sugar
S. ½ cup roast almonds

PREPARATION

Mix F, G, H together. Add 1 teaspoon water. Stir up well before using. Mix O, P, Q, R and add ½ cup water. Stir up well before using.

COOKING

1. Put A in very hot skillet. Add B and C.
2. Add D, E. Stir-fry until light brown. Add preparation F, G, H.
3. Add I, J, K, L, M. Stir-fry 3 minutes, stirring constantly.
4. Add N. Cover and cook 5 minutes.
5. Add preparation O, P, Q, R. Stir-fry until gravy thickens and is smooth. Add S.

Serve with boiled rice.

Serves 3.

Note: When black mushrooms are used, soak them in warm water for 10 to 15 minutes before dicing. Turkey, beef, roast pork, veal or lamb may be substituted for chicken; the name of the dish changes accordingly: Diced Cut Turkey with Almonds, or Diced Cut Beef with Almonds, etc.

228. DICED CUT CHICKEN MEAT WITH WALNUTS
(*Hop-Ho Guy Din*)

Follow basic recipe No. 227, using walnuts instead of almonds.

229. DICED CUT CHICKEN MEAT WITH PEAS
(*Ching-Dow Guy Din*)

Follow basic recipe No. 227, adding 1 cup frozen peas to vegetables. Peas should be cooked in boiling water 2 minutes, then rinsed with cold water and drained.

230. DICED CUT CHICKEN GIBLETS
(*Guy Foo-Chee Din*)

Follow basic recipe No. 227, using 1 set of chicken giblets (heart, liver and gizzard), cleaned and diced; 1 cup diced lean raw pork instead of chicken meat.

231. DICED CUT CHICKEN MEAT WITH
PINEAPPLE (*Boo-Lo Guy Din*)

Follow basic recipe No. 227, adding 1 cup each frozen peas and pineapple, diced, to vegetables.

232. DICED CUT CHICKEN WITH OLIVE PIT MEAT
(*Lom-Yen Guy Din*)

Follow basic recipe No. 227, adding 1 cup olive pit meat. (Boil olive pit meat for 15 minutes. Rinse in cold water. Peel off skin and fry in deep fat until light brown. (Olive pit meat may be purchased in any Chinese grocery store in Chinatown.)

233. DICED CUT CHICKEN WITH ASSORTED VEGETABLES (*Qur-Toy Guy Din*)

Follow basic recipe No. 227, adding 1 cup each diced cut pea pods, string beans and broccoli.

234. CHICKEN MEAT WITH SUBGUM (*Subgum Guy Pan*)

A. 1 tablespoon peanut oil or lard
B. 1 teaspoon salt
C. 1 clove garlic
D. 1 lb. chicken meat (fresh-killed), cut in thin slivers
E. ½ cup fresh lean pork, cut in thin slivers
F. 2 teaspoons light soy sauce
G. 1 teaspoon rice wine
H. 1 teaspoon fresh ginger, shredded very fine
I. 2 fresh tomatoes, medium size, cut in wedges (about 8 pieces each)
J. 2 green peppers, small size. Remove seeds and cut in wedges (about 10 pieces each)
K. 1 cup celery, sliced
L. 1 cup onions, sliced (or in wedges)
M. 1 cup Chinese cabbage, sliced
N. 1 cup snow pea pods
O. ¼ cup water chestnuts, peeled and sliced
P. ½ cup bamboo shoots, sliced
Q. ½ cup black or white mushrooms, sliced
R. 1 cup soup stock
S. 1 tablespoon cornstarch
T. 1 teaspoon sugar
U. 1 teaspoon seasoning powder
V. 1 teaspoon heavy soy sauce
W. dash of pepper

PREPARATION

Mix F, G, H and 1 tablespoon of water together. Stir well before using. Mix S, T, U, V, W and add ½ cup water. Stir well before using.

COOKING

1. Put A in hot skillet.
2. Add B, C.
3. Add D, E. Stir-fry 2 minutes, until meat is light brown.
4. Add F, G, H preparation. Stir-fry 1 minute.
5. Add I, J, K, L, M, N, O, P, Q and stir-fry thoroughly 3 minutes.
6. Add R. Cover and cook 5 minutes.
7. Add S, T, U, V, W preparation; stir thoroughly until gravy thickens and is smooth.
Serve with boiled rice.

Serves 2.

235. CHICKEN MEAT WITH ASSORTED VEGETABLES AND MUSHROOMS
(*Chow Moo-Koo Guy Pan*)

BASIC RECIPE

A. 1 tablespoon peanut oil
B. ½ teaspoon salt
C. 1 clove garlic, mashed
D. 1 lb. raw chicken meat (fresh-killed), sliced thin
E. ¼ cup fresh lean pork, sliced very thin (optional)
F. 1 tablespoon light soy sauce
G. 1 teaspoon rice wine
H. 1 teaspoon sugar
I. dash of pepper
J. few drops of sesame seed oil
K. 1 cup Chinese fresh cabbage, sliced
L. 1 cup celery, sliced thin
M. ½ cup bamboo shoots, sliced
N. ¼ cup water chestnuts, peeled and sliced thin
O. ½ cup black or white mushrooms, sliced thin

P. 1 cup soup stock
Q. 1 tablespoon cornstarch
R. 1 teaspoon seasoning powder
S. 1 teaspoon heavy soy sauce

PREPARATION

Mix F, G, H, I, J together. Stir well before using. Mix Q, R, S and ½ cup cold water together. Stir well before using.

COOKING

1. Put A in very hot skillet. Add B and C.
2. Add D, E and stir-fry until pieces of meat are brown. Then add F, G, H, I, J preparation.
3. Add K, L, M, N, O and stir-fry thoroughly about 3 minutes.
4. Add P. Cover and cook 2 minutes.
5. Add Q, R, S preparation and stir-fry until gravy thickens and is smooth.

Serves 2 or 3.

236. CHICKEN MEAT WITH SNOW PEA PODS
(*Sheet-Dow Guy Pan*)

Use basic recipe No. 235, adding 1½ cups snow pea pods (Chinese) to vegetables.

237. CHICKEN MEAT WITH WALNUTS
(*Hop-Hoo Guy Pan*)

Use basic recipe No. 235, adding 1 cup walnut meats, roasted or fried, to vegetables.

238. CHICKEN MEAT WITH PINEAPPLE
(*Boo-Lo Guy Pan*)

Use basic recipe No. 235, adding 1½ cups canned pineapple, sliced, to vegetables.

239. CHICKEN MEAT WITH BLACK FUNGUS
(*Yu-Ye Guy Pan*)

Use basic recipe No. 235, adding ¼ cup dried fungus. Soak in warm water about 15 minutes. Rinse in cold water several times, and drain. Slice and add same time as other vegetables.

240. STUFFED CHICKEN WINGS
(*Loong Chun Fung Yet*)

A. 16 chicken wings (lower parts only), boned
B. ¼ lb. Virginia ham, cooked and shredded
C. ¼ lb. bamboo shoots (celery may be substituted), shredded
D. 2 tablespoons light soy sauce
E. ½ teaspoon garlic powder
F. 1 teaspoon rice wine
G. 1 teaspoon ginger, shredded very fine
H. 1 teaspoon heavy soy sauce
I. 1 tablespoon oyster sauce
J. 1 tablespoon cornstarch
K. 1 teaspoon seasoning powder
L. 1 teaspoon sugar
M. ¼ teaspoon salt
N. 1 cup peanut oil

PREPARATION

Stuff B, C into A. Steam for 40 minutes. Rub half of D over chicken wings. Mix remaining D, E, F, G. Add 1 tablespoon water. Mix H, I, J, K, L, M together well. Add ½ cup water. Stir up well before using.

COOKING

1. Put N in very hot skillet; heat to about 375°.
2. Put A in oil. Fry until both sides are light brown. Then pour off excess oil.
3. Add D, E, F, G preparation. Stir-fry 1 minute.
4. Add H, I, J, K, L, M preparation. Stir-fry until gravy thickens. Serve with potatoes or boiled rice.

Serves 2.

241. GOLD COIN CHICKEN or CHINESE COMBINATION SANDWICH (*Gam-Tien Guy*)

A. 1½ lbs. fat pork, boiled 5 minutes, rinsed in cold water. Repeat operation 4 times. Slice in 20 pieces.
B. 10 tablespoons sugar
C. 1 chicken, 4 lbs., cleaned
D. 1½ lbs. raw lean pork
E. ½ cup light soy sauce
F. 1 tablespoon heavy soy sauce
G. 1 teaspoon seasoning powder
H. 1 teaspoon garlic, mashed
I. 1 tablespoon sweet vegetable sauce
J. 1 tablespoon rice wine or 4 tablespoons sherry wine
K. 1 tablespoon honey
L. 2 teaspoons salt
M. ½ teaspoon pepper
N. 1½ lbs. Virginia ham, cooked, sliced thin
O. 1 head lettuce
P. ½ lb. sweet pickles, sliced
Q. 40 pieces toast

PREPARATION AND COOKING

Combine 8 tablespoons B with A. Let stand overnight or longer. Mix E, F, G, H, I, J, K, L, M. Add rest of B. Mix well together. Soak C, D in this second preparation 60 minutes or longer, then put in 400° oven and roast 10 minutes. Reduce heat to 250°. After 25 minutes, remove chicken. Cook pork 20 minutes longer. Cool and slice. Make sandwich as follows: slice of toast at bottom; then lettuce, slice lean pork, slice fat pork, slice chicken, sliced pickles, and top with slice of toast. Trim edges to make round.

Makes 20 sandwiches.

DUCK

In China, duck is not commonly included in daily family menus. In restaurants, good cafés and hotels, however, duck dishes are at the top of the bill of fare.

The preparation of duck for Chinese dishes is a long and somewhat difficult task. Properly done, roast duck especially, it is a most delicious dish.

Prepared roast duck can be bought in any large city in China, and in most grocery stores in the Chinatowns of America.

---

242. ROAST DUCK, CANTONESE STYLE
(*Shu Op or Four-Op*)

A. 1 fresh-killed duck, 5 to 6 lbs., washed, cleaned, back slit, all intestines removed (save giblets for another dish)
B. 1 tablespoon Chinese salt cabbage
C. 2 tablespoons rose or rice wine
D. 2 tablespoons light soy sauce
E. 1 tablespoon sugar
F. 1 teaspoon fresh ginger, mashed
G. 2 tablespoons dried tangerine skin, soaked in warm water for 45 minutes and cleaned
H. 2 cloves garlic, mashed
I. 1 tablespoon brown bean sauce
J. 1 fresh leek (white part only), chopped
K. 2 fresh scallions (white part only) or ½ small onion, chopped
L. 3 cups soup stock
M. 1 teaspoon salt
N. ¼ cup heavy soy sauce
O. ½ cup honey

PREPARATION AND COOKING

Dry A with a clean towel. Tie up neck with string and hang up until skin is dry; this generally takes about 2 hours. Mix B, C, D, E, F, G, H, I, J, K, L, M. Add 1 teaspoon of N and 1 teaspoon of O. Boil all ingredients in pot for 25 minutes over low heat. Meantime, preheat oven to 400°. Break both joints of legs and wings and make a few slits in side, but not through the skin. Pour prepared mixture into duck (must be boiling). Then sew up the slit so that no juice or mixture leaks out. Mix rest of N and O with 1 pint boiling water. Hang up duck, pour this mixture over the duck 4 or 5 times, or more.

Place the duck on a rack in a pan with 1 inch of water on bottom. Roast 15 to 20 minutes (at 400°), until duck is golden brown. Then lower the heat to 250°. Roast 40 to 50 minutes or more, until duck is done.

Serves 4.

Note: When serving, cut thread and let mixture out. Strain into bowl or pot. Keep warm. Pour mixture over the duck, when serving. This recipe may be used for wild duck and goose.

243. DRIED DUCK (*Lup op*)

A. 1 young duck, about 5 lbs., washed, cleaned and opened at breast (save giblets for other dishes)
B. ½ cup light soy sauce
C. 1 tablespoon heavy soy sauce
D. 1 teaspoon sugar
E. 1 tablespoon honey
F. ½ teaspoon pepper
G. ¼ teaspoon cinnamon powder
H. ¼ cup rice wine
I. ½ cup coarse salt

PREPARATION AND COOKING

Use a sharp knife; slash both legs and breast of A. Mix B, C, D, E, F, G, H. Rub I over the duck, inside and out. Put duck on table and place a weight of 50 or 100 lbs. on it, so that duck flattens out. Leave for 5 or 6 hours, or more. Rinse with cold water once or twice, to get some of the salt out. Brush prepared mixture over duck inside and out. Let stand 10 to 12 hours so that mixture penetrates the meat.

Cover the duck with a piece of cheesecloth; cut a hole in each side. Thread a strong string through the holes. Hang out in open air. Dry in the sun. It takes approximately 16 to 17 days, depending on the weather. After duck is dried, cut into 4 pieces. Cover with rice. This preserves it for 6 to 12 months. (This type of dried duck should be made in winter or fall.)

Steam until soft or place on top of rice, when boiled rice is almost done or steam until soft, then grind with beef or pork to make hamburg or pork sausage.

Serves 6.

Note: Duck bones make an excellent base for soup stock.

244. OIL-PRESERVED SALT DUCK (*You Dim Lup op*)

Use method and ingredients as in recipe No. 243, but let hang only until 50 percent dry. Put in peanut oil in a glass jar, chopping duck into small pieces to fit jar. This will preserve it usually for 6 months or longer. (This type of preserved duck is made during the summertime.)

To cook, rinse in cold water, then boil for 20 minutes.

245. DRIED DUCK'S MEAT (*Op Yoke Pen*)

A. 1 duck, about 6 lbs., cleaned and boned
B. ½ cup light soy sauce
C. 1 tablespoon heavy soy sauce
D. 1 teaspoon salt
E. 1 teaspoon sugar
F. 1 tablespoon honey
G. 2 tablespoons rice wine

PREPARATION

Dry A with clean towel. Mix B, C, D, E, F, G together in a large bowl. Soak A in this mixture overnight. Dry and preserve as instructed in recipe No. 243.

246. PEKINESE DUCK (*Kur Loo Op, Pekin Style*)

A. 1 young duck, 5 to 6 lbs., washed and cleaned
B. 1 cup honey
C. 2 cups boiling water
D. 1 teaspoon salt
E. 1 teaspoon Chinese spice
F. 1 tablespoon rose or rice wine
G. 1 tablespoon Chinese sweet vegetable sauce
H. 1 teaspoon Chinese hot sauce
I. 1 teaspoon sugar
J. 1 teaspoon vinegar
K. ½ teaspoon sesame seed oil

PREPARATION AND COOKING

Cut slit in back of A and under the neck; remove all intestines. (Save giblets for other dishes.) Mix B, C. Mix D, E. Stir-fry over low heat 15 minutes. Mix F, G, H, I, J, K together. Dip A in boiling water for about ½ minute. Hang duck up; brush B, C preparation over it 3 or 4 times, until skin of duck is thoroughly saturated. Rub D, E preparation inside duck. Then hang up to allow skin to dry hard; takes 10 to 12 hours. Take down and rub F, G, H, I, J, K preparation inside duck.

Roast duck in 450° oven for 20 minutes. Lower heat to 250° and roast for 40 minutes or more.

To serve, cut all the duck skin into 1-inch by 2½-inch strips and serve on plate with Chinese "thousand floor" bread. Or serve it on very thin bread or toast. Chop meat up to serve on another plate with duck sauce.

Serves 5.

Note: Actually, Pekinese Duck is supposed to be barbecued. If you have no barbecue equipment, roast it in oven.

247. STEAMED DUCK, WEST LAKE STYLE
(*Si-Woo Chun Op*)

A. 1 young duck, 5 to 6 lbs., washed, cleaned, breast slit open, all intestines removed (save giblets for some other dish)
B. 2 teaspoons light soy sauce
C. 1½ tablespoons heavy soy sauce
D. 1 teaspoon thyme
E. 1 teaspoon anise
F. 4 slices fresh ginger
G. 1 teaspoon cassia herb (optional)
H. 1 tablespoon rice wine
I. 1 teaspoon honey
J. 1 tablespoon salt
K. ½ cup bamboo shoots, shredded very fine
L. ½ cup Chinese black mushrooms, soaked in warm water for 15 minutes, shredded very fine
M. ½ cup tender part of celery, shredded very fine (about 2 inches long)
N. 1 tablespoon cornstarch
O. 1 teaspoon seasoning powder
P. ½ cup cooked Virginia ham, shredded very fine (about 2½ inches long)
Q. 1 cup Chinese parsley, chopped in pieces about 1½ inches long

PREPARATION

Mix B with ½ tablespoon of C; rub all over skin of A. Dry inside of duck with clean towel. Fry duck in deep oil until light brown. Then rinse in cold water. Place duck in deep bowl or pan. Put rest of C, D, E, F, G, H, I, J on top of duck, and add enough boiling water to cover. Mix N, O together with ½ cup water. Stir up well before using.

COOKING

1. Place a rack on bottom of large pot containing about 3 inches of boiling water. Then put the bowl containing prepared duck on rack. Cover and steam (medium heat) for 1½ hours. Add water frequently to pot so that there is always 3 inches of water.
2. Take out duck. Let it cool. Then remove all bones. Save the juice, but strain it.
3. Place duck flat on another deep plate (skin up). Steam another

15 minutes, or until tender. Cover and keep warm. You may put back some of the drained juice to steam with duck. (Use rest of drained juice to cook with other ingredients.)

4. Put juice in hot frying pan, add K, L, M. Cover and cook 10 minutes.
5. Add cornstarch preparation gradually, cooking until gravy is smooth.
6. Pour mixture over duck and sprinkle P on top. Put lettuce all around plate and add Q as garnish.

Serves 6.

Note: Cooking time is halved and flavor of dish is improved if pressure cooker is used for steamed duck or chicken. If desired, duck may be rubbed with soy sauce before frying in deep fat. If you have a big family, or if you like stuffing very much, make double or more of the amount called for in recipe and, after stuffing the duck, place remainder of stuffing in bottom of bowl. Put duck on top of this and steam together.

248. STEAMED DUCK GARNISHED WITH LETTUCE
(*Sang-Toy Par Op*)

Use same method and ingredients as in recipe No. 247. Eliminate ham, and add head lettuce at bottom of duck for second steaming, and garnish with more lettuce around plate.

249. STEAMED DUCK WITH SPINACH
(*Boo-Toy Par Op*)

Use same method and ingredients as in recipe No. 247. Eliminate ham, and add 1 lb. fresh cleaned spinach at bottom of duck for second steaming. Garnish with leaves of lettuce.

Note: Broccoli, asparagus, Chinese celery cabbage or mustard green, onion, salted celery, dumpling or mushrooms may be substituted for lettuce or spinach. As usual, name of dish changes accordingly.

250. STEAMED DUCK WITH OLD TANGERINE SKIN (*Gor-Pe Op*)

Use same method and ingredients (except for following) as in recipe No. 247. Eliminate ham, mushrooms, bamboo shoots and cornstarch and seasoning powder. Add ¾ cup old tangerine skin. Soak in water for 30 minutes. Clean inside of skin. Cook at same time with Chinese herbs. After straining, take tangerine skin out and put on top of duck for second steaming.

Note: Sauce or juice must be tasted; if too salty or not salty enough, season before serving.

251. STEAMED DUCK WITH ASSORTED NUTS (*Quor-Do Chun Op*)

A. 1 fresh-killed duck, 5 to 6 lbs., washed, cleaned, back split, and intestines removed
B. ¼ cup Virginia ham, diced
C. ¼ cup white nuts
D. ¼ cup water chestnuts, peeled and diced
E. 4 pieces Chinese red dates
F. ¼ cup black or white mushrooms, diced
G. ¼ cup bamboo shoots, diced
H. ¼ cup chestnuts or American mixed nuts
I. 1 teaspoon seasoning powder
J. 1 teaspoon salt
K. 2 cups soup stock
L. 1 head lettuce
M. 1 cup Chinese parsley

COOKING

1. Cook all ingredients except A, L, M until chestnuts are tender.
2. Fry A in deep fat until light brown. Rinse in cold water.
3. Stuff cooked ingredients into duck, and sew up or truss duck.
4. Put duck in large bowl.
5. Put a rack in a large pot containing 3 inches of boiling water. Then put bowl containing duck on rack. Steam over low heat for 2 hours, or until duck is tender. Add water frequently so pot never has less than 3 inches boiling water. Garnish with L, M and serve.

Serves 6.

252. STEAMED DUCK WITH EIGHT JEWELS
(*But-Chen Chun Op*)

A. 1 fresh-killed duckling, 5 to 6 lbs., washed, cleaned, back split, intestines removed (save giblets for other dishes)

B. ½ cup glutinous rice, washed until water is clear, soaked in water 10 or more hours

C. 2 tablespoons barley, cleaned and soaked in water with glutinous rice

D. 6 dried almond meats (dried apricots may be substituted)

E. 12 fresh chestnuts, shelled, cooked until tender

F. 12 white nuts, shelled

G. ¼ cup canned lotus seeds

H. 1 tablespoon dried dragon's eye meat or golden seedless raisins

I. ½ cup water chestnuts, peeled, diced

J. 1 teaspoon sugar

K. 1 teaspoon salt

L. 1 teaspoon seasoning powder

M. 2 tablespoons rice wine

N. 1 fresh scallion (white part only), chopped very fine

O. 1 head lettuce and 1 cup Chinese parsley

PREPARATION AND COOKING

Fry A in deep fat until light brown. Rinse in cold water. Mix B, C, D, E, F, G, H, I, J, K, L, M, N and stuff into duck. Add 1 cup water or soup stock. Sew up or truss duck, and place in a large bowl. Place a rack on bottom of a large pot containing 3 inches boiling water. Place bowl on rack. Cover and steam 2 hours over medium heat, or until duck is tender. Garnish with O.

Serves 6.

253. STEAMED DUCK WITH FIVE KINDS OF SAUCE
(*Ng Din Chun Op*)

A. 1 fresh-killed duckling, 5 to 6 lbs., washed, cleaned, breast split open and intestines removed; clean and dice giblets to make sauce for garnish

B. 2 tablespoons brown bean sauce, mashed

C. 2 tablespoons sweet vegetable sauce

D. 1 teaspoon hot sauce

E. 1 tablespoon oyster sauce

F. 1 tablespoon duck sauce

G. 1 tablespoon light soy sauce

H. 1 teaspoon heavy soy sauce

I. 1 teaspoon honey

J. 1 teaspoon salt

K. pinch of pepper and Chinese spice

L. 2 heads lettuce, sliced (save 4 large leaves for garnish on sides of plate, slices for bottom)

M. 1 teaspoon seasoning powder

N. 1 cup Chinese parsley, chopped

PREPARATION

Mix B, C, D, E, F, G, H, I, J, K. Rub mixture over duck, inside and out. Put duck in bowl and keep in refrigerator overnight (there will be some excess juice in bowl; save it to make sauce).

COOKING

1. Put a rack in a large pot containing 3 inches boiling water.

2. Place bowl containing duck on rack. Cover and steam 1½ hours (pressure cooker with 15 to 18 lbs., steam for 45 minutes).

3. Bone duck, or chop through bone into small pieces; place them on plate lined with L.

4. Use juice you saved; add ½ cup water, 1 teaspoon cornstarch and M. Mix well.

5. Cook giblets in a pan with ½ cup of water for 15 minutes. Add cornstarch preparation gradually. Stir frequently until gravy thickens, then pour over duck.

Garnish with N.

Serves 6.

254. STEAMED DUCK WITH FIVE KINDS OF SAUCE AND POTATOES (*Ng-Din Shee-Doy Chun Op*)

Use same method and ingredients as in recipe No. 253. Add 3 lbs. potatoes, peeled and cut into wedges. Put potatoes in bottom of bowl, duck on top.

255. STEAMED DUCK WITH FIVE KINDS OF SAUCE AND TARO (*Ng-Din Wu-Doy Chun Op*)

Use same method and ingredients as in recipe No. 253. Add 3 lbs. taro.

256. STUFFED DUCK WITH EIGHT PRECIOUS INGREDIENTS (*But-Bor Chun Op*)

A. 1 fresh-killed duckling, 5 to 6 lbs., washed, cleaned, back split and intestines removed (save giblets for other dishes)
B. ¼ cup Virginia ham, chopped
C. ¼ cup Chinese pork sausage, chopped
D. ¼ cup dried or preserved duck meat, chopped
E. 1 piece preserved or dried duck's liver, chopped
F. 3 medium size dried oysters, soaked in warm water overnight, cleaned and chopped
G. 4 large sized dried scallops, soaked in warm water overnight, chopped
H. 2 tablespoons dried shrimps, soaked in warm water overnight, chopped
I. ½ cup fresh or canned crab or lobster meat, chopped with above 7 ingredients
J. ½ cup glutinous rice, soaked in water overnight
K. ¼ cup water chestnuts, peeled and chopped
L. ½ cup black or white mushrooms, diced
M. 1 teaspoon seasoning powder
N. 1 teaspoon salt
O. ½ teaspoon garlic powder
P. 1 tablespoon rice wine
Q. 1 teaspoon sugar or honey
R. 1 cup quick-frozen peas, cooked in boiling water 1½ minutes, rinsed in cold water and put aside for garnish
S. 1 head lettuce and 1 cup Chinese parsley, also for garnish

PREPARATION AND COOKING

Mix all ingredients from B to Q. Rub light soy sauce over duck's skin. Fry duck in deep fat until light brown. Rinse in cold water. Stuff mixed preparation into duck. Sew up or truss. Place in bowl. Add about 1 cup soup stock or water.

See recipe No. 253 for cooking instructions.

Garnish with lettuce on all sides of bowl, peas all around duck and parsley on top of duck.

Serves 6.

257. CRISPY DUCK WITH FIVE SPICES
(*Eng Hong Op*)

A. 1 fresh-killed duckling, 5 to 6 lbs., washed and cleaned, breast split open, intestines removed, gizzard and liver cleaned
B. 2 tablespoons light soy sauce
C. 1 tablespoon thyme
D. 1 teaspoon anise
E. 1 teaspoon salt
F. 1 tablespoon honey
G. 1 tablespoon heavy soy sauce
H. 3 cups water (boiling)
I. 1 tablespoon 5 aroma spices
J. 1 tablespoon brown bean sauce, mashed
K. ½ cup water chestnut flour or all purpose flour
L. ¼ cup cornstarch
M. 1 head lettuce and 1 cup Chinese parsley, for garnish

PREPARATION

Rub B over skin of A. Fry A in deep fat until golden brown. Rinse in cold water. Put duck and giblets in a large bowl; add C, D, E, F, G, H.

COOKING

1. Put bowl on rack in pot with 3 inches boiling water in bottom. Cover and steam 60 to 75 minutes. Strain. Save the juice for gravy for future use.
2. Remove duck when cool, and bone it.
3. Mix I, J. Rub on duck inside and out.

4. Sift K, L together. Rub all over duck.
5. Fry duck in deep fat until golden brown and crisp. Line a large
   bowl or deep plate with M. Chop duck into 1-inch by 2-inch
   pieces and place on top of lettuce; garnish with parsley and
   giblets. Serve with duck sauce and hot sauce mixed.

Serves 6.

258. COLD DUCK WITH CHINESE SAUERKRAUT
(*Leong Ben Op Yoke*)

A. 1 lb. cooked duck meat (roast, boiled or broiled), shredded
   fine
B. 1 cup sweet potatoes, peeled, shredded very fine
C. 1 cup cabbage, shredded fine
D. 1 cup carrots, peeled, shredded fine
E. 1 cup Chinese white turnips, shredded fine
F. 1 cup cucumber, peeled, shredded fine
G. ½ cup green pepper, shredded fine
H. 1 cup sugar
I. 1 cup vinegar
J. ½ teaspoon salt
K. ½ teaspoon hot sauce
L. 1 tablespoon ketchup
M. 1 tablespoon salad oil
N. few drops sesame seed oil
O. pinch of cinnamon powder
P. dash of pepper

PREPARATION

Mix B, C, D, E, F, G together thoroughly. Add H, I, J, K, L, M,
N, O, P. Mix thoroughly. Keep in cool place for 24 hours, then
turn all ingredients over so they can soak thoroughly for another
24 hours. Place the prepared mixture in a plate. Add A on top.
Garnish with lettuce and red cherries.

Serves 2.

Note: This makes an excellent dish for hot-weather menus.

259. COLD ROAST DUCK WITH PINEAPPLE
(*Boo-Loo Leong Ben Op*)

A. 1 lb. roast duck meat, sliced
B. 2 cups lettuce, sliced
C. 1 cup canned pineapple juice
D. 2 teaspoons cornstarch
E. 1 cup canned pineapple, sliced

PREPARATION

Mix C, D together; cook slowly until sauce thickens. Arrange B in a deep plate. Place A on top of lettuce. Pour cornstarch mixture over duck. Put E on top; chill in refrigerator before serving.

Serves 2.

260. BRAISED DUCK WITH MUSHROOMS
(*Tung Koo Min Op*)

A. 2 tablespoons peanut oil or lard
B. 1 teaspoon salt
C. 2 cloves garlic, mashed
D. 1 fresh-killed duckling, 5 to 6 lbs., wash and clean, then chop through the bone into pieces about 1 inch by 2 inches
E. 2 cups mushrooms (black or white), sliced into halves
F. 1 cup bamboo shoots, sliced about same size as mushrooms
G. 1 cup water chestnuts, peeled and sliced
H. 1 tablespoon light soy sauce
I. 1 teaspoon rice wine or 2 tablespoons sherry wine
J. 1 teaspoon fresh ginger, shredded fine
K. 2 cups of soup stock
L. 1½ tablespoons cornstarch
M. 1 teaspoon seasoning powder
N. 1 teaspoon sugar
O. 1 teaspoon heavy soy sauce
P. dash of pepper

PREPARATION

Mix H, I, J; add 1 tablespoon water. Stir well before using. Mix L, M, N, O, P together; add ¾ cup water. Stir well before using.

COOKING

1. Put A in very hot skillet; add B and C.
2. Add D. Stir-fry 5 minutes; then add E, F, G. Stir-fry 2 minutes.
3. Add H, I, J preparation. Stir-fry 2 minutes.
4. Add K. Cover and cook until boiling; then lower heat and let simmer 40 minutes, or until tender.
5. Add L, M, N, O, P preparation. Stir-fry thoroughly until gravy thickens and is smooth. Serve with boiled rice or potatoes; garnish with lettuce and parsley.

Serves 4.

Note: Duck's giblets could be cooked with duck if you do not want to save them for some other dish. Suggestions: Make Giblet Foo Yong, Chop Suey or Chow Yoke.

261. BRAISED DUCK WITH SWEET BEAN CURD STICKS (*Tiem-Yok Min Op*)

A. 2 tablespoons peanut oil
B. 1 tablespoon salt
C. 2 cloves garlic, crushed
D. 1 fresh killed duckling, 5 to 6 lbs., washed and cleaned, breast opened, intestines, giblets and heart removed; chop duck through bone in pieces about 1 inch by 2 inches
E. ¼ lb. dried sweet bean curd stick, soaked in warm water 30 minutes or longer; chop in pieces about 2 or 2½ inches
F. 1 cup Chinese white nuts, shelled and cooked 15 minutes; remove soft skin
G. 1 doz. red dates, soaked in water 30 minutes
H. 1 cup black mushrooms, soaked in warm water 30 minutes, sliced
I. ½ cup water chestnuts, peeled and sliced
J. ½ cup bamboo shoots, sliced
K. 1 tablespoon light soy sauce
L. 1 teaspoon rice wine or 2 tablespoons sherry wine
M. 1 teaspoon fresh ginger, shredded
N. 2 cups soup stock
O. 1½ tablespoons cornstarch
P. 1 teaspoon seasoning powder
Q. 1 teaspoon sugar
R. 1 teaspoon heavy soy sauce
S. dash of pepper

PREPARATION

Mix K, L, M together; add 1 tablespoon water. Stir well before using. Mix O, P, Q, R, S together with ½ cup water. Stir well before using.

COOKING

1. Put A in hot skillet. Add B, C.
2. Add D. Stir-fry 5 minutes.
3. Add E, F, G, H, I, J. Stir thoroughly 2 minutes.
4. Add K, L, M preparation. Stir-fry 2 minutes.
5. Add N. Cover and cook until boiling; lower heat, simmer 35 minutes.
6. Add O, P, Q, R, S preparation and stir thoroughly until gravy thickens.

Serves 6.

262. STIR-FRY DUCK MEAT WITH ASSORTED VEGETABLES AND MUSHROOMS (*Chow Op Pan*)

Use same method and ingredients as in recipe No. 235, using duck meat instead of chicken.

263. STIR-FRY DUCK MEAT WITH FUNGUS AND ASSORTED VEGETABLES (*Yee-Ye Op Pan*)

Use same method and ingredients as in recipe No. 239, using duck meat instead of chicken.

264. FRIED BONELESS DUCK IN BATTER, KIM MON STYLE (*Kim Mon Op*)

Use same method and ingredients as in recipe No. 205, using duck meat instead of chicken.

265. BREADED BONELESS DUCKLING WITH ALMONDS AND SWEET SAUCE (*Wor-Shu Chun Op*)

A. 1 fresh-killed duck, 5 to 6 lbs., washed and cleaned, breast split, intestines removed (save giblets for other dishes)
B. 1 teaspoon thyme
C. 1 teaspoon anise
D. 1 piece dried orange rind (optional)
E. 4 sliced ginger roots
F. 1 tablespoon salt
G. 1 tablespoon sugar
H. 1 tablespoon honey
I. 1 tablespoon rose or rice wine
J. 1 clove garlic, mashed
K. ½ teaspoon pepper
L. 1 tablespoon heavy soy sauce
M. 1 cup water chestnut flour or cracker meal
N. 1 tablespoon cornstarch
O. 1 teaspoon seasoning powder
P. 1 head lettuce, sliced
Q. 1 tablespoon cooked Virginia ham, chopped very fine
R. 2 tablespoons roasted almonds, smashed
S. 1 cup Chinese parsley, cut in 2-inch long pieces

PREPARATION

Place A in deep bowl or pot. Put B, C, D, E, F, G, H, I, J, K, L on top. Pour boiling water over all, covering ingredients and duck.

COOKING

1. Place bowl containing prepared duck on rack in large pot with about 3 inches of boiling water. Cover and steam 45 minutes.
2. When duck is cool, remove all bones. Strain sauce. Put sauce aside.
3. Rub M thoroughly over duck.
4. Fry duck in deep fat until golden brown.
5. Chop up in small pieces.
6. Arrange P on a deep plate. Then put duck on top of lettuce.
7. Cook sauce (which had been strained) until boiling. Then mix N, O with ½ cup water. Stir well. Add gradually to sauce. Stir until gravy thickens. Pour over duck.
8. Top with Q, R, S.

Serves 6.

266. DUCK STUFFED WITH GLUTINOUS RICE
(*Wor-Shu Noo-Mei Op*)

Use same method and ingredients as in recipe No. 225, using duck meat instead of chicken.

267. DUCK STUFFED WITH BIRD'S NEST
(*Yen-Wor Chun Op*)

Use same method and ingredients as in recipe No. 226, using duck meat instead of chicken.

268. COMBINATION SALTED AND FRESH DUCK MEAT WITH MUSHROOM SAUCE (*Yon Yonng Op*)

A. 2 lbs. fresh-cooked duck meat, sliced ¼ inch thick by 2 inches wide

B. 1 lb. dehydrated duck or salted duck, sliced ⅛ inch thick by 1½ inches wide

C. 1½ tablespoons cornstarch

D. 1 teaspoon seasoning powder

E. 1 teaspoon honey

F. 2 tablespoons butter (drawn)

G. 1 cup mushrooms, diced

PREPARATION AND COOKING

Put 1 piece A on a deep plate and place 1 piece B over it; repeat until all duck meat is used (spread all around the plate). Place plate in a large pot, with a rack on bottom, containing 3 inches boiling water. Cover and steam for 45 minutes; drain juice from plate; add about ¾ cup water; mix with C, D, E, F, G. Stir constantly until smooth, not too thick. Pour mixture over duck. Garnish with lettuce and parsley.

Serves 3 or 4.

269. WHOLE WINTER MELON STUFFED WITH DUCK'S MEAT AND VARIETIES
(*Dong-Gar Op Chung*)

Use same method and ingredients as in recipe No. 27, adding 4 cups duck meat, ½ cup pork and ¼ cup ham.

Note: Here are some other suggestions for dishes in which duck can be used: Use giblet, heart and breast to make soup. Use the rest of the duck for a stir-fry or fried-in-batter concoction. Use the bones to make sweet and sour, or stir-fry with black bean sauce. Recipes for all these are to be found in this book.

SQUAB

270. FRIED SQUAB CHINESE, FAMILY STYLE
(*Jow Bok Opp*)

A. 2 young squabs about 8 to 10 weeks old; slit back, remove intestines, clean giblets
B. 3 tablespoons light soy sauce
C. 1 teaspoon heavy soy sauce
D. 1 tablespoon brown bean sauce, mashed
E. 1 tablespoon rice wine
F. 1 teaspoon fresh ginger, crushed
G. 1 teaspoon garlic powder
H. ¼ teaspoon pepper
I. 1 small head of lettuce

PREPARATION

Mix B, C, D, E, F, G, H together well. Rub mixture over A inside and out; let soak about 30 minutes or more.

COOKING

1. Put prepared squabs in a bowl. Put bowl on rack in a pot containing 3 inches boiling water.
2. Cover and steam 45 minutes, or until tender. If you have any mixture left, rub on outside of skin again.
3. Chop each squab into four parts. Fry in deep fat until golden brown. Fry giblets in same pan.
   Serve in lettuce-lined plate with a piece of lemon for each serving.

Serves 2.

271. CRISPY BONELESS SQUAB WITH ALMONDS AND SWEET SAUCE (*Wor-Shu Bok Opp*)

Use same method and ingredients as in recipe No. 265, using 2 or more squabs instead of duck.

272. STEAMED SQUAB, WEST LAKE STYLE (*Si-Woo Bok Opp*)

Use same method and ingredients as in recipe No. 247, using 3 or more squabs instead of duck.

273. WHOLE WINTER MELON STUFFED WITH SQUAB AND VARIETIES (*Dong Gar Bok Opp Chung*)

Use same method and ingredients as in recipe No. 27, using 6 to 8 squabs. Add 1 cup diced pork and ¼ cup more Virginia ham.

274. POT ROAST SQUABS WITH SOY SAUCE (*Loo Bok-Opp*)

A. 6 squabs or pigeons, cleaned, back slit and intestines removed
B. 1 tablespoon thyme
C. 1 teaspoon anise
D. 1 tablespoon fresh ginger root, crushed
E. 1 quart best light soy sauce
F. ½ cup best heavy soy sauce
G. 2 heads of lettuce
H. 1 cup Chinese parsley, chopped

COOKING

1. Wrap B, C in a piece of cheesecloth and tie with a string.
2. Put B, C, D, E, F in a large pot over medium heat; bring to a boil, then lower heat.
3. Add A. Let simmer one hour, or until squabs are tender. (If sauce does not cover the squabs, add some soup stock, 1 tablespoon honey and 1 tablespoon seasoning powder.)
4. Serve in deep plate lined with G. Garnish with H.

Serves 6.

Note: Excess juice may be saved for cooking other dishes, such as pot roast chicken, pork, beef, veal, turkey or lamb.

275. FRIED BONELESS SQUAB WITH STRAW OR GRASS MUSHROOMS (*Tao-Koo Wat Bok Opp Kew*)

Use same method and ingredients as in recipe No. 201, using squab instead of chicken.

276. STIR-FRY SQUAB WITH OYSTER SAUCE (*Chow Bok Opp Lok*)

Use same method and ingredients as in recipe No. 208, using squab instead of chicken.

277. MINCED SQUAB MEAT WITH VEGETABLES (*Bok Opp Soong*)

A. 1 tablespoon peanut oil
B. 1 teaspoon salt
C. 1 clove garlic
D. 2 squabs, bone and grind meat
E. 1 cup lean pork, ground with squab meat
F. 1 tablespoon Virginia ham, ground
G. 1 tablespoon light soy sauce
H. 1 teaspoon rice wine
I. ½ teaspoon ginger, chopped very fine
J. 1 teaspoon sugar

к. ¼ cup water chestnuts, chopped very fine
l. ½ cup imported black mushrooms, soaked in water for 15 minutes, diced
m. ½ cup Chinese cabbage (white part only), diced very fine
n. ¼ cup bamboo shoots, diced very fine
o. ½ cup celery, diced very fine
p. ¼ cup onion, diced very fine
q. 1 fresh scallion (white part only), chopped very fine
r. ¾ cup soup stock
s. 1 tablespoon cornstarch
t. 1 teaspoon seasoning powder
u. few drops sesame oil
v. 1 teaspoon heavy soy sauce
w. ¼ teaspoon pepper
x. 1 head lettuce
y. 1 cup chopped Chinese parsley

PREPARATION

Mix G, H, I, J together well; add 1 tablespoon water. Stir well before using. Mix S, T, U, V, W together. Add ½ cup water. Stir well before using.

COOKING

1. Put A in hot skillet; add B and C.
2. Add D, E, F. Stir-fry 3 minutes. Add G, H, I, J preparation and stir-fry thoroughly 2 minutes.
3. Add K, L, M, N, O, P, Q. Stir-fry thoroughly for another minute.
4. Add R. Cover and cook 3 minutes.
5. Add S, T, U, V, W preparation. Stir-fry constantly until juice is fairly thick. Serve in a deep plate lined with X. Garnish with Y.

Serves 3 or 4.

278. DICED CUT SQUAB MEAT WITH VEGETABLES AND ALMONDS (*Chow Bok Opp Din*)

Use same method and ingredients as in recipe No. 227, using 2 cups squab meat instead of chicken, and adding 1 cup frozen peas and asparagus tips. Pea pods, broccoli or string beans could be added also, if desired.

279. STEAMED SQUAB WITH ASSORTED NUTS
(*Quor-Do Bok Opp*)

Use same method and ingredients as in recipe No. 251, using 6 squabs instead of a duck.

280. SQUAB EN CASSEROLE, MANDARIN STYLE
(*Quor-Do Woi Opp*)

A. 2 squabs, dressed and cleaned, rubbed with light soy sauce and a pinch of garlic powder
B. 1 cup imported black mushrooms, large ones cut in halves
C. ½ cup white nuts, shelled and soaked in boiling water for 5 minutes, soft skin removed
D. ½ dozen Chinese red dates, stones removed
E. ½ cup chestnut meats
F. ½ cup water chestnuts, peeled and cut in halves
G. 1 teaspoon sugar
H. ½ teaspoon fresh ginger root, crushed
I. 1 tablespoon soy sauce
J. ½ cup rice wine or 1 cup sherry wine
K. 1 teaspoon salt
L. 1 teaspoon seasoning powder
M. 1½ cups boiling soup stock

PREPARATION AND COOKING

Fry A in deep fat until golden brown. Rinse with cold water. Put squabs in a casserole; then add all ingredients from B to M. Cook in moderate oven 30 minutes, or until squabs are tender. Serve with boiled rice.

Serves 2.

LOBSTER

---

281. FRIED LOBSTER WITH MEAT SAUCE, CHINESE STYLE (*Chow Loong-Har*)

A. 1 tablespoon peanut oil
B. ½ teaspoon salt
C. 1 tablespoon black bean sauce, washed and mashed
D. 2 cloves garlic, mashed
E. few drops sesame seed oil (optional)
F. dash of pepper
G. ½ lb. fresh raw pork, chopped very fine
H. 1 live lobster, 1½ to 2 lbs.; cut through shell in half, then cut crosswise in 1 inch pieces, crack claws and cut in half
I. 1 teaspoon light soy sauce
J. 1 teaspoon rice wine or 2 tablespoons sherry wine
K. 1 teaspoon fresh ginger root, shredded fine
L. 1 teaspoon sugar
M. 1 cup soup stock
N. 1 egg, beaten
O. 1 tablespoon scallion, chopped fine
P. 1 teaspoon seasoning powder
Q. 1 tablespoon cornstarch

PREPARATION

Mix C, D, E, F together and add 1 tablespoon water. Stir well before using. Mix I, J, K, L with ⅛ cup water. Stir well before using. Mix P, Q together in ½ cup water. Stir well before using.

COOKING

1. Put A in very hot skillet.
2. Add B.
3. Add C, D, E, F preparation. Stir-fry ½ minute.
4. Add G. Stir-fry until light brown (about 2 minutes).
5. Add H. Stir-fry thoroughly 2 minutes.
6. Add I, J, K, L preparation. Stir-fry 1 minute.
7. Add M. Cover and cook 2 minutes.
8. Add N, O. Stir-fry ½ minute.
9. Add P, Q preparation. Stir-fry thoroughly until gravy thickens.
10. Serve hot with boiled rice.

Serves 2.

282. STUFFED LOBSTER WITH MEAT SAUCE
(*Yonk Loong-Har*)

A. 1 live lobster, about 1½ to 2 lbs.
B. 1 cup raw lean pork or chicken meat, chopped very fine
C. 1 teaspoon black beans, washed clean and mashed
D. 2 cloves garlic, crushed
E. 1 tablespoon Virginia ham or Chinese pork sausage, chopped very fine
F. 1 fresh scallion (white part only), chopped very fine
G. 2 eggs, beaten
H. 1 teaspoon seasoning powder
I. ½ teaspoon salt
J. 1½ tablespoons peanut oil

PREPARATION AND COOKING

Clean and split A in half, retaining shell. Split claws in half. Put lobster in deep dish, shell side down. Mix B, C, D, E, F, G, H, I together and pour over lobster.

This dish may be broiled, baked or steamed. To broil, pour J over prepared lobster and broil 25 minutes. To bake, put in moderate oven 350° about 35 minutes. When done, pour smoking hot J over before serving. To steam, take same time as for baking, and pour hot oil over when done.

Serves 1.

283. STEAMED LOBSTER (*Jen Loong-Har*)

A. 1 live lobster, about 1½ to 2 lbs.
B. ½ teaspoon salt
C. 1 teaspoon seasoning powder
D. pinch garlic powder
E. dash of pepper
F. 1 teaspoon rice wine or 2 tablespoons sherry wine
G. 1 teaspoon fresh ginger root, crushed
H. 1 teaspoon light soy sauce
I. 2 tablespoons peanut oil
J. ⅛ teaspoon sesame seed oil

PREPARATION

Clean and split A in half. Split claws in half. Put lobster in deep dish, shell side down. Mix all ingredients from B through H and pour over A.

COOKING

1. Steam 15 minutes.
2. Heat I, J until smoking; pour over lobster when done; serve hot.
3. Garnish with lettuce.

Serves 1.

284. FRIED LOBSTER IN BATTER, CHINESE STYLE (*Soo-Jow Loong-Har*)

A. 1 live lobster, about 2 lbs., cooked and shelled
B. 1 tablespoon oyster sauce
C. 1 teaspoon rice wine or 2 tablespoons sherry wine
D. 1 teaspoon fresh ginger root, crushed
E. 2 teaspoons seasoning powder
F. 1 teaspoon garlic powder
G. 1 teaspoon salt
H. 2 eggs
I. ¼ cup water chestnut flour or cornstarch
J. ¼ cup all purpose flour
K. 10 to 12 strips bacon
L. 1 head lettuce, sliced

PREPARATION

Cut A into 10 or 12 pieces. Mix B, C, D; add ½ of E, ½ F and ½ G. Soak lobster in this preparation 10 minutes or more. Beat up H and add I, J. Beat again. Add rest of E, F, G. Mix well. Wrap A, piece by piece, in K, then dip in egg mixture. Fry in deep fat until golden brown. Serve in lettuce-lined plate; garnish with sliced lemon and tomatoes.

Serves 2.

285. FRIED LOBSTER MEAT IN BATTER WITH ASSORTED VEGETABLES (*Soo-Jow Loong-Har Kew*)

A. 2 teaspoons seasoning powder
B. 2 tablespoons oyster sauce
C. 2 teaspoons rice wine or 4 tablespoons sherry wine
D. 1 teaspoon fresh ginger, crushed
E. 1 lb. lobster meat (freshly cooked, raw or canned), cut crosswise in about 1 inch pieces
F. 2 eggs, beaten
G. ½ cup water chestnut flour or cornstarch
H. ½ cup all purpose flour
I. 1 tablespoon peanut oil, add a few drops sesame seed oil
J. 1 teaspoon salt
K. 1 clove garlic, crushed
L. 1 cup mushrooms (French or Chinese), sliced
M. 1 cup pea pods (large ones, cut in half)
N. 1 cup Chinese cabbage (white part only), sliced
O. ½ cup celery (tender part only), sliced
P. ½ cup onion, sliced
Q. ¼ cup water chestnuts, peeled and sliced
R. ½ cup bamboo shoots, sliced
S. ½ cup soup stock
T. 1 tablespoon cornstarch
U. 1 teaspoon sugar
V. 1 teaspoon heavy soy sauce

PREPARATION

Mix A, B, C, D. Divide into 2 parts (add 1 tablespoon water to each portion). Soak E in half of mixture 10 minutes or more. Beat F, G, H together to form a smooth paste. Mix T, U, V together; add ½ cup water. Stir well before using.

COOKING

1. Dip soaked lobster in egg batter and fry in deep fat until golden brown. Set aside.
2. Put I in very hot skillet; then add J and K.
3. Add L, M, N, O, P, Q, R. Stir-fry thoroughly 3 minutes.
4. Add other half of A, B, C, D mixture and stir for another minute.
5. Add S. Cover and cook 3 minutes.
6. Add fried lobster.
7. Add T, U, V preparation. Stir-fry constantly until gravy thickens and is smooth. Serve immediately. Garnish with lettuce leaves.

Serves 5.

286. FRIED LOBSTER MEAT IN BATTER WITH BLACK MUSHROOMS AND MEAT
(*Hon-Shu Loong-Har Kew*)

A. 2 teaspoons light soy sauce
B. 2 teaspoons rice wine or 4 tablespoons sherry wine
C. 1 teaspoon fresh ginger root, crushed
D. 1 lb. fresh-cooked lobster meat, cut into 1½ inch cubes
E. 2 eggs, beaten
F. ¼ cup water chestnut flour or cornstarch and ½ cup all purpose flour
G. 1 tablespoon peanut oil and few drops sesame seed oil
H. 1 teaspoon salt
I. 1 clove garlic, crushed
J. ¾ cup meat (pork, beef, veal, lamb, chicken, turkey, ham or liver), shredded fine
K. ½ cup Chinese black mushrooms, soaked in warm water 15 minutes, shredded fine
L. ¾ cup each kind of vegetable (bamboo shoots, broccoli, Chinese cabbage and celery) (tender part only), shredded fine
M. ¼ cup water chestnuts, peeled and shredded fine
N. ½ cup soup stock
O. 1 tablespoon cornstarch with ½ cup water
P. dash of pepper
Q. 1 teaspoon seasoning powder
R. 1 teaspoon heavy soy sauce
S. 1 teaspoon sugar

PREPARATION

Mix A, B, C together; divide into 2 parts. Soak D in half of mixture 10 minutes or more. Beat E, F well together; add a pinch of salt and pepper and a dash of seasoning powder. Mix O, P, Q, R, S together. Stir well before using.

COOKING

1. Dip soaked lobster in egg batter and fry in deep fat until golden brown. Set aside.
2. Put G in hot skillet; add H and I.
3. Add J, K, L, M. Stir-fry thoroughly 3 minutes.
4. Add other half of mixture. Stir-fry another minute.
5. Add N. Cover and cook 5 minutes.
6. Add fried lobster meat and O, P, Q, R, S preparation. Stir-fry constantly until gravy thickens and is smooth.
   Garnish with lettuce leaves.

Serves 2.

287. SWEET AND SOUR LOBSTER, PLAIN SAUCE
(*Tiem-Shoon Loong-Har Kew*)

A. 1 tablespoon lemon juice
B. 1 teaspoon seasoning powder
C. 1 teaspoon light soy sauce
D. 1 lb. cooked lobster meat
E. 2 eggs, beaten
F. ¾ cup all purpose flour
G. ½ cup sugar
H. ½ cup vinegar
I. 1½ tablespoons cornstarch
J. 1 tablespoon heavy soy sauce
K. ½ teaspoon garlic powder
L. ½ teaspoon fresh ginger, shredded fine

PREPARATION

Mix A, B, C together; pour over D. Let soak for 5 minutes. Beat up E, F together to form a smooth paste; add pinch salt and dash pepper. Dip soaked lobster in egg batter and fry in deep fat until golden brown. Put in a deep plate. Mix I, J, K, L with ½ cup water. Stir well before using.

COOKING

1. Place ½ cup water in a hot skillet; add G and boil 1 minute. Add H, boil another minute.
2. Add cornstarch preparation gradually. Stir until sauce thickens and is smooth. Pour over prepared lobster.

Note: This is the basic recipe for all sweet and sour fish.

288. SWEET AND SOUR LOBSTER MEAT WITH SUBGUM SAUCE (*Subgum Loong-Har Kew*)

Follow recipe No. 287. Cook the following ingredients with water 5 minutes before adding sugar and vinegar: 1 cup mixed sweet pickles, cut in wedges; ½ cup green pepper, cut in wedges; ½ cup fresh tomatoes, cut in wedges; ½ cup carrots, cut in wedges (optional).

289. SWEET AND SOUR LOBSTER WITH PINEAPPLE (*Boo-Loo Loong-Har Kew*)

Follow recipe No. 287, adding 1½ cups pineapple, sliced, to sauce.

290. SWEET AND SOUR LOBSTER WITH LICHEE (*Lichee Tiem-Shoon Loong-Har Kew*)

Follow recipe No. 287, adding 1 can preserved lichee nuts to sauce.

291. DICED CUT LOBSTER MEAT WITH VEGETABLES (*Chow Loong-Har Din*)

A. 1 tablespoon peanut oil
B. 1 teaspoon salt
C. 1 clove garlic, crushed
D. ½ cup Chinese black mushrooms, soaked in warm water 15 minutes, diced
E. ½ cup white mushrooms, diced
F. ¾ cup celery, diced
G. ¾ cup Chinese cabbage (white part only), diced
H. ½ cup onion, diced
I. ½ cup bamboo shoots, diced
J. ¼ cup water chestnuts, peeled, diced
K. 1 lb. cooked lobster meat, diced
L. 1 teaspoon light soy sauce
M. 1 teaspoon rice wine or 2 tablespoons sherry wine
N. 1 teaspoon fresh ginger, shredded very fine
O. ½ cup soup stock
P. 1 tablespoon cornstarch with ½ cup water and a dash of pepper
Q. 1 teaspoon sugar
R. 1 teaspoon seasoning powder
S. 1 teaspoon heavy soy sauce
T. ¼ cup roasted almonds, crushed
U. ½ cup fresh or frozen peas, cooked in boiling water 2 minutes

PREPARATION

Mix L, M, N and add 1 tablespoon water. Mix P, Q, R, S together with ½ cup water. Stir well before using.

COOKING

1. Put A in very hot skillet; add B and C.
2. Add D, E, F, G, H, I, J. Stir-fry thoroughly 2 minutes.
3. Add K. Stir another minute.
4. Add L, M, N preparation. Stir 1 minute.
5. Add O. Cover and cook 3 minutes.
6. Add P, Q, R, S preparation. Stir constantly until gravy thickens and is smooth.

Serve with boiled rice, and garnish with T, U.

Serves 2.

Note: If desired, you may use American vegetables, such as broccoli, asparagus, carrots, turnip, green pepper, tomatoes, as substitutes for peas, Chinese cabbage and Chinese mushrooms.

292. LOBSTER MEAT WITH VERMICELLI
(*Loong-Har Fon-Soo*)

A. 2 cups soup stock

B. 3 oz. dried vermicelli, soaked in warm water 25 minutes or more, rinsed with cold water, drained, then cut into 5 or 6 inch pieces

C. ½ cup imported black mushrooms, shredded very fine

D. ½ cup celery (tender part only), shredded very fine, about 2 inches long

E. 1 cup lobster meat, cooked in boiling water 2 minutes, rinsed with cold water, shredded very fine

F. 2 teaspoons light soy sauce

G. 1 teaspoon rice wine or 2 tablespoons sherry wine

H. 1 teaspoon fresh ginger, shredded very fine

I. ¼ teaspoon pepper

J. ¼ teaspoon garlic powder

K. 1 teaspoon seasoning powder

L. ¾ teaspoon salt

M. 2 fresh scallions (white part only), shredded very fine

COOKING

1. Bring A to a boil.
2. Add B. Cover and cook 4 minutes.
3. Add C, D and cook 3 minutes.
4. Add E, F, G, H, I, J, K, L. Cook another 3 minutes.
5. When serving, add M as garnish.

293. FRIED LOBSTER MEAT WITH SUBGUM
SAUCE (*Subgum Loong-Har*)

A. 1 tablespoon peanut oil
B. 1 teaspoon salt
C. 1 clove garlic, crushed
D. 1 lb. lobster meat, diced
E. 1 teaspoon light soy sauce
F. 1 teaspoon rice wine or 2 tablespoons sherry wine
G. 1 teaspoon fresh ginger, chopped very fine
H. 1 cup white mushrooms, diced
I. 1 cup green peppers, diced
J. 1 cup tomatoes, diced
K. 1 cup celery, diced
L. 1 cup onion, diced
M. ¼ cup water chestnuts, peeled, diced
N. ½ cup bamboo shoots, diced
O. 1 cup Chinese cabbage (white part only), diced
P. 1 tablespoon cornstarch
Q. 1 teaspoon sugar
R. dash of pepper
S. 1 teaspoon seasoning powder
T. 1 teaspoon heavy soy sauce
U. 1 cup soup stock

PREPARATION

Mix E, F, G together; add 1 tablespoon water. Mix P, Q, R, S, T together; add ½ cup water. Stir well before using.

COOKING

1. Put A in hot skillet; add B and C.
2. Add D. Stir-fry 1 minute.
3. Add E, F, G preparation. Stir another minute.
4. Add H, I, J, K, L, M, N, O. Stir thoroughly 2 minutes.
5. Add U. Cover and cook 3 minutes.
6. Add P, Q, R, S, T preparation. Stir constantly until gravy thickens and is smooth.
   Serve with boiled rice.

Serves 2.

294. LOBSTER CHOP SUEY (*Loong-Har Dep Suey*)

Use same method and ingredients as in recipe No. 198, substituting canned or fresh lobster for chicken.

295. LOBSTER CHOW MEIN (*Loong-Har Chow Mein*)

Use same method and ingredients as in recipe No. 186, using lobster meat instead of pork.

296. SUBGUM LOBSTER CHOW MEIN
(*Subgum Loong-Har Chow Mein*)

Use same method and ingredients as in recipe No. 188, using lobster meat instead of pork.

SHRIMP

---

297. SHRIMP WITH LOBSTER SAUCE
(*Har-Doy Loong-Har Wu*)

A. 1 tablespoon peanut oil
B. ½ teaspoon salt
C. 2 cloves garlic, crushed
D. 1 tablespoon black bean sauce, washed and mashed
E. 1 lb. fresh shrimp, shelled and split down the back; clean out all the dark veins
F. 1 cup raw pork, ground fine
G. 1 teaspoon fresh ginger, shredded very fine
H. 1 teaspoon sugar
I. 1 teaspoon light soy sauce
J. 1 teaspoon rice wine or 2 tablespoons sherry wine
K. 1½ cups soup stock or water
L. 1 egg, beaten
M. 3 scallions (white part only), chopped fine
N. 1 teaspoon seasoning powder
O. 1 teaspoon heavy soy sauce
P. 2 tablespoons cornstarch
Q. dash of pepper

PREPARATION

Rinse E in boiling water; rinse with cold water and drain. Mix G, H, I, J together and add 1 tablespoon water. Stir well before using. Mix N, O, P, Q together; add ½ cup water. Stir well before using.

COOKING

1. Put A in hot skillet; add B, C, D. Stir, so that they blend well, about ½ minute.

[182]

2. Add E. Stir-fry 1 minute.
3. Add F. Stir-fry 2 minutes.
4. Add G, H, I, J preparation. Stir-fry 1 minute.
5. Add K. Cover and cook 3 minutes.
6. Add L, M. Mix well and stir-fry 1 minute.
7. Add N, O, P, Q preparation. Stir-fry until sauce thickens.

Serves 2.

298. BUTTERFLY SHRIMP (*Wu Dep Har*)

A. 1 tablespoon light soy sauce
B. 1 teaspoon rice wine
C. 1 teaspoon fresh ginger, crushed
D. 1 lb. fresh jumbo shrimp, shelled, split slightly in back and cleaned
E. 3 eggs, beaten
F. ½ cup all purpose flour
G. ¼ cup water chestnut flour
H. 1 teaspoon seasoning powder
I. ¾ teaspoon salt
J. dash of pepper
K. ½ teaspoon garlic powder
L. 1 tablespoon sour milk
M. 1 head lettuce (use 4 best leaves for garnishing and slice or shred the rest)

PREPARATION AND COOKING

Mix A, B, C together and soak D in this mixture 15 minutes or more. Mix E, F, G, H, I, J, K, L together and beat until a smooth paste is formed. Dip soaked shrimp in this batter, one by one; fry in deep fat until golden brown. Serve in deep lettuce-lined plate. Garnish with shredded lettuce and slices of lemon.

Serves 2.

299. BUTTERFLY SHRIMP WITH BACON
(*Wor-Hep Har*)

A. 1 teaspoon fresh ginger, crushed
B. 1½ tablespoons light soy sauce
C. 1 teaspoon rice wine or 2 tablespoons sherry wine
D. dash of pepper
E. ½ teaspoon garlic powder
F. 1½ teaspoons seasoning powder
G. 1 lb. fresh jumbo shrimp, shelled, split slightly in back and cleaned
H. strips of bacon (1 strip for each shrimp)
I. 3 eggs, beaten
J. ½ cup water chestnut flour or cornstarch
K. ½ cup all purpose flour
L. ½ cup mixed nuts, roasted, crushed to a powder
M. 1 teaspoon salt

PREPARATION AND COOKING

Mix A, B, C, D, E and ½ F together. Soak G in this mixture 10 minutes or more. Wrap each shrimp in strip of H. Beat I, J, K together until a smooth paste is formed. Add L and remaining F and M. Beat well. Dip prepared shrimp in batter and fry in deep fat until golden brown. Serve with hot sauce and ketchup mixture or with sweet vegetable sauce and hot mustard mixture; garnish with lettuce.

Serves 2.

300. BUTTERFLY SHRIMP WITH VEGETABLES
(*Hon-Shu Har-Kew*)

A. 1 tablespoon peanut oil (add few drops sesame seed oil)
B. 1 teaspoon salt
C. 1 clove garlic, crushed
D. 1 cup fresh pea pods, cut crosswise in half
E. 1 cup bamboo shoots, sliced thin
F. 1½ cups Chinese cabbage (white part only), sliced thin
G. 1 cup celery (tender part only), sliced thin
H. ½ cup water chestnuts, peeled and sliced thin
I. ½ cup onion, sliced thin
J. ½ cup Chinese mushrooms (or French or fresh mushrooms)

K. 2 tablespoons light soy sauce
L. 2 teaspoons rice wine or 4 tablespoons sherry wine
M. 1 teaspoon fresh ginger, shredded very fine
N. 2 scallions (white part only), split in half, cut in 1 inch pieces
O. 1 cup soup stock
P. 1 lb. fresh jumbo shrimp, shelled, split slightly in back and cleaned
Q. 1 cup all purpose flour
R. 2 eggs, beaten
S. 1½ teaspoons heavy soy sauce
T. 1½ tablespoons cornstarch
U. 1½ teaspoons seasoning powder
V. 1 teaspoon sugar
W. dash of pepper

PREPARATION

Rinse P in boiling water, then in cold, and drain. Mix K, L, M together and add 1 tablespoon water and a few drops sesame seed oil (optional). Soak in this mixture for 10 minutes or more. Mix S, T, U, V, W together with ½ cup water. Stir well before using. Beat Q, R vigorously; add a pinch of salt and 1 teaspoon sour milk and beat to form a smooth paste. Remove shrimp from liquid mixture, dip in batter, and fry in hot deep peanut oil until golden brown; set aside.

COOKING

1. Put A in hot skillet; add B, C.
2. Add D, E, F, G, H, I, J. Stir-fry 3 minutes.
3. Add K, L, M preparation and stir-fry 2 minutes.
4. Add N.
5. Add O. Cover and cook 3 minutes, then remove cover and stir thoroughly.
6. Add fried shrimp. Stir thoroughly.
7. Add S, T, U, V, W preparation. Stir-fry until gravy thickens and is smooth.

Serve with boiled rice.

Serves 2 or 3.

301. STUFFED SHRIMP, ROYAL STYLE
(*Yong Wong Gong Har*)

A. 1 lb. fresh shrimp, shelled, split slightly in back and cleaned

B. 2½ lbs. filet of pike (haddock or sea bass), chopped very fine

C. 2 oz. dried shrimp or oyster, soaked in warm water 8 hours or more, chopped very fine

D. 3 strips bacon, chopped very fine

E. 2 tablespoons Virginia ham, chopped very fine

F. 2 tablespoons Chinese sausage (optional), chopped very fine

G. ¾ cup cornstarch

H. ½ teaspoon pepper

I. 3 cloves garlic, chopped very fine

J. 1½ teaspoons seasoning powder

K. 3 fresh scallions (white part only), chopped very fine

L. 1½ teaspoons salt

M. ½ teaspoon fresh ginger, chopped very fine

N. 3 eggs, beaten

O. 1 cup Chinese preserved mixed fine shredded fruit

P. 2 lbs. caul fat, cut into 4 by 6 inch pieces

PREPARATION AND COOKING

Mix ingredients B through N (save some beaten egg for later use); beat with heavy large spoon until a smooth paste is formed. Grease hands with peanut oil. Roll each shrimp in the prepared mixture, then wrap with a piece of P; brush end of fat with some beaten egg, to fasten tight. Repeat operation until shrimp are used up. Fry shrimp in deep hot peanut oil until golden brown. Place in lettuce-lined plate, sprinkle with O, and garnish with Chinese chopped parsley.

Serves 2 or 3.

302. PHENIX TAIL SHRIMP (*Fung-Mai Har*)

A. 1 lb. fresh shrimp, shelled (keep tails on), split slightly in back and cleaned

B. 2½ lbs. filet of pike (haddock or sea bass), chopped very fine

C. 2 oz. dried oyster, soaked in warm water 8 hours or more, cleaned, chopped very fine

D. 3 strips bacon, chopped very fine
E. 2 tablespoons Virginia ham, chopped very fine
F. 2 tablespoons Chinese sausage or dried duck meat (optional), chopped very fine
G. ¾ cup cornstarch
H. ½ teaspoon pepper
I. 2 cloves garlic, mashed
J. 1½ teaspoons seasoning powder
K. 3 fresh scallions (white part only), chopped very fine
L. 1 teaspoon salt
M. ½ teaspoon fresh ginger, chopped very fine
N. 2 eggs, beaten
O. 2 cups cornmeal

PREPARATION AND COOKING

Mix ingredients B through M; beat well with large heavy spoon until a paste is formed (if necessary, add 1 or 2 eggs). Grease hands with peanut oil. Roll each shrimp in about 3 tablespoons of the prepared mixture (leaving tail exposed); dip in N and roll in O. Repeat operation until all shrimp are used up.

Fry in deep hot peanut oil until golden brown. Place in lettuce-lined plate and garnish with sliced lemon and chopped Chinese parsley.

Serves 2 or 3.

303. FRIED SHRIMP, LOO-FOUL STYLE
(*Loo-Foul Har*)

A. 1 tablespoon honey
B. 1 teaspoon lemon juice
C. 1 teaspoon rice wine or 2 tablespoons sherry wine
D. 1 teaspoon fresh ginger, crushed
E. 1 lb. fresh jumbo shrimp, shelled, split slightly in back and cleaned
F. 2 eggs, beaten
G. 1 teaspoon seasoning powder
H. ¾ teaspoon salt
I. dash of pepper
J. ½ teaspoon garlic powder
K. ½ cup all purpose flour
L. ¼ cup cornstarch
M. ½ cup milk

PREPARATION AND COOKING

Mix together A, B, C, D. Soak E in this mixture 15 minutes or more. Beat F, G, H, I, J, K, L, M together until a smooth paste is formed. Dip E in paste. Fry in hot deep peanut oil until light brown. When cool, refrigerate until ready to serve. Dip in paste again. Fry until golden brown. Serve with lemon, duck sauce or tartar sauce.

Serves 2.

304. CAUL FAT WRAPPED SHRIMP WITH CHINESE BACON AND HAM (*Mon-Yu Yuen-Young Har*)

A. 1 lb. fresh jumbo shrimp, shelled, split in half and cleaned
B. ½ lb. Chinese bacon, or substitute American bacon, sliced very thin
C. ¼ lb. Virginia ham, sliced very thin
D. 2 lbs. caul fat, cut into 4 by 6 inch pieces

PREPARATION AND COOKING

Take a half shrimp; add one piece of ham, the other half of shrimp, then a piece of bacon. Wrap up in a piece of caul fat. Repeat operation until all shrimp are finished. Fry in deep fat until golden brown. Garnish with lettuce and sliced tomatoes. Or, bake in moderate oven 25 minutes, and garnish with cooked spinach or peas. Serves 2.

Note: Caul fat may be ordered from your butcher or from any pork store.

305. STEAMED SHRIMP ROLLS (*Har Quon*)

A. 1 lb. fresh shrimp, shelled, split in back, cleaned and chopped very fine
B. 1 cup Chinese sausage or bacon, chopped fine
C. 1 cup Virginia ham, chopped very fine
D. ½ lb. filet of haddock, chopped fine
E. 1 teaspoon fresh ginger, chopped very fine
F. 2 fresh scallions (white part only), chopped very fine
G. 1 teaspoon seasoning powder

H. 1 teaspoon garlic powder
I. ½ teaspoon pepper
J. 1 tablespoon rice wine
K. 1 teaspoon salt
L. 1 tablespoon peanut oil
M. ½ teaspoon sesame oil
N. 1 tablespoon light soy sauce
O. 6 eggs with 4 tablespoons water, a pinch of seasoning powder and salt, beaten vigorously 10 minutes

PREPARATION

Chop A, B, C, D, E, F together. Add G, H, I, J, K, L, M, N and mix thoroughly. Grease a large 8 or 10 inch frying pan, and place 3 tablespoons O mixture, or just enough to cover pan to form a layer on bottom, and cook one side over low flame until done. Remove from pan and repeat operation until egg layers are done. Spread the two prepared mixtures over the egg layer, about ¾ inches thick, then roll up the same way as you would a jelly roll.

COOKING

1. Place all shrimp rolls in a deep plate. Place on rack in a large pot with 2 inches of boiling water in bottom. Cover and steam 20 to 30 minutes.
2. Serve, sliced about 1 inch thick, in a lettuce-lined plate, garnished with parsley and tomatoes.

306. SHRIMP PAGODA (*Har Hop*)

A. 1 lb. fresh shrimp, shelled, split in back slightly, cleaned, sliced thin
B. 1 lb. fish meat (pike, sea bass, halibut or swordfish), sliced about ⅛ inch thick (about the size of a silver dollar)
C. 1 teaspoon heavy soy sauce
D. 4 tablespoons light soy sauce
E. 1 teaspoon fresh ginger, crushed
F. ¼ teaspoon pepper
G. 1 teaspoon garlic powder
H. 1 tablespoon rice wine or 2 tablespoons sherry wine
I. 2 teaspoons salt
J. 2 teaspoons seasoning powder
K. ½ lb. bacon, sliced thin
L. ½ lb. Virginia ham, sliced thin

PREPARATION AND COOKING

Mix C, D, E, F, G, H, I, J. Place A, B in the prepared mixture. Let them soak thoroughly. Place 1 slice shrimp at bottom of a deep plate, 1 slice ham on top of shrimp, 1 slice fish on top of ham, and 1 slice bacon on top of fish, to make one pagoda. Repeat construction of pagodas. Put a toothpick through the center of each; continue to build until all ingredients are used up. This makes approximately 35 pagodas. Place plate on rack in large pot with 3 inches boiling water in bottom and steam for 25 to 35 minutes. Or, bake in moderate oven 20 to 30 minutes. Serve hot with boiled rice.

Serves 4 or 5.

307. SWEET AND SOUR SHRIMP, PLAIN SAUCE
(*Tiem-Shoon Har Kew*)

Use same method and ingredients as in recipe No. 287, using shrimp instead of lobster.

308. SWEET AND SOUR SHRIMP WITH SUBGUM
SAUCE (*Subgum Tiem-Shoon Har Kew*)

Use same method and ingredients as in recipe No. 287, using shrimp instead of lobster, and adding 1 cup mixed sweet pickles cut in wedges, ½ cup green pepper, cut in wedges, and ½ cup fresh tomatoes, cut into wedges.

309. SWEET AND SOUR SHRIMP WITH PINEAPPLE
(*Boo-Loo Tiem-Shoon Har Kew*)

Use same method and ingredients as in recipe No. 287, using shrimp instead of lobster, and adding 1½ cups sliced pineapple.

310. SWEET AND SOUR SHRIMP WITH LICHEE
(*Lichee Tiem-Shoon Har Kew*)

Use same method and ingredients as in recipe No. 287, using shrimp instead of lobster, and adding 1 can preserved lichee nuts.

311. DICED CUT SHRIMP WITH VEGETABLES AND ALMONDS (*Chow Har Din*)

Use same method and ingredients as in recipe No. 139, using shrimp instead of pork.

312. DICED CUT SHRIMP WITH STRING BEANS
(*Dow-Doi Har Din*)

Use same method and ingredients as in recipe No. 139, using shrimp instead of pork, and adding 1½ cups diced string beans and 1 cup diced onions.

Note: Broccoli, asparagus or pea pods could be added to both the above recipes.

313. STIR-FRY SHRIMP WITH BEAN CURD
(*Dow-Foo Chow Har*)

Use same method and ingredients as in recipe No. 96A, using shrimp instead of pork.

314. SHRIMP WITH VERMICELLI (*Fon-Soo Har*)

Use same method and ingredients as in recipe No. 292, substituting shrimp for lobster.

315. SHRIMP WITH CURRY SAUCE (*Kur-Lee Har*)

Use same method and ingredients as in recipe No. 95, substituting shrimp for pork.

316. BATTER-FRY SHRIMP WITH CURRY
(*Kur-Lee Har Kew*)

Use same method and ingredients as in recipe No. 95, using shrimp instead of pork, and frying shrimp in batter, as instructed in recipe No. 298.

317. STIR-FRY SHRIMP WITH SHREDDED MEAT
AND VEGETABLES (*Som-Soo Har Kew*)

A. 1½ tablespoons peanut oil
B. 1 teaspoon salt
C. 2 cloves garlic, crushed
D. 1 lb. fresh shrimp, shelled, split in half, cleaned
E. 1 cup cooked meat (pork, beef, veal, ham, lamb, chicken, or turkey), shredded
F. 2 teaspoons light soy sauce
G. 1 teaspoon rice wine or 2 tablespoons sherry wine
H. 1 teapoon sugar
I. 1 teaspoon ginger, shredded very fine
J. 1 cup imported black mushrooms, soaked in warm water 15 minutes, shredded
K. 1 cup each of any of 3 vegetables (Chinese cabbage, broccoli, celery, bamboo shoots, asparagus, pea pods, onion, green pepper, cauliflower or bean sprouts)
L. ¼ cup water chestnuts, peeled and sliced, shredded
M. ½ cup soup stock
N. 1 tablespoon cornstarch
O. 1 teaspoon seasoning powder
P. 1 teaspoon heavy soy sauce
Q. ¼ teaspoon pepper

PREPARATION

Mix F, G, H, I; add 1 tablespoon water. Stir well before using.
Mix N, O, P, Q together with ½ cup water. Stir well before using.

COOKING

1. Put A in hot skillet. Add B and C.
2. Add D. Stir-fry 1 minute.
3. Add E. Stir-fry ½ minute.
4. Add F, G, H, I preparation. Stir-fry 1 minute.
5. Add J, K, L. Stir-fry thoroughly 2 minutes.
6. Add M. Cover and cook 3 minutes.
7. Add N, O, P, Q preparation. Stir thoroughly and constantly until gravy thickens and is smooth.

Serve with boiled rice.

Serves 3.

318. STIR-FRY SHRIMP WITH BEAN SPROUTS
(*Gar-Toy Chow Har*)

BASIC RECIPE

A. 1 tablespoon peanut oil
B. 1 teaspoon salt
C. 1 clove garlic, crushed
D. ½ lb. fresh shrimp, shelled, split in half and cleaned
E. 1 teaspoon light soy sauce
F. 1 teaspoon rice wine or 2 tablespoons sherry wine
G. 1 teaspoon ginger, shredded very fine
H. 1 teaspoon sugar
I. 1 lb. bean sprouts
J. 1 tablespoon preserved sweet pickles, shredded fine
K. ½ cup soup stock
L. 1 teaspoon heavy soy sauce
M. 1 tablespoon cornstarch
N. 1 teaspoon seasoning powder
O. ¼ teaspoon pepper

PREPARATION

Mix E, F, G, H; add 1 tablespoon water. Stir well before using.
Mix L, M, N, O with ½ cup water. Stir well before using.

COOKING

1. Put A in hot skillet. Add B and C.
2. Add D. Stir-fry 1 minute.
3. Add E, F, G, H preparation. Stir-fry ½ minute.
4. Add I, J. Stir-fry thoroughly 2 minutes.
5. Add K. Cover and cook 3 minutes.
6. Add L, M, N, O preparation. Stir-fry thoroughly and constantly until gravy thickens and is smooth.

Serves 3.

Note: You may add any of your favorite vegetables, if you wish.

319. STIR-FRY SHRIMP WITH BROCCOLI
(*Kai-Liang Chow Har*)

Follow basic recipe No. 318, substituting ½ lb. broccoli for half the bean sprouts.

320. STIR-FRY SHRIMP WITH PEA PODS
(*Shut-Dow Chow Har*)

Follow basic recipe No. 318, substituting ½ lb. pea pods for half the bean sprouts.

321. STIR-FRY SHRIMP WITH STRING BEANS
(*Dow-Doi Chow Har*)

Follow basic recipe No. 318, substituting ½ lb. string beans, cut 2 inches long, for half the bean sprouts.

322. STIR-FRY SHRIMP WITH THREE KINDS OF BAMBOO SHOOTS (*Sam-Shoon Chow Har*)

Use same method and ingredients as in recipe No. 112, using shrimp instead of pork.

323. STIR-FRY SHRIMP WITH ASSORTED VEGETABLES (*Kar-Toy Chow Har*)

Follow basic recipe No. 318, using 2 cups bean sprouts, 1 cup each of green pepper, tomatoes, celery, onion, and ¼ cup mushrooms, sliced.

324. SHRIMP CHOP SUEY (*Har Dep*)

Follow basic recipe No. 318, using 1 cup each of bean sprouts, onion, celery and ¼ cup each of bamboo shoots, mushrooms and water chestnuts. Slice all vegetables.

325. SHRIMP CHOW MEIN (*Har Chow Mein*)

Use same method and ingredients as in recipe No. 186, using shrimp instead of pork and crisp noodles instead of soft-fry noodles.

326. FRIED SHRIMP WITH TOMATO KETCHUP (*Kur-Chip Wong Har*)

BASIC RECIPE

A. 1 tablespoon peanut oil
B. ½ teaspoon salt
C. 2 cloves garlic, crushed
D. 1 lb. fresh jumbo shrimp, shelled, split slightly and cleaned
E. 1 tablespoon soy sauce
F. 1 teaspoon rice wine or 2 tablespoons sherry wine
G. 1 teaspoon sugar
H. 1 teaspoon fresh ginger, shredded very fine
I. ½ teaspoon pepper
J. 3 tablespoons tomato ketchup
K. ½ cup soup stock
L. 1 teaspoon heavy soy sauce
M. 1 teaspoon seasoning powder
N. 1 tablespoon cornstarch

PREPARATION

Mix E, F, G, H, I; add 1 tablespoon water. Stir well before using.
Mix L, M, N with ½ cup water. Stir well before using.

COOKING

1. Put A in hot skillet or a large frying pan. Add B and C.
2. Add D. Stir-fry thoroughly 2 minutes.
3. Add E, F, G, H, I preparation. Stir-fry ½ minute.
4. Add J. Stir-fry another ½ minute.
5. Add K. Stir-fry 2 minutes.
6. Add L, M, N preparation. Stir-fry until gravy thickens and is smooth.

   Serve hot with boiled rice.

Serves 2.

Note: Shrimp may be fried with shell. It will take 4 to 5 minutes in 2 tablespoons peanut oil.

327. FRIED SHRIMP WITH BLACK BEAN SAUCE
(*Dow-Shee Wong-Har*)

Follow basic recipe No. 326, using mashed black bean sauce instead of tomato ketchup.

328. FRIED SHRIMP WITH OYSTER SAUCE
(*Hoo-You Wong Har*)

Follow basic recipe No. 326, using oyster sauce instead of tomato ketchup.

CONCH

---

329. BRAISED CONCH WITH MUSHROOMS
(*Hong-Sher Hong-Lor*)

A. 1 tablespoon peanut oil
B. 1 teaspoon salt
C. 1 clove garlic, crushed
D. 4 large-size conchs
E. 1 cup imported black mushrooms, soaked in warm water 15 minutes, sliced (American mushrooms may be substituted)
F. 1 cup bamboo shoots, cut into 1 inch cubes
G. 1 cup celery, cut about 1 inch crosswise
H. 1 cup onion, cut in wedges
I. 2 teaspoons light soy sauce
J. 1 teaspoon rice wine or 2 tablespoons sherry wine
K. 1 teaspoon ginger, shredded very fine
L. 1 tablespoon leek, chopped very fine
M. 1½ cups soup stock
N. 1 tablespoon cornstarch
O. 1 teaspoon seasoning powder
P. 1 teaspoon sugar
Q. ¼ teaspoon pepper
R. 10 drops sesame seed oil

PREPARATION

Remove D from shells. Wash in hot water, rinse in cold water; cut in halves, then crosswise and lengthwise into 1 inch cubes. Place in a deep pan or pot; cover with 2 quarts water and add 1 tablespoon baking powder. Cover and cook 45 minutes, or until tender. Rinse with cold water; drain. Mix I, J, K, L together; add 1 tablespoon water. Stir well before using. Mix N, O, P, Q, R together with ½ cup water: stir well before using.

1. Put A in hot skillet, add B and C.
2. Add D. Stir-fry ½ minute.
3. Add E, F, G, H. Stir thoroughly 2 minutes.
4. Add I, J, K, L preparation. Stir-fry 2 minutes.
5. Add M. Cover and cook 2 minutes.
6. Add N, O, P, Q, R preparation. Stir-fry constantly until gravy thickens and is smooth.

Serves 2.

330. STIR-FRY CONCH WITH VEGETABLES
(*Chow Hong-Lor Pen*)

A. 1 teaspoon peanut oil
B. 1 teaspoon salt
C. 1 clove garlic, crushed
D. 4 large-size conchs
E. 1 cup Chinese barbecued pork, sliced thin
F. ½ cup black or white mushrooms
G. ¼ cup water chestnuts, peeled, sliced
H. 1 cup Chinese pea pods (broccoli or asparagus may be substituted)
I. ½ cup bamboo shoots, sliced very thin
J. 1 cup bean sprouts
K. ½ cup onion, sliced
L. 1 teaspoon light soy sauce
M. 1 teaspoon rice wine or 2 tablespoons sherry wine
N. 1 teaspoon ginger, shredded very fine
O. 10 drops sesame seed oil
P. ½ cup soup stock
Q. 1 tablespoon cornstarch
R. 1 teaspoon seasoning powder
S. ¼ teaspoon pepper
T. 1 teaspoon sugar
U. 1 teaspoon heavy soy sauce

PREPARATION

Remove D from shells. Wash in warm water; cut in halves. Cook 1 hour, or until tender (add 1 tablespoon baking powder to water). Rinse in cold water; slice thin. Mix L, M, N, O together; add 1 tablespoon water. Stir well before using. Mix Q, R, S, T, U together with ½ cup water. Stir well before using.

COOKING

1. Put A in hot skillet; add B and C.
2. Add D, E. Stir-fry ½ minute.
3. Add F, G, H, I, J, K. Stir-fry thoroughly 2 minutes.
4. Add L, M, N, O preparation. Stir-fry thoroughly 1 minute.
5. Add P. Cover and cook 3 minutes.
6. Add Q, R, S, T, U preparation. Stir constantly until gravy thickens and is smooth.

Serves 3.

331. SWEET AND SOUR CONCH WITH PLAIN SAUCE (*Tiem-Shoon Hong-Lor*)

A. 1 cup water
B. ½ cup sugar
C. ½ cup vinegar
D. 4 large-size conchs
E. 1 teaspoon light soy sauce
F. 1 teaspoon rice wine or 2 tablespoons sherry wine
G. 1 teaspoon ginger, shredded very fine
H. ¼ teaspoon sesame seed oil
I. ¾ cup all purpose flour
J. 2 eggs, beaten
K. ½ teaspoon seasoning powder
L. ¼ teaspoon pepper
M. ¼ teaspoon salt
N. 1 tablespoon cornstarch
O. 1½ teaspoons heavy soy sauce

PREPARATION

Remove D from shells. Wash with hot water, then boil, adding 2 tablespoons baking powder to water, for 1 hour, or until tender. Cut into 1 inch cubes. Mix E, F, G, H together; add 1 tablespoon water. Stir well before using. Beat I, J vigorously until a smooth paste is formed. Add K, L, M and mix well together. Mix N, O together with ½ cup water. Stir well before using. Soak cooked conchs in E, F, G, H preparation for 15 minutes or more.

COOKING

1. Dip prepared D in egg mixture; fry in deep fat until golden brown. Place in a deep plate.
2. Pour A into hot skillet; add B and C. Cook until sugar dissolves.
3. Add cornstarch preparation gradually and stir constantly until sauce thickens and is smooth; pour over conchs and serve. Garnish with Chinese parsley.

Serves 2.

332. SWEET AND SOUR CONCH WITH SUBGUM SAUCE (*Subgum Tiem-Shoon Hong-Lor*)

Use same method and ingredients as in recipe No. 331. Add the following ingredients after sugar dissolves: 1 cup tomatoes, cut in wedges or diced; 1 cup green peppers, cut in wedges or diced; 1 cup mixed sweet pickles. Cook 3 or 4 minutes before adding cornstarch preparation.

333. SWEET AND SOUR CONCH WITH PINEAPPLE (*Bo-Lo Tiem-Shoon Hong-Lor*)

Use same method and ingredients as in recipe No. 331, adding 2 cups cubed pineapple to sauce.

334. FRIED CONCH IN BATTER WITH VEGETABLES (*Sod-Jow Hong-Lor Kew*)

A. 1 tablespoon peanut oil
B. 1 teaspoon salt
C. 1 clove garlic, crushed
D. 4 large-size conchs
E. 1 cup black mushrooms, soaked in warm water 15 minutes, sliced
F. 1 cup bamboo shoots, sliced
G. 1 cup celery, sliced

H. ¼ cup water chestnuts, peeled and sliced
I. ½ cup pea pods, sliced
J. 2 teaspoons light soy sauce
K. 1 teaspoon rice wine or 2 tablespoons sherry wine
L. 1 teaspoon ginger, shredded very fine
M. 10 drops sesame seed oil
N. dash of pepper
O. ¾ cup all purpose flour
P. 2 eggs, beaten
Q. ½ teaspoon seasoning powder
R. ½ cup soup stock
S. 1 tablespoon cornstarch
T. 1 teaspoon seasoning powder
U. 1 teaspoon sugar
V. 1 teaspoon heavy soy sauce

PREPARATION

Remove D from shells. Wash in hot water. Cook 1 hour, or until tender, adding 2 tablespoons baking powder to water. Cut into 1 inch cubes. Mix J, K, L, M, N together with 1 tablespoon water. Divide into 2 parts. Soak D in half of mixture for 15 minutes or longer. Beat O, P; add pinch of salt and seasoning powder and beat until a paste is formed. Dip D in this preparation and fry in deep fat until golden brown. Mix S, T, U, V together with ½ cup water. Stir well before using.

COOKING

1. Put A in hot skillet; add B and C.
2. Add E, F, G, H, I. Stir-fry thoroughly 2 minutes.
3. Add second half of J, K, L, M, N preparation and stir-fry 1 minute.
4. Add R. Cover and cook 3 minutes.
5. Add prepared conchs. Stir thoroughly ½ minute.
6. Add cornstarch preparation gradually. Stir constantly until gravy thickens and is smooth.

Serves 2 or 3.

Note: One cup of any one of the following vegetables may be added to this recipe: broccoli, asparagus, Chinese cabbage, mushrooms, mustard greens.

SNAILS

335. SAUTE SNAILS WITH BLACK BEAN SAUCE IN SHELL (*Chow Tien-Low*)

A. 2 tablespoons peanut oil
B. 1 teaspoon salt
C. 4 cloves garlic, crushed
D. 2 tablespoons black bean sauce, washed and cleaned
E. 1 tablespoon do-soo (herb) (optional)
F. 2 lbs. live snails (keep snails in clear water for 24 hours or more; change water every 5 or 6 hours; cut off the point of the shell)
G. 1 tablespoon light soy sauce
H. 1 teaspoon rice wine or 2 tablespoons sherry wine
I. 1 tablespoon hot sauce
J. 1 teaspoon ginger, shredded very fine
K. 1 cup soup stock
L. 1 tablespoon cornstarch
M. 1½ teaspoons seasoning powder
N. ¼ teaspoon pepper
O. ½ teaspoon curry powder

PREPARATION

Mix C, D, E together with 1 tablespoon water. Mix G, H, I, J; add 1 tablespoon water. Stir well before using. Mix L, M, N, O together with ½ cup water. Stir well before using.

COOKING

1. Put A in hot skillet; add B.
2. Add C, D, E preparation. Stir ½ minute.
3. Add F. Stir-fry thoroughly 3 minutes.

4. Add G, H, I, J preparation and stir another minute.
5. Add K. Cover and cook 2 minutes. Lower heat, sauté 20 minutes.
6. Add L, M, N, O preparation. Stir constantly until gravy thickens and is smooth.

Serves 4.

336. SAUTE SNAILS WITH CURRY SAUCE IN SHELL (*Kur-Lee Tien-Low*)

Use same method and ingredients as in recipe No. 335, substituting 1 tablespoon curry sauce for black bean sauce. (See recipe No. 95 for curry sauce.)

337. SNAIL MEAT WITH LOBSTER SAUCE (*Tien-Low Loong Har Wu*)

Use same method and ingredients as in recipe No. 297, using snails instead of shrimp.

CLAMS

338. STEAMED CLAMS OR RAZOR CLAMS
(*Cho-Hing*)

A. 3 dozen clams or razor clams (in shells)
B. 2 tablespoons light soy sauce
C. 1 teaspoon fresh ginger, shredded very fine
D. 1 teaspoon rice wine
E. 1 teaspoon seasoning powder
F. 1 head fresh leek, chopped very fine

PREPARATION AND COOKING

Put A in a bowl; put bowl on rack in a large pot with 3 inches boiling water in bottom. Steam 15 minutes, or until bivalves open. Remove clams from shell and place in deep plate. Mix B, C, D, E, F together, and pour over clams. Use the same steam pot and steam 5 to 7 minutes.

Serve with boiled rice or potatoes.

Serves 2.

339. STIR-FRY CLAM MEAT WITH CURRY SAUCE
(*Kur-Lee Hing-Yoke*)

Use same method and ingredients as in recipe No. 95, using shelled clams instead of pork.

340. FRIED CLAMS IN BATTER WITH VEGETABLES (*Hon-Shu Hing-Yoke*)

Use same method and ingredients as in recipe No. 285, using clams instead of lobster.

[204]

341. SWEET AND SOUR CLAMS
(*Tiem-Shoon Hing-Yoke*)

Use same method and ingredients as in recipe No. 287, using clams instead of lobster.

342. CLAMS WITH LOBSTER SAUCE
(*Hing-Yoke Loong Har Wu*)

Use same method and ingredients as in recipe No. 297, using clams instead of shrimp.

343. STEAMED CLAMS WITH SHRIMP SAUCE, VILLAGE STYLE (*Hom-Har Cho Hing-Yoke*)

A. 1 lb. shelled clams
B. 2 tablespoons shrimp sauce
C. 1 fresh leek (white part only), chopped very fine

COOKING

1. Put clams in deep bowl. Pour B on top of clams; then sprinkle C on top of sauce.
2. Put bowl on rack in large pot with about 3 inches boiling water in bottom. Steam 5 to 7 minutes.

OYSTERS

344. FRIED OYSTERS, CHINESE STYLE
(*Soo-Jow Hoo-Shee*)

A. 1 tablespoon light soy sauce
B. 1 teaspoon heavy soy sauce
C. ½ teaspoon ginger, mashed very fine
D. 1 teaspoon rice wine or 2 tablespoons sherry wine
E. 1 dozen raw oysters
F. 1 cup mixed nuts, crushed into powder
G. 1 dozen strips bacon, sliced very thin
H. 1 dozen pieces Virginia ham or Chinese sausage
I. 2 scallions (white part only), cut crosswise 1½ inches
   long, then into halves (12 pieces)
J. ½ cup all purpose flour
K. 1 egg
L. pinch of salt, pepper and seasoning powder

PREPARATION AND COOKING

Mix A, B, C, D together. Soak E in this mixture 15 minutes or more. Dip E into F. Wrap a strip of bacon around 1 oyster, 1 piece ham and 1 piece scallion. Beat J, K, L together, beating vigorously to form a paste. Dip prepared oysters in this mixture. Fry in deep fat until golden brown. Serve with lemon, and garnish with parsley and lettuce.

Serves 2.

345. DRIED OYSTERS WRAPPED WITH CAUL FAT
(*Mon-Yu Ho-Shee*)

A. 1 teaspoon ginger
B. 1 lb. fish filet (pike, haddock or sea bass)
C. 2 cloves garlic, crushed
D. 2 fresh scallions (white part only), split
E. 1 cup fresh shrimps
F. 1 cup raw pork
G. ½ teaspoon pepper
H. 1 teaspoon salt
I. 1 teaspoon seasoning powder
J. ½ teaspoon sesame oil
K. 1 tablespoon peanut oil
L. 12 pieces dried oysters, soaked in cold water for 24 hours or more, cleaned thoroughly until all sand is out
M. 12 pieces caul fat, cut 4 inches x 8 inches
N. 1 egg, beaten

PREPARATION AND COOKING

Grind A, B, C, D, E, F together. Add G, H, I, J, K and mix thoroughly. Roll each oyster in about 3 tablespoons of above mixture; repeat until all are coated. Wrap each L in one piece M. Before rolling up, brush N all around edge of caul fat. Fry in deep hot oil until golden brown. Serve with sliced lemon and tomatoes, garnish with lettuce.

Serves 2.

346. STUFFED GREEN PEPPER WITH DRIED OYSTER MIXTURE (*Ho-Shee-Soong Yong Lard-Dew*)

Use same ingredients as in recipe No. 345, eliminating caul fat and beaten egg, and adding 6 large green peppers. Cut peppers in half, remove seeds. Grind all ingredients together and stuff into peppers. Steam or bake in moderate oven 25 to 30 minutes.

Serves 2 or 3.

347. DRIED OYSTER EGG ROLLS (*Hoo-Shee Guen*)

Follow recipe No. 62. Add 1 dozen dried oysters, medium size, soaked in cold water 24 hours (until soft), shredded very fine, and 2 tablespoons oyster sauce to the filling mixture.

348. MINCED DRIED OYSTERS WITH ASSORTED VEGETABLES (*Chow Hoo-Shee Soong*)

A. 1½ tablespoons peanut oil
B. 1 teaspoon salt
C. 1 clove garlic, crushed
D. 1 dozen dried oysters, soaked in cold water 24 hours; cleaned thoroughly until all sand is out and chopped very fine
E. 1 cup raw pork, chopped very fine
F. 1 cup celery, chopped very fine
G. 1 cup Chinese cabbage (white part only), chopped fine
H. ½ cup bamboo shoots, chopped fine
I. ½ cup water chestnuts, peeled and chopped fine
J. 1 cup pea pods, chopped very fine (broccoli or asparagus may be substituted)
K. 1 fresh scallion (white part only), chopped very fine
L. 1 tablespoon light soy sauce
M. 1 teaspoon rice wine or 2 tablespoons sherry wine
N. 1 teaspoon ginger, shredded very fine
O. 1 teaspoon sugar
P. ¼ teaspoon sesame oil
Q. ½ cup soup stock
R. 1 tablespoon cornstarch
S. 1 teaspoon seasoning powder
T. pinch of pepper
U. 1 teaspoon hot sauce
V. 1 teaspoon heavy soy sauce
W. 1 tablespoon oyster sauce

PREPARATION

Mix L, M, N, O, P together; add 1 tablespoon water. Stir well before using. Mix R, S, T, U, V together with ½ cup water. Stir well before using.

COOKING

1. Put A in very hot skillet; add B and C.
2. Add D, E. Stir-fry 2 minutes.
3. Add F, G, H, I, J. Stir-fry thoroughly 3 minutes.
4. Add K.
5. Add L, M, N, O, P preparation. Stir-fry 1 minute.
6. Add Q. Cover and cook 3 minutes, stirring thoroughly.
7. Add R, S, T, U, V, W preparation. Stir-fry constantly until gravy thickens and is smooth.
   Serve hot with boiled rice or toast, or use as sandwich filling.

Serves 2 or 3.

349. STIR-FRY SLICED DRIED OYSTERS WITH ASSORTED VEGETABLES (*Chow Hoo-Shee-Pen*)

Use same method and ingredients as in recipe No. 348, slicing the oysters and vegetables instead of chopping them.

350. DICED CUT DRIED OYSTERS WITH ASSORTED VEGETABLES (*Chow Hoo-Shee Din*)

Use same method and ingredients as in recipe No. 291, using dried oysters, properly soaked and cleaned, instead of lobster.

Note: String beans, asparagus or frozen peas may be added to the previous three recipes.

SCALLOPS

---

351. BUTTERFLY SCALLOPS (*Soo-Jow Kong Yu-Cho*)

Use same method and ingredients as in recipe No. 298, using scallops instead of shrimp.

352. BUTTERFLY SCALLOPS WITH BACON
(*Wor-Hep Kong Yu-Cho*)

Use same method and ingredients as in recipe No. 299, using scallops instead of shrimp.

353. STUFFED SCALLOPS, ROYAL STYLE
(*Wong-Kung Kong Yu-Cho*)

Use same method and ingredients as in recipe No. 301, using scallops instead of shrimp.

Note: Scallops may be cut into cubes. Do not split.

354. DICED CUT SCALLOPS WITH ALMONDS
AND VEGETABLES (*Chow Kong Yu-Cho Din*)

Use same method and ingredients as in recipe No. 139, using scallops instead of pork.

355. SWEET AND SOUR SCALLOPS
(*Tiem-Shoon Kong Yu-Cho*)

Use same method and ingredients as in recipe No. 287, using scallops instead of lobster.

Note: For other variations, follow recipes Nos. 288, 289, 290, using scallops instead of lobster.

356. BUTTERFLY SCALLOPS WITH VEGETABLES
(*Soo-Jow Yu-Cho Kew*)

Use same method and ingredients as in recipe No. 204, using scallops instead of chicken.

357. SCALLOP CHOP SUEY (*Kong-Yu-Cho Dep Suey*)

Use same method and ingredients as in recipe No. 198, using scallops instead of chicken.

ABALONE

---

358. STIR-FRY ABALONE WITH SOY SAUCE
(*Hong-Shu Bow-Pu*)

A. 1 tablespoon peanut oil
B. ½ teaspoon salt
C. 1 clove garlic
D. 1 can abalone, cut in 1 inch cubes (save stock from can)
E. 1 cup lean raw pork, chopped very fine
F. ½ cup mushrooms, chopped very fine
G. ¼ cup water chestnuts, peeled, chopped very fine
H. ½ cup bamboo shoots, diced fine
I. 2 teaspoons light soy sauce
J. 1 teaspoon rice wine or 2 tablespoons sherry wine
K. 1 teaspoon ginger, chopped very fine
L. ½ teaspoon sesame seed oil
M. ½ cup abalone stock (saved from can)
N. 1 tablespoon cornstarch
O. 1 teaspoon seasoning powder
P. 1 teaspoon sugar
Q. 1 teaspoon heavy soy sauce

PREPARATION

Mix I, J, K, L together; add 1 tablespoon water. Stir well before using. Mix N, O, P, Q together with ½ cup water. Stir well before using.

COOKING

1. Put A in very hot skillet; add B and C.
2. Add D, E. Stir-fry 1 minute.
3. Add F, G, H. Stir-fry 2 minutes.
4. Add I, J, K, L preparation. Stir-fry 1 minute.

5. Add M. Cover and cook 1 minute.
6. Add N, O, P, Q preparation (stirred up well), and stir constantly until gravy thickens and is smooth.

Serve with boiled rice.

Serves 2.

359. STIR-FRY ABALONE WITH OYSTER SAUCE
(*Hoo-Yu Bow-Pu*)

Use same method and ingredients as in recipe No. 358, using 2 tablespoons oyster sauce instead of light soy sauce.

360. STIR-FRY SHREDDED ABALONE WITH THREE KINDS SHREDDED MEATS AND VEGETABLES
(*Som-Soo Bow-Yu*)

A. 1 tablespoon peanut oil
B. ½ teaspoon salt
C. 1 clove garlic
D. 1 can abalone, shredded very fine (save stock from can)
E. ½ cup roast pork (beef, veal or lamb may be substituted), shredded very fine
F. ½ cup cooked chicken or turkey meat, shredded very fine
G. ¼ cup cooked Virginia ham or bacon shredded very fine
H. 2 teaspoons light soy sauce
I. 1 teaspoon rice wine or 2 tablespoons sherry wine
J. 1 teaspoon ginger, shredded fine
K. ½ cup bamboo shoots, shredded very fine
L. ½ cup black mushrooms, soaked in warm water 15 minutes, then shredded fine
M. 1½ cups celery (tender part only), shredded very fine
N. ½ cup abalone stock (saved from can)
O. 1 tablespoon cornstarch
P. 1 teaspoon seasoning powder
Q. 1 teaspoon sugar
R. 1 teaspoon heavy soy sauce
S. 1 tablespoon oyster sauce

PREPARATION

Mix H, I, J together; add 1 tablespoon water. Stir well before using. Mix O, P, Q, R, S together with ½ cup water. Stir well before using.

COOKING

1. Put A in hot skillet; add B and C.
2. Add D, E, F, G. Stir-fry ½ minute.
3. Add H, I, J preparation. Stir-fry ½ minute.
4. Add K, L, M. Stir-fry 1 minute.
5. Add N. Cover and cook 2 minutes.
6. Add O, P, Q, R, S preparation. Stir-fry thoroughly until gravy thickens and is smooth.
   Serve with boiled rice.

Serves 2.

361. STIR-FRY ABALONE WITH ASSORTED VEGETABLES (*Chow Bow-Yu Pen*)

Use same method and ingredients as in recipe No. 235, using sliced abalone instead of chicken meat.

SQUID

---

362. STIR-FRY DRIED SQUID WITH MUSHROOMS AND ASSORTED VEGETABLES
(*Chow Dew-Pan Yu*)

A. 1 tablespoon peanut oil
B. 1 teaspoon salt
C. 1 clove garlic, crushed
D. 1 lb. dried squid
E. 2 teaspoons light soy sauce
F. 1 teaspoon rice wine or 2 tablespoons sherry wine
G. 1 teaspoon ginger, shredded fine
H. ¼ teaspoon sesame oil
I. 1 cup celery, sliced thin crosswise
J. ½ cup onion, sliced
K. ½ cup Chinese pea pods
L. ½ cup bamboo shoots, sliced thin
M. ½ cup black or white mushrooms, sliced thin
N. 1 cup Chinese cabbage (white part only), sliced thin crosswise (broccoli, asparagus or celery cabbage may be substituted)
O. ¼ cup water chestnuts, peeled and sliced thin
P. ½ cup soup stock
Q. 1 tablespoon cornstarch
R. 1 teaspoon seasoning powder
S. 1 teaspoon sugar
T. 1 teaspoon heavy soy sauce

PREPARATION

Soak D in water for 24 hours or more. Pull out center bones and take off black skin; clean inside. Cut off tentacles, then split open and slash lengthwise and crosswise on inside; then cut into 1½ or 2 inch squares (they will roll up like balls when fried). Mix E, F, G, H together; add 1 tablespoon water. Stir well before using. Mix Q, R, S, T together with ½ cup water. Stir well before using.

COOKING

1. Put A in very hot skillet; add B and C.
2. Add D (plus tentacles previously removed). Stir-fry ½ minute, or until pieces of squid roll up like balls.
3. Add E, F, G, H preparation. Stir-fry 1 minute. Take squid out of skillet. Add I, J, K, L, M, N, O. Stir-fry thoroughly 2 minutes.
4. Add P. Cover and cook 3 minutes. Return squid to skillet and add Q, R, S, T preparation. Stir until gravy thickens and is smooth.

Serves 2 or 3.

Note: Fresh squid may be used, if desired; use same method for cleaning.

Note: 1 tablespoon oyster sauce may be added to all seafood dishes.

363. STIR-FRY DRIED SHREDDED SQUID WITH THREE KINDS OF MEATS AND VEGETABLES
(*Som-Soo Dew-Pen*)

Prepare dried squid as instructed in preceding recipe. Use same method and ingredients as in recipe No. 360, using squid instead of abalone.

364. STIR-FRY FRESH SQUID WITH CURRY SAUCE
(*Kur-Lee Sen-Yu*)

Use same method and ingredients as in recipe No. 95, using squid instead of pork. Prepare squid as instructed in recipe No. 362.

365. SWEET AND SOUR FRESH SQUID
(*Tiem-Shoon Sen-Yu*)

Use same method and ingredients as in recipe No. 287, using squid instead of lobster. Prepare squid as instructed in recipe No. 362.

366. FRIED FRESH SQUID IN BATTER WITH ASSORTED VEGETABLES (*Hong-Shu Sen-Yu*)

Use same method and ingredients as in recipe No. 285, using squid instead of lobster. Prepare squid as instructed in recipe No. 362.

CRABS

367. CRABMEAT FRITTERS WITH SHREDDED VEGETABLES (*Sum-Soo Hi-Kew*)

A. 1 tablespoon peanut oil
B. ½ teaspoon salt
C. 1 clove garlic
D. 1 cup celery (tender part only), shredded very fine
E. ¾ cup imported black mushrooms, soaked in warm water 15 minutes, shredded very fine
F. 1 cup Chinese cabbage (white part only), shredded very fine
G. 1 cup bamboo shoots, shredded very fine
H. ¼ cup water chestnuts, peeled and shredded very fine
I. 1 cup Chinese pea pods, shredded
J. 1 teaspoon light soy sauce
K. 1 teaspoon rice wine or 2 tablespoons sherry wine
L. 1 teaspoon ginger, shredded very fine
M. ½ teaspoon sesame seed oil
N. ½ cup soup stock
O. 1 tablespoon cornstarch
P. 1 teaspoon seasoning powder
Q. 1 teaspoon heavy soy sauce
R. 1 teaspoon sugar
S. 3 eggs
T. ½ cup all purpose flour
U. 1 lb. fresh or canned crabmeat, chopped
V. 1 teaspoon seasoning powder
W. ¼ teaspoon pepper
X. ½ teaspoon garlic salt

PREPARATION

Beat S, T vigorously with electric beater or by hand 10 minutes; add U. Add V, W, X, beat again 2 minutes. Form into cakes, using

1 tablespoon to a fritter, and fry in deep fat until golden brown. Set aside in large deep lettuce-lined plate. Mix J, K, L, M together; add 1 tablespoon water. Stir well before using. Mix O, P, Q, R together with ½ cup water. Stir well before using.

COOKING

1. Put A in hot skillet; add B, C.
2. Add D, E, F, G, H, I. Stir-fry 3 minutes.
3. Add J, K, L, M preparation. Stir-fry 1 minute.
4. Add N. Cover and cook 2½ minutes.
5. Add O, P, Q, R preparation. Stir-fry constantly until gravy thickens. Pour over crab fritters and serve hot.

Garnish with Chinese parsley and crushed mixed nuts.

Serves 3 or 4.

368. FRIED SOFT SHELL CRABS IN BATTER WITH MUSHROOMS AND VEGETABLES
(*Soo-Jow Yuen-Hock Hi*)

A. 1 tablespoon peanut oil
B. ½ teaspoon salt
C. 1 clove garlic
D. 1 cup imported black mushrooms, soaked in warm water 15 minutes, shredded
E. 1 cup bamboo shoots, shredded
F. ¼ cup water chestnuts, peeled and shredded
G. 1½ cups Chinese cabbage (white part only), shredded
H. 1½ cups Chinese pea pods, shredded (broccoli or asparagus may be substituted)
I. 2 tablespoons light soy sauce
J. 1 tablespoon rice wine or 2 tablespoons sherry wine
K. 1 teaspoon ginger, crushed
L. ¼ teaspoon sesame seed oil
M. 1 teaspoon garlic powder
N. ½ cup soup stock
O. 1 tablespoon cornstarch
P. 1 teaspoon sugar
Q. 1 teaspoon seasoning powder
R. 1 teaspoon heavy soy sauce
S. 2 eggs
T. ½ cup all purpose flour
U. 6 soft shell crabs, cut in 4 pieces each

PREPARATION

Mix I, J, K, L, M together; add 1 tablespoon water. Soak U in this preparation 10 minutes or more. Mix O, P, Q, R together with ½ cup water. Stir well before using. Beat S, T vigorously 10 minutes; add pinch of salt, seasoning powder, pepper and beat again for 1 minute. Remove crabs from mixture (saving what is left of this preparation) and dip soaked crab pieces in egg mixture. Fry in deep hot fat until golden brown. Set aside in deep lettuce-lined plate.

COOKING

1. Put A in hot skillet; add B and C.
2. Add D, E, F, G, H. Stir-fry 2 minutes.
3. Add what is left of I, J, K, L, M mixture. Stir-fry 2 minutes.
4. Add N. Cover and cook 2 minutes.
5. Add O, P, Q, R preparation. Stir-fry until gravy thickens. Pour over crabs. Serve with vinegar or sliced lemon.

Serves 3.

369. FRIED HARD SHELL CRABS WITH MEAT SAUCE (*Yoke Wu Chow-Hi*)

Use same method and ingredients as in recipe No. 281, using 6 crabs instead of lobster. Remove shell of crab and chop off feet; crack claws, then cut crab into 4 pieces.

Serves 2.

370. STUFFED CRABS WITH MEAT SAUCE (*Yonk Hi*)

Use same method and ingredients as in recipe No. 282, using 6 crabs instead of lobster. Prepare crabs as instructed in preceding recipe.

FISH

---

371. STEAMED FISH WITH SOY SAUCE
(*Bok Suey Yu*)

A. 1 to 2 lbs. sea bass, black bass, porgy, shad, pike, white-fish or mackerel, cleaned thoroughly
B. 1 teaspoon salt
C. 1 teaspoon seasoning powder
D. 2 tablespoons light soy sauce
E. 4 tablespoons peanut oil, add a few drops sesame oil
F. 1 clove garlic, crushed
G. 1 tablespoon chopped cooked Virginia ham or bacon
H. 4 tablespoons Chinese preserved sweet pickle and ginger, shredded very fine
I. 2 fresh scallions (white part only), cut into sections 2 inches long, then split into 4 or 5 pieces

COOKING

1. Put A in deep plate.
2. Place a rack in a large pot containing 3 inches boiling water; put plate on rack. Cover and steam 20 minutes or until fish is done.
3. Drain all liquid from plate; add B.
4. Sprinkle C, D over fish.
5. Heat E until smoking; add F; turn off heat. Let oil cook garlic 1 minute; then pour over fish.
6. Sprinkle G, H, I on top of each serving.

Serves 2.

372. STEAMED FISH WITH BROWN BEAN SAUCE
(*Mien-Shee Jing Yu*)

A. 1 lb. fish (porgy, sea bass, black bass, pike, whitefish, mackerel, halibut); whole fish or cut in sections, as you desire, washed and cleaned thoroughly, and dried
B. 1½ tablespoons brown bean sauce, mashed
C. 1 tablespoon chopped leek
D. 1 teaspoon ginger, shredded very fine
E. 1 teaspoon seasoning powder
F. 2 tablespoons peanut oil, add a few drops sesame seed oil
G. 1 clove garlic, crushed

COOKING

1. Put A in deep plate.
2. Mix B, C, D, E together.
3. Rub mixture on surface of fish.
4. Place a rack in a large pot containing 3 inches boiling water; put plate on rack. Cover and steam 20 minutes, or until fish is done.
5. Heat F with G until oil starts to smoke. Pour oil over fish and serve at once.

Serves 2.

Note: Black beans may be substituted for brown bean sauce; black beans should be soaked in water for 10 minutes, cleaned and mashed.

373. STEAMED FISH WITH SHRIMP SAUCE
(*Hom-Har Jing Yu*)

A. 1 to 2 lbs. fish (sea bass, black bass, porgy, etc.)
B. 1½ tablespoons shrimp sauce
C. 1 tablespoon leek, chopped fine
D. 1 teaspoon ginger, shredded fine
E. 1 teaspoon scallions, chopped fine
F. 1½ tablespoons peanut oil
G. 1 teaspoon seasoning powder

COOKING

1. Put A in deep plate.
2. Mix rest of ingredients (B through G) together.
3. Rub mixture on surface of fish.
4. Place plate on rack in pot with 3 inches boiling water. Cover and steam 20 minutes, or until fish is done.

Serves 2.

374. FRIED FISH WITH SOY SAUCE (*Dinn Yu*)

A. 2 tablespoons peanut oil
B. 1 lb. fish (porgy, sea bass, smelts, sturgeon, shad, halibut, mackerel, haddock, pike, etc.), washed, cleaned and dried
C. 1 teaspoon salt
D. 1 tablespoon light soy sauce
E. 1½ teaspoons rice wine or 2 tablespoons sherry wine
F. 1 teaspoon ginger, shredded fine
G. 1 tablespoon leek, chopped fine
H. 1 teaspoon scallions, chopped fine
I. 1 teaspoon seasoning powder
J. few drops sesame seed oil
K. pinch of pepper
L. ½ cup soup stock or water

PREPARATION

Rub B with C. Mix D, E, F, G, H, I, J, K together well.

COOKING

1. Put A in hot skillet.
2. Put B in skillet. Fry on both sides until light brown.
3. Add prepared mixture and L. Cover and cook 15 minutes, or until fish is done.

Serves 2.

375. FRIED FISH WITH TOMATOES
(*Fon-Kur Gee-Yu*)

Use same method and ingredients as in recipe No. 374, adding 1½ cups tomatoes, cut in wedges.

376. FRIED FISH WITH BEAN CURD
(*Dow-Foo Gee-Yu*)

Use same method and ingredients as in recipe No. 374, adding 2 cups bean curd, cut in 1 inch squares.

Note: Egg plant, carrot, Chinese turnip, bitter melon, pickled mustard greens or Chinese cabbage may also be added to this fried fish recipe.

377. BRAISED FISH WITH BLACK MUSHROOMS
(*Mien Yu*)

A. 1½ tablespoons peanut oil
B. 1 teaspoon salt
C. 1 clove garlic
D. 2 lbs. fish (porgy, sea bass, sturgeon, shad, whitefish, mackerel, haddock, etc.) cleaned, washed and dried
E. 1 tablespoon light soy sauce
F. 1 teaspoon rice wine or 2 tablespoons sherry wine
G. 1 teaspoon shredded ginger
H. 1 teaspoon sugar
I. 1 tablespoon chopped leek
J. 1 teaspoon seasoning powder
K. ¼ teaspoon pepper
L. few drops of sesame seed oil
M. 1 teaspoon chopped scallions
N. 1 cup imported black mushrooms, soaked in warm water for 15 minutes, shredded
O. ½ cup Chinese or American bacon, shredded
P. 6 pieces Chinese red dates, soaked in warm water, stones removed, shredded
Q. ¼ cup water chestnuts, peeled, shredded
R. ½ cup bamboo shoots, shredded
S. 1 cup sweet bean stick, soaked in warm water for 25 minutes, shredded

PREPARATION

Mix E, F, G, H, I, J, K, L, M together.

COOKING

1. Put A in very hot skillet. Add B and C.
2. Add D. Fry on both sides until light brown; then add prepared mixture and 1½ cups water.
3. Add N, O, P, Q, R, S. Cover and bring to a boil. Lower heat; simmer 20 minutes, adding water if needed.
   Garnish with lettuce and parsley.

Serves 2 or 3.

378. FIVE WILLOW SWEET AND SOUR FISH
(*Eng-Liu Yu*)

A. 2 lbs. fish (sea or black bass, pike, white mullet, carp, haddock, mackerel, porgy and bluefish are best suited for making sweet and sour fish); washed and cleaned
B. 2 cups water
C. 4 tablespoons sugar
D. 4 tablespoons vinegar
E. 1 teaspoon seasoning powder
F. 1 teaspoon rice wine or 2 tablespoons sherry wine
G. 1 tablespoon cornstarch, dissolve in ½ cup water
H. 2 cups Chinese mixed pickles, shredded very fine (American mixed sweet pickles may be substituted) Add ½ cup each of shredded green pepper, carrots and tomatoes

COOKING

1. Put A in deep plate. Place plate on rack in pot with 3 inches boiling water. Cover and steam about 20 minutes or until fish is done (if any juice is left in plate, pour out and save to make sweet and sour gravy).
2. Pour B in hot skillet; add C, D.
3. Mix E, F with G and water and add to skillet slowly; stir until gravy becomes translucent.
4. Add H. Cook 3 minutes. Pour sauce over fish and serve at once. Garnish with chopped parsley, lettuce or split scallions cut into 2 inch sections.

Serves 2 or 3.

379. FIVE WILLOW SWEET AND SOUR FISH IN BATTER (*Eng-Liu Hong Shu Yu*)

Use same method and ingredients as in recipe No. 378, but fry fish first dipped in batter made with 2 eggs, beaten, and ½ cup all purpose flour.

380. FRIED FISH IN BATTER, SIWO STYLE (*Siwo Yu*)

A. 1½ teaspoons salt
B. 2 lbs. fish (sea or black bass, white mullet, haddock, mackerel, porgy or bluefish), washed and cleaned
C. 2 eggs, beaten vigorously
D. ¾ cup all purpose flour
E. ¾ cup black mushrooms, soaked in warm water for 15 minutes, shredded
F. 1 cup bamboo shoots, shredded
G. ¼ cup water chestnuts, peeled, shredded
H. 1½ cups celery, shredded
I. 1 teaspoon light soy sauce
J. 1 teaspoon rice wine or 2 tablespoons sherry wine
K. 1 teaspoon ginger, shredded
L. ¼ teaspoon pepper
M. 1 tablespoon cornstarch
N. 1 teaspoon sugar
O. 1 teaspoon seasoning powder
P. 1 teaspoon heavy soy sauce
Q. ½ cup soup stock

PREPARATION

Rub A over B. Dip fish in C, then in D, making sure that surface is well floured. Mix I, J, K, L together; add 1 tablespoon water. Stir well before using. Mix M, N, O, P together with ½ cup water. Stir well before using.

COOKING

1. Fry prepared fish in deep fat until golden brown. Set aside in deep lettuce-lined dish.
2. Put 1 tablespoon peanut oil in hot skillet; add ½ tablespoon salt.
3. Add E, F, G, H. Stir-fry 2 minutes.

4. Add I, J, K, L preparation. Stir thoroughly 2 minutes.
5. Add Q. Cover and cook 2 minutes.
6. Add cornstarch preparation. Stir constantly until gravy thickens and is smooth; pour over fish.
Garnish with 1 cup chopped parsley.

Serves 2 or 3.

381. FISH CAKES (*Yu Beng*)

A. 2 tablespoons peanut oil
B. 2 lbs. filet of pike, flounder, bass, haddock or sole
C. 1 cup raw pork
D. 2 fresh scallions (white part only), chopped
E. 1 clove garlic, crushed
F. ¼ cup Virginia ham
G. 1 oz. dried shrimps, soaked in warm water 30 minutes
H. 1 teaspoon ginger, crushed
I. 1 teaspoon dried tangerine skin, soaked in warm water 1 hour and cleaned
J. 1 teaspoon Chinese salt cabbage, soaked in warm water 10 minutes, rinsed with cold water 2 or 3 times
K. 3 tablespoons all purpose flour
L. ¾ teaspoon pepper
M. 1½ teaspoons seasoning powder
N. ½ teaspoon sesame seed oil
O. 1 teaspoon salt
P. 1 tablespoon light soy sauce
Q. 1 teaspoon rice wine

PREPARATION

Grind B, C, D, E, F, G, H, I, J in meat grinder. Add K, L, M, N, O and blend thoroughly. Divide mixture into eight parts and shape like hamburger cakes. Mix P and Q together with 1 tablespoon water. Stir well before using.

COOKING

1. Put A in hot skillet. Fry cakes as you would hamburgers, until golden brown on both sides.
2. Add P, Q mixture. Cover and cook 2 minutes.

Serve with boiled rice or potatoes.

Serves 4.

Note: If any cakes are left over, they will keep in refrigerator for days. These fish cakes may be sliced and used in a fish cake chop suey; or they may be used in a stir-fry dish with any kind of vegetable: broccoli, asparagus, Chinese or American cabbage, bean sprouts, etc.

382. STIR-FRY FISH WITH VEGETABLES
(*Chow Yu Pen*)

A. 2 tablespoons peanut oil
B. 2 teaspoons salt
C. ¾ lb. bean sprouts
D. 2 tablespoons Chinese preserved sweet pickle, shredded fine
E. 1 tablespoon Chinese preserved ginger, shredded very fine
F. 1 fresh scallion (white part only), cut in 2 inch long sections and split into 4
G. 1 clove garlic, crushed
H. 1 lb. filet of pike, sliced ¼ inch thick
I. 1 tablespoon light soy sauce
J. 1 teaspoon rice wine or 2 tablespoons sherry wine
K. 1 teaspoon fresh ginger, shredded
L. 1 teaspoon sugar
M. 1½ teaspoons seasoning powder
N. ½ teaspoon pepper
O. 1 teaspoon heavy soy sauce
P. 10 drops sesame seed oil
Q. 1 tablespoon cornstarch

PREPARATION

Mix I, J, K, L, M, N, O, P together; add 1 tablespoon water. Stir well before using. Add ¾ cup water to dissolve Q. Stir well before using.

COOKING

1. Put half of A in very hot skillet; add half of B.
2. Add C, D, E, F. Stir-fry 1 minute. Add ¼ cup water. Cover and cook 3 minutes. Set aside in deep plate.
3. Reheat skillet, and when very hot, put in remaining A and B; add G.
4. When oil starts to smoke, add H. Stir-fry about 1 minute.
5. Add I, J, K, L, M, N, O, P preparation. Stir-fry 2 minutes. Add cornstarch mixture, and when gravy becomes translucent, pour into plate with other cooked ingredients.
Garnish with chopped parsley.

Serves 2 or 3.

383. FRIED FISH IN BATTER WITH ASSORTED VEGETABLES (*Soo-Jow Yu Kew*)

Use same method and ingredients as in recipe No. 285, using fish instead of lobster: 1 lb. swordfish, halibut, pike, bass, haddock, etc. Slice, or cut in cubes, as you prefer.

EELS

---

384. SAUTE BONELESS EELS WITH SWEET BEAN STICK (*Wai Bok-Seng*)

A. 2 tablespoons peanut oil
B. 1 teaspoon salt
C. 1 clove garlic, crushed
D. 1 medium-size eel (from 1½ to 2½ lbs.)
E. 2 teaspoons light soy sauce
F. 1 teaspoon rice wine or 2 tablespoons sherry wine
G. 1 teaspoon shredded ginger root
H. ¼ teaspoon sesame seed oil
I. dash of pepper and garlic powder
J. 1 cup bacon, shredded
K. 12 doz. Chinese red dates (soaked in warm water 15 minutes, stones removed, shredded)
L. ½ cup imported black mushrooms (soaked in warm water 15 minutes, shredded)
M. 2 cups Chinese sweet bean stick
N. ¼ cup water chestnuts, peeled and shredded
O. ½ cup bamboo shoots, shredded
P. 1 tablespoon leek, chopped
Q. 3 cups soup stock

PREPARATION

Boil D with 2 or 3 slices ginger root 25 to 30 minutes. Rinse with cold water; remove bones and chop into sections about 1½ inches long. Mix E, F, G, H, I together; add 1 tablespoon water. Stir well before using.

COOKING

1. Put A in very hot skillet. Add B and C.
2. Add D. Fry on both sides until light brown. Add prepared mixture. Cover and cook ½ minute.

3. Add J, K, L, M, N, O, P.
4. Add Q. Cover and cook until boiling. Lower heat and let simmer until water is almost gone (about ½ cup soup stock left).

Serves 2 or 3.

385. FRIED EEL MEAT IN BATTER WITH ASSORTED VEGETABLES (*Hong-Shu Bok-Seng*)

Prepare eels as instructed in recipe No. 384, then follow recipe No. 368, using eel meat instead of crabs. Garnish with parsley.

386. SWEET AND SOUR EELS WITH SUBGUM (*Subgum Tiem-Shoon Bok-Seng*)

Prepare eels as instructed in recipe No. 384, then follow basic recipe No. 287 for sweet and sour gravy and recipe No. 293 for subgum sauce, using eel meat instead of lobster.

387. EEL MEAT WITH VERMICELLI (*Fon-Soo Seng*)

Prepare eels as instructed in recipe No. 384; shred meat. Follow recipe No. 292, using eel meat instead of lobster.

EGG FOO YONG

---

388. CHICKEN EGG FOO YONG (*Guy Foo-Yong Don*)

BASIC RECIPE

A. ½ cup cooked chicken meat, chopped
B. ½ cup onion, chopped
C. ½ cup bean sprouts
D. ¼ cup scallions, chopped
E. 1 teaspoon seasoning powder
F. ½ teaspoon salt
G. ¼ teaspoon pepper
H. 4 eggs, beaten
I. ¼ cup mushrooms, chopped
J. ¼ cup celery, chopped
K. ¼ teaspoon garlic powder

PREPARATION AND COOKING

1. Pour about 1 to 1½ inches of oil or lard into frying pan, and heat to 350°.
2. Mix all ingredients together thoroughly; divide into 3 or 4 portions, and fry (like omelet) in hot oil until golden brown on both sides.
3. Drain on towel.
   Serve with brown gravy and boiled rice.

Serves 1 or 2.

Note: There are a great number of foo yong dishes, all of which follow this basic recipe. Any kind of fish or meat may be used instead of chicken: lobster, shrimp, crabmeat, roast pork, ham, veal, lamb, beef, etc. As usual, the name of the dish changes according to the main ingredient used.

The above also applies to the following recipe, No. 389, which is the basic recipe for subgum foo yong, and to recipe No. 391, basic recipe for foo yong, Cantonese style.

389. CHICKEN SUBGUM EGG FOO YONG
(*Subgum Yong Don*)

BASIC RECIPE

A. 1 cup cooked chicken meat, diced
B. ½ cup celery, diced
C. ½ cup onion, diced
D. ½ cup mushrooms, diced
E. ½ cup bamboo shoots, diced
F. ¼ cup water chestnuts, peeled and diced
G. ½ cup cooked green pepper, diced
H. ½ cup tomatoes, diced
I. 1 fresh scallion (white part only), chopped
J. 1 teaspoon seasoning powder
K. 1 teaspoon salt
L. ¼ teaspoon pepper
M. ½ teaspoon garlic powder
N. 6 eggs, beaten

PREPARATION AND COOKING

1. Pour about 1 to 1½ inches of oil or lard into frying pan, and heat to 350°.
2. Mix all ingredients together thoroughly; divide into 5 or 6 portions, and fry (like omelet) in hot oil until golden brown on both sides.
3. Drain on towel.

Serve with brown gravy and boiled rice.

Serves 2 or 3.

390. VEGETABLE EGG FOO YONG
(*Kur-Toy Yong Don*)

A. 1 cup fresh cooked peas (broccoli, asparagus, green pepper, tomatoes, mushrooms or celery), chopped or diced
B. ½ cup bean sprouts
C. ½ cup onion, diced or sliced
D. 1 teaspoon seasoning powder
E. 1 teaspoon salt
F. ¼ teaspoon pepper
G. ¼ teaspoon garlic powder
H. 4 eggs, beaten

PREPARATION AND COOKING

1. Pour about 1 to 1½ inches of oil or lard into frying pan, and heat to 350°.
2. Mix all ingredients together thoroughly; divide into 3 or 4 portions, and fry (like omelet) in hot oil until golden brown on both sides.
3. Drain on towel.

Serve with brown gravy and boiled rice.

Serves 1 or 2.

391. EGG FOO YONG, CANTONESE STYLE
(*Kwong-Chow Yong Don*)

BASIC RECIPE

A. 6 eggs, beaten
B. 1 teaspoon seasoning powder
C. 1 teaspoon salt
D. ½ cup black or white mushrooms, shredded
E. ¼ teaspoon pepper
F. ½ teaspoon garlic powder
G. 3 cups bean sprouts
H. 1 fresh scallion (white part only), chopped

PREPARATION AND COOKING

1. Blend A, B, C, D, E, F together.
2. Pour 1½ tablespoons peanut oil in very hot skillet.

3. Add G. Stir-fry 1 minute. Add ½ cup water or soup stock. Cover and cook 3 minutes.
4. Add prepared mixture and H. Stir thoroughly, then press flat. Fry until one side is light brown; turn and fry other side.

Serve hot with boiled rice.

Serves 2.

EGGS

---

392. STEAMED EGGS (CUSTARD) (*Jing-Don*)

BASIC RECIPE

A. 6 eggs
B. 2 cups water or milk
C. 1 teaspoon seasoning powder
D. 1 teaspoon salt
E. ¼ teaspoon pepper
F. ¾ teaspoon rice wine
G. 1 teaspoon light soy sauce or oyster sauce
H. few drops sesame seed oil

PREPARATION AND COOKING

1. Blend the above ingredients in a large mixing bowl; beat thoroughly and vigorously.
2. Pour mixture into deep plate, or into individual custard cups. Put plate or cups on rack in large pot with 3 inches of boiling water in bottom. Cover and steam over low heat 30 to 40 minutes, or until eggs are set. Add 1 tablespoon hot cooked peanut oil before serving.

Serves 3.

Note: This is another egg dish which lends itself to much variation. Add ¾ cup chopped chicken meat, shrimp, lobster, pork or ham, etc., to this basic recipe.

393. FRIED EGGS IN DEEP FAT WITH OYSTER SAUCE (*Ho-Yu Hoo-Bow Don*)

A. 6 eggs
B. 2 tablespoons oyster sauce

COOKING

1. Pour about 1 inch peanut oil into small frying pan and heat to 350°. Fry A one by one until light brown around the edges. Put them into deep lettuce-lined plate.
2. Pour B over eggs and serve hot.

Serves 3.

394. FRIED EGGS IN DEEP FAT, LIANG-FAR STYLE (*Liang-Far Don*)

A. 1 tablespoon peanut oil
B. 1 teaspoon salt
C. 1 clove garlic, crushed
D. 1 cup bamboo shoots, shredded fine
E. 1½ cups celery, shredded very fine
F. 1 cup black imported mushrooms, soaked in water 15 minutes, shredded fine
G. ¼ cup water chestnuts, peeled, shredded
H. 1 cup pea pods, shredded very fine (Chinese cabbage, broccoli or asparagus may be substituted)
I. 1 teaspoon light soy sauce
J. 1 teaspoon rice wine or 2 tablespoons sherry wine
K. 1 teaspoon seasoning powder
L. 1 teaspoon sugar
M. ½ cup soup stock
N. 1 tablespoon cornstarch
O. 1 teaspoon heavy soy sauce
P. 6 eggs

PREPARATION

Mix I, J, K, L together; add 1 tablespoon water. Stir well before using. Mix N, O together with ¾ cup water. Stir well before using. Pour about 1 inch of peanut oil into small frying pan, and heat to 350°. Fry eggs, one by one, until light brown. Set aside in deep lettuce-lined plate.

COOKING

1. Put A in very hot skillet. Add B and C.
2. Add D, E, F, G, H. Stir-fry 2 minutes.
3. Add I, J, K, L preparation. Stir-fry thoroughly 2 minutes.
4. Add M. Cover and cook 3 minutes.
5. Add N, O gradually. Stir-fry until gravy becomes translucent. Pour over fried eggs. Garnish with scallions or parsley.

Serves 3.

395. SCRAMBLED EGGS WITH FROZEN PEAS
(*Ting-Dow Chow Don*)

A. 6 eggs, beaten with 1 cup water
B. 1 teaspoon seasoning powder
C. pinch of pepper and garlic powder
D. 1 teaspoon light soy sauce
E. 1½ tablespoons peanut oil
F. 1 teaspoon salt
G. 1 cup frozen peas, cooked in boiling water 2 minutes, rinsed with cold water and drained

PREPARATION AND COOKING

1. Add B, C, D to A. Blend well.
2. Put E and a few drops of sesame seed oil in very hot skillet. Add F.
3. Add G. Stir-fry 2 minutes.
4. Add egg mixture. Stir-fry or scramble until eggs are cooked.

Serves 2 or 3.

Note: One cup cooked diced asparagus, pea pods, broccoli, green peppers, Chinese cabbage, bamboo shoots, string beans, scallions or onions may be used in scrambled egg dishes.

396. SCRAMBLED EGGS WITH BACON
(*Yin-Yoke Chow Don*)

A. ½ tablespoon peanut oil
B. ½ teaspoon salt

c. ½ cup diced or shredded Chinese or American bacon, ham, chicken, beef, veal, lamb, pork, Chinese or American sausages, turkey, lobster, shrimps, crabmeat or fish meat
d. 1 teaspoon seasoning powder
e. pinch of pepper and garlic powder
f. 1 teaspoon light soy sauce
g. 6 eggs, beaten with 1 cup water or milk

PREPARATION AND COOKING

1. Put A and a few drops sesame seed oil in hot skillet. Add B.
2. Add C. Stir-fry until almost done.
3. Mix D, E, F well with G and pour in skillet.
4. Stir-fry or scramble until eggs are cooked.

Serves 2 or 3.

Note: Any leftover cooked meat is suitable for this dish.

397. BOILED EGGS WITH SOY SAUCE (*Van-Don*)

a. 6 eggs (ducks' eggs are best), boiled 45 minutes, shelled
b. 1 cup best light soy sauce
c. 1 tablespoon honey
d. 1 tablespoon heavy soy sauce
e. 2 teaspoons seasoning powder
f. 1 leek, chopped into sections about 1 to 2 inches long
g. 1 teaspoon dried tangerine rind, soaked in warm water for 30 minutes, cleaned
h. 1 teaspoon salt
i. 2 cloves garlic, crushed
j. 8 cups water

COOKING

1. Mix all ingredients except A in pot. Bring to a boil.
2. Add A. Bring to boil again, then lower heat and simmer 3 hours. Add water if needed.
3. Slice eggs into a lettuce-lined plate. Serve hot or cold. Garnish with sliced tomatoes and parsley.
   Serve with duck sauce or ketchup with hot sauce mixture.

Serves 2 or 3.

398. BOILED EGGS WITH TEA (*Don-Char*)

A. 6 eggs, boiled 45 minutes, shelled
B. 2 tablespoons tea (Moo-Yu Char, Jasmine or Lichee)
C. ½ cup rock sugar

COOKING

1. Pour 8 cups water in pot; bring to a boil.
2. Add B and boil 15 minutes. Strain tea leaves (make sure liquid is clear).
3. Add A. Bring tea to boiling point again, then reduce heat and let simmer for 2 hours.
4. Add C. Simmer another hour.

Serve eggs hot or cold.

Serves 3.

Note: So-called hundred-year-old eggs are among the rare delicacies imported from China. These would be served as an entree at a formal party or banquet. The lime-treated eggs, cleaned, shelled and sliced, are served with sweet and sour mixed pickles. The salt-treated eggs are cleaned and cooked 25 minutes; they are then shelled and sliced (or halved) and served with cooked peanut oil.

VEGETABLES

---

399. STEAMED BLACK MUSHROOMS
(*Ching-Toon Don-Koo*)

A. ¼ lb. imported black thick dried mushrooms, or 2 lbs. fresh mushrooms (soak dried mushrooms in warm water for 15 minutes, rinse several times in cold water; boil fresh mushrooms with salt and crushed garlic for 15 minutes, rinse several times in cold water)
B. 3 tablespoons rock sugar or honey
C. ½ lb. chicken fat
D. 1 tablespoon seasoning powder
E. 3 tablespoons rice wine or rose wine
F. 10 cups super soup stock
G. 1 teaspoon ginger, sliced

COOKING

1. Put all ingredients in a pot. Bring to a boil, then lower heat and let simmer 1½ hours. Add more soup stock if necessary.
2. Line a big bowl with lettuce leaves. Set the small mushrooms at bottom, large ones on top; strain juice and pour 1 cup over mushrooms.
3. Place a rack on bottom of large pot with 3 or 4 inches of boiling water. Put bowl with mushrooms on rack. Cover. Steam 15 minutes.
Serve hot.

Serves 6.

400. STIR-FRY BLACK MUSHROOMS
(*Hong-Shu Don-Koo*)

A. 1½ tablespoons peanut oil; add a drop of sesame oil
B. 1 teaspoon salt
C. 1 clove garlic
D. 2 oz. dried black mushrooms, soaked in warm water for 15 minutes, sliced
E. ½ cup water
F. 1 tablespoon light soy sauce
G. 1 teaspoon sugar
H. 1 teaspoon seasoning powder
I. 1 teaspoon rice wine or 2 tablespoons sherry wine
J. 1 teaspoon cornstarch

PREPARATION

Mix E, F, G, H, I, J together. Stir well before using.

COOKING

1. Put A in very hot skillet; add B and C.
2. Add D. Stir-fry 5 minutes. Add ¼ cup water. Cover and cook 5 minutes.
3. Add prepared mixture. Stir-fry thoroughly. When boiling, lower heat; let simmer until gravy becomes translucent.
   Serve hot with boiled rice or potatoes.

Serves 2 or 3.

401. STIR-FRY STRAW MUSHROOMS
(*Hong-Shu Tao-Kou*)

Follow preceding recipe No. 400.

Use 2 oz. straw mushrooms. Rinse mushrooms with cold water once or twice, then soak in large bowl with 2 cups hot water. Stir mushrooms with chopstick or fork. Let set 5 minutes, then pick mushrooms out and put them in clean bowl. When sand has sunk to bottom of bowl, pour off top water slowly into another bowl. Repeat this operation 3 or 4 times to be sure all sand is out, or strain with a piece of cheesecloth. Use water for cooking.

Serves 2 or 3.

402. STIR-FRY CHINESE CABBAGE (*Chow-Bok-Toy*)

BASIC RECIPE

A. 1½ tablespoons peanut oil or butter
B. 1 teaspoon salt
C. 1 clove garlic, crushed
D. 1 lb. Chinese cabbage, washed and cleaned; cut leaves into 1 inch sections with the stem slanting about 45°; drain
E. ½ cup water
F. 1 teaspoon light soy sauce
G. 1 teaspoon seasoning powder
H. 1 teaspoon sugar
I. ½ teaspoon crushed ginger
J. 1 teaspoon rice wine or 2 tablespoons sherry wine
K. 1 teaspoon cornstarch

PREPARATION

Mix E, F, G, H, I, J, K together. Stir well before using.

COOKING

1. Put A in very hot skillet; add B and C.
2. Put white part and stem of D in skillet. Stir-fry 2 minutes. Add green leaves; stir another minute.
3. Add prepared mixture. Stir thoroughly 1 minute. Cover and cook 2 minutes.

Serves 2 or 3.

Note: Following this basic recipe, any number of dishes can be made with almost any kind of vegetable being used instead of Chinese cabbage: mustard greens, pea pods, green peas, celery, onions, green peppers, American cabbage, etc. If broccoli or asparagus is used, cook in boiling water 2 minutes and rinse in cold water before adding to skillet. Broccoli should be cooked 5 minutes (and 2 teaspoons sugar should be used instead of 1); asparagus should be cooked 6 minutes.

403. STIR-FRY ASSORTED VEGETABLES, CHINESE STYLE (*Chow Dep Suey*)

Follow basic recipe No. 402, using at least 2 and not more than 5 different kinds of vegetables. If more than a pound (in all) is used, make more sauce in proportion.

404. SPINACH WITH CHINESE WHITE CHEESE (*Foo-Yu Bow-Toy*)

Follow basic recipe No. 402, using 1 lb. fresh spinach, washed and cleaned, instead of cabbage, and add 3 cakes white cheese to the prepared mixture of soy sauce, etc.

405. STRING BEANS WITH CHINESE WHITE CHEESE (*Foo-Yu Dow-Doy*)

Follow basic recipe No. 402, using 1 lb. fresh string beans, cleaned and chopped into 1½ inch pieces, instead of cabbage, and add 4 cakes white cheese to the prepared mixture of soy sauce, etc. Before putting string beans in skillet, cook in boiling water for 3 minutes, then rinse in cold water.

406. BEAN CURD WITH SOY SAUCE (*Shee-Yu Doy-Foo*)

A. 6 cakes bean curd
B. 3 tablespoons best light soy sauce
C. 1 teaspoon seasoning powder and pinch of pepper
D. 4 tablespoons peanut oil, heated until smoking
E. 2 fresh scallions (white part only), cut into 1½ inch sections, then split
F. ½ cup parsley

PREPARATION AND SERVING

1. Cut A into 4 slices each and place on deep plate, or divide into 2 portions and place on individual plates.

2. Mix B, C together. Pour over A.
3. Pour D over bean curd. Garnish with E and F. Serve hot or cold.
Serves 2.

407. BEAN CURD WITH OYSTER SAUCE
(*Hoo-Yu Dow-Foo*)

Follow recipe 406, using oyster sauce instead of soy sauce.

408. BEAN CURD WITH SHRIMP SAUCE
(*Hom-Har Dow-Foo*)

Follow recipe 406, using cooked shrimp sauce instead of soy sauce.
Note: Steam 2 tablespoons shrimp sauce in a bowl for 10 minutes.

409. FRIED BEAN CURD WITH MUSHROOMS
(*Hong-Shu Dow-Foo*)

A. 6 cakes bean curd
B. 1½ cups black or white mushrooms, shredded (soak black
   mushrooms in warm water 15 minutes)
C. 1 teaspoon light soy sauce
D. 1 teaspoon sugar
E. 1 teaspoon seasoning powder
F. 1 teaspoon rice wine or 2 tablespoons sherry wine
G. 1 teaspoon salt
H. pinch of pepper
I. ½ cup water
J. 1 tablespoon cornstarch
K. ½ teaspoon heavy soy sauce

PREPARATION

Cut A into 4 pieces each. Fry in deep fat until light brown. Put in
deep plate. Mix C, D, E, F together; add ½ cup water. Stir well
before using. Mix I, J, K together. Stir well before using.

COOKING

1. Soak B in C, D, E, F preparation; cook in frying pan 5 minutes.
2. Add cornstarch preparation slowly and cook until mixture becomes translucent. Then pour sauce over A.
   Garnish with chopped parsley.

Serves 2.

410. SAUTE POTATOES WITH BLACK BEAN SAUCE
(*Dow-Shee See-Doy*)

Use same method and ingredients as in recipe No. 137, eliminating the pork and adding 2 more cups potatoes and 1 more tablespoon black beans.

411. SAUTE 3 KINDS OF BAMBOO SHOOTS WITH CHINESE RED CHEESE (*Som-Soon Nam-Yu*)

A. 1 tablespoon peanut oil
B. 1 clove garlic, crushed
C. 1 cup bamboo shoots, cut into wedges
D. 1 cup dried bamboo shoots, soaked in cold water overnight; cut off hard ends, chop into sections
E. 1 cup dried golden shoots, soaked in cold water overnight; cut off hard ends, chop into sections
F. 1 cake red cheese, mashed

COOKING

1. Put A and a few drops of sesame seed oil in hot skillet; add B.
2. Add C, D, E. Stir-fry 2 minutes.
3. Add F. Stir 1 minute. Add 2 cups water. Bring to a boil, reduce heat very low and let simmer 1 hour. Add more water if necessary.

Serves 2.

412. SWEET AND SOUR MUSTARD GREENS
(*Tiem-Shoon Kai-Toy*)

A. 1 lb. sweet and sour mustard greens, cut into sections, squeezed dry
B. 1½ tablespoons peanut oil
C. ½ cup water
D. 2 tablespoons sugar
E. 2 tablespoons vinegar
F. 1 tablespoon cornstarch

PREPARATION

Mix C, D, E together. Mix F with ½ cup with water. Stir well before using.

COOKING

1. Put A in hot skillet. Stir-fry 10 to 15 minutes, until very dry, then add B. Stir thoroughly.
2. Add C, D, E preparation and stir 2 minutes.
3. Add cornstarch preparation and stir-fry until gravy thickens and is smooth.

Serves 2.

413. EGGPLANT WITH SHRIMP SAUCE
(*Hom-Har Che-Kar*)

A. 1½ tablespoons peanut oil
B. 1 clove garlic, crushed
C. 1 big eggplant (about 2 lbs.), peeled, cut lengthwise into 8 sections, then cut into 1½ inch wedges or cubes
D. 3 tablespoons shrimp sauce
E. 1 teaspoon seasoning powder
F. 1½ cups soup stock or water

COOKING

1. Put A in very hot skillet. Add B.
2. Add C. Stir-fry 1 minute.
3. Add D. Stir-fry 1 minute, then add E and F. Bring to a boil. Reduce to low heat and cook 25 minutes, or until juice thickens. Serve with boiled rice.

Serves 2.

414. CHINESE VEGETARIAN'S GREAT VARIETIES
(*Loo Hon Ji*)

A. ½ cup peanut oil

B. 2 tablespoons salt

C. 5 cloves garlic, crushed

D. ¼ lb. rice noodles (vermicelli), soaked in water 15 minutes, cut in 6 inch long pieces

E. 1 cup dried tiger lilies, soaked in water 30 minutes; cut off hard ends

F. 5 cakes bean curd

G. ¼ lb. bean stick

H. 1 cup hair seaweed

I. 2 tablespoons dried cloud fungus, soaked in water 30 minutes, rinsed several times in cold water

J. 1 cup Chinese white nuts (fresh or canned); if fresh, crack shells, boil 10 minutes, rinse in cold water, peel

K. 1 cup black mushrooms, soaked in water 30 minutes, shredded (white mushrooms may be substituted)

L. 1 cup gold bamboo shoots, soaked in water overnight; cut off hard ends

M. 2 cups bamboo shoots, shredded

N. 1 cup each of 4 or 5 different fresh vegetables, sliced: Chinese cabbage, pea pods, bean sprouts, green peppers, celery, onions, mustard greens, broccoli, asparagus, cauliflower, spinach, etc.

O. ½ cup light soy sauce

P. 2 tablespoons seasoning powder

Q. 2 tablespoons sugar

R. 2 teaspoons pepper

S. 5 tablespoons rice wine or 1/3 cup sherry wine

T. 2 teaspoons fresh ginger, shredded very fine

U. 4 cups soup stock

V. 4 tablespoons black beans

W. 4 tablespoons cornstarch

X. 1 tablespoon heavy soy sauce

PREPARATION

Cut F into 4 slices each; fry in deep fat until light brown, then cut again into fine slices. Fry G in deep fat until light brown; cut in sections 2 or 3 inches long. Soak H 30 minutes; rinse several times in cold water; cook in oil and garlic 30 minutes, then pull apart into small bunches. Mix O, P, Q, R, S, T together with ½ cup water. Stir well before using. Mix W, X together with 1 cup water. Stir well before using.

COOKING

1. Put A in very hot large skillet or pot; add B and C.
2. Add D, E. Stir-fry 2 minutes.
3. Add prepared F, G, H and I, J, K, L, M. Stir constantly and fry 5 or 6 minutes.
4. Add N. Stir-fry 5 more minutes.
5. Add O, P, Q, R, S, T preparation. Stir thoroughly 2 minutes.
6. Add U and V. Cover and cook 10 minutes.
7. Add cornstarch preparation. Stir until gravy thickens and is smooth.

Serves 10 or more.

Note: If you do not have a large enough pot to hold all these ingredients, cook 3 or 4 ingredients separately, then mix them up before serving.

COOKIES AND CAKES

415. ALMOND COOKIES (*Heong-Yen Beng*)

A. 4 cups pastry flour
B. 1 teaspoon baking powder
C. 2 cups lard or vegetable shortening
D. 2 cups sugar
E. 1 egg, beaten
F. 1 tablespoon almond paste (optional)
G. 1 teaspoon almond extract
H. 1 teaspoon vanilla extract
I. 2 tablespoons almonds

PREPARATION AND BAKING

1. Sift A, B together.
2. Add C, D, E, F. Mix well. Add G, H.
3. Knead until dough is firm.
4. Flatten dough with rolling pin until ½ inch thick. Cut dough with cookie cutter. Put one piece I in center of each cookie.
5. Place cookies on pan about 1½ inches apart.
6. Bake in hot oven, 450°, about 10 minutes, or until cookies start to brown. Reduce heat to 250° or 300°, and bake 20 minutes more.

Makes about 20 cookies.

416. WALNUT COOKIES (*Hop-Hoo Soo Beng*)

A. 4 cups pastry flour
B. 1 teaspoon baking powder
C. 2 cups soft shortening
D. 2 cups sugar

E. 1 egg, beaten
F. 1 tablespoon corn syrup
G. 1 teaspoon vanilla extract
H. 1 teaspoon almond extract
I. 1 cup walnut meats, chopped

PREPARATION AND BAKING

1. Sift A, B together.
2. Add C, D, E, F, G, H.
3. Knead until dough is firm.
4. Flatten dough with a rolling pin until ¾ inch thick. Cut dough with a cookie cutter (about 2 inches in diameter).
5. Place on baking pan 2 inches apart.
6. Put 3 or 4 pieces I on top of each cookie.
7. Bake in hot oven, 450°, for 15 minutes, or until cookies are a delicate brown. Reduce heat to 250° and bake for 25 minutes more.

Makes about 1 dozen cookies.

417. PEANUT COOKIES (*Far-Sang Beng*)

A. 4 cups roasted peanuts, chopped very fine
B. 4 cups lard or shortening
C. 2 cups brown sugar
D. ½ cup corn syrup
E. ¼ cup peanut butter
F. 4 cups pastry flour
G. 1 teaspoon baking powder

PREPARATION AND BAKING

1. Mix A, B, C, D, E together.
2. Sift in F, G.
3. Knead until mixture is firm.
4. Cut dough with cookie cutter any size you like.
5. Bake in moderate oven 30 minutes, or until cookies are deep brown.

Makes about 2 dozen cookies.

418. RICE COOKIES (*Mei Beng*)

A. 6 eggs
B. 1 cup confectioners sugar
C. 1 cup rice flour
D. 1 teaspoon banana or lemon extract

COOKING

1. Beat A with electric or hand beater 2 minutes. Add B gradually, beating again 10 minutes. Add C gradually and D, beating 2 minutes.
2. Drop by tablespoons on electric grill; toast ½ minute on each side, or until light brown; repeat operation until dough is used up.

Makes about 5 dozen cookies.

419. FORTUNE COOKIES (*Tiem-Yu Beng*)

Follow recipe No. 418, using all purpose flour instead of rice flour. When cookies are done, and still hot, place a strip of fortune-teller paper in center of each cookie and fold up from 3 sides.

420. COCOANUT ROLLS (*Yer-Soo Don-Qon*)

Follow recipe No. 418, using all purpose flour instead of rice flour. When cookies are done, and still hot, place 1 tablespoon shredded cocoanut on each cookie and roll up.

421. PUFFED GLUTINOUS RICE CAKES
(*Tung-Mei Beng*)

A. 1 lb. glutinous rice, cooked, cooled and spread until absolutely dried by heat
B. 3 cups water
C. 2 cups sugar
D. 1 cup heavy corn syrup

COOKING

1. Fry A in deep fat until light brown and puffed.
2. Boil B, C 15 minutes.
3. Add D. Boil slowly until thick, about 30 minutes (50° in candy and jelly thermometer).
4. Line a pan with sesame seed, then put A over it, about 2 inches deep.
5. Pour B, C, D preparation over A.
   When cool, cut into squares.

422. WESTERN COWBOY CAKES (*Sai Kay Mar*)

A. 4 cups pastry flour
B. 1 teaspoon salt
C. 1 tablespoon baking powder
D. ½ cup sugar
E. 6 large eggs, beaten
F. 2 cups sugar
G. 3 cups water
H. 1 cup heavy corn syrup

COOKING

1. Sift A, B, C together.
2. Mix D, E together and add to dry ingredients. Knead until firm; roll dough very thin with a rolling pin on floured table and dust some flour on surface, then roll up and cut into small bits. Fry in deep fat until light brown.
3. Boil F, G 15 minutes.
4. Add H, gradually boiling until thick, about 30 minutes (45° in candy and jelly thermometer).
5. Line a pan with sesame seed, then put fried preparation over it, about 2 inches deep.
6. Pour prepared syrup over all.
   When cool, cut into squares.

423. STEAMED SPONGE CAKE (*Gai Don Gor*)

A. 6 large eggs, separated
B. 1½ cups granulated or confectionery sugar
C. 1½ cups all purpose flour
D. ½ teaspoon baking powder
E. 1 teaspoon lemon extract
F. ½ teaspoon vanilla

COOKING

1. Beat egg whites vigorously 25 minutes, or until stiff (electric beater 15 minutes). Add B gradually, beat another 5 minutes.
2. Add egg yolks, beat 5 minutes. Add lemon and vanilla.
3. Sift C and D together and add to above preparation. Mix thoroughly.
4. Put mixture in small bamboo steam-tier or colander with piece of paper on bottom.
5. Put steam-tier or colander on rack in bottom of large pot with 3 or 4 inches of boiling water. Steam 25 minutes.
6. Cut into 2 inch squares and serve hot or cool.

424. CHINESE TEA CAKE WITH PIE CRUST (*Soo-Beng*)

1. Mix the following ingredients together. Cover up with damp cloth 30 minutes:
   A. 6 cups pastry flour
   B. 3 cups shortening
   C. ½ cup hot water

2. Mix the following ingredients together well:
   D. 4 cups pastry flour
   E. 2½ cups soft shortening

3. Divide 1 and 2 into 30 parts each.

4. Flatten 1. Wrap in 2, one by one, until dough is used up.

5. Roll each 4 into a long thin strip with a rolling pin, then roll it up with your hand and fold up again like a ball.

6. Flatten 5. Fill dough with some kind of sweet filling, such as crushed cooked black beans, green beans, soy beans, lima beans,

dates, figs, jelly, jam, crushed pineapple, cooked apples, seedless raisins, etc.

7. Flatten again. Bake in slow oven 20 minutes; turn and bake another 10 minutes in slow oven (about 300°).

Makes about 30 cakes.

425. MISTRESS OR WIFE CAKES (*Law-Poo Beng*)

Follow recipe No. 424 to make crust.

Use the following ingredients to make filling: 2 cups sugar dried sweet winter melon, chopped fine; 1 cup Chinese cooked cake flour; ¾ cup sugar; ½ cup cooked fat pork, chopped fine; ¾ cup shortening; 1 teaspoon banana extract.

Makes about 30 cakes.

426. MIXED NUT CAKES (*Subgum Soo-Beng*)

Follow recipe No. 424 to make crust.

Use the following ingredients to make filling: 1½ cups mixed roasted nuts, chopped; ¾ cup sugar; 4 tablespoons Chinese cooked cake flour; 4 tablespoons cooked pork fat; 4 tablespoons corn syrup.

Makes about 30 cakes.

Note: You may add cooked Virginia ham, chopped; the cake would then be called Subgum Hom Yoke Soo Beng.

427. STEAMED ROLLS WITH SWEET OR MEAT FILLING (*Hom Yoke Bow*)

A. 1 cake fresh yeast
B. 6 cups bread flour

PREPARATION

1. Dissolve A in cup of warm water.
2. Put B on board; make a hole in center.
3. Put yeast mixture in center hole.
4. Knead dough; add water if needed.
5. Add 2 tablespoons peanut oil while you knead dough, to avoid sticking. Knead until dough is smooth and elastic.
6. Place dough in large bowl. Cover with damp cloth and let rise in warm, draft-free spot until 3 or 4 times its original size.
7. Take dough out and knead again. If sticky, use a little more oil.
8. Divide dough into equal parts, about 35 to 40 ordinary-size rolls.
9. Roll dough around like a ball.

FILLING

1. For sweet filling, use the same kind of filling as noted in recipe No. 424.
2. For meat filling: use meat ball, see recipe No. 117; or use chopped Chinese roast pork and add some Chinese salted cabbage; or use chopped Chinese sausage.
3. Place rolls in warm place 30 to 40 minutes, until they rise to double original size.

COOKING

1. Put rolls in a bamboo-tier or colander.
2. Place rack in bottom of large pot or Chinese cooking pan with 3 or 4 inches boiling water; put tier or colander on rack, steam 15 to 20 minutes.
   Serve hot.

Serves 10.

SAUCES

---

428. DUCK SAUCE (*Soo-Moy Ding*)

A. 4 cups fresh plums, skins and stones removed, mashed
B. 3 cups fresh or dried apricots
C. 2 cups apples, pears, pineapples, strawberries, or peaches
D. 1 cup vinegar
E. 2 cups sugar
F. 1 cup chopped pimentos

PREPARATION AND COOKING

1. Mash A, B, C together; add D, E, F.
2. Put in pot and bring to boiling point; lower heat and let simmer 1½ hours.
3. Preserve in airtight jar. Keep in cool place for about a month.
4. When ready to use, add a little water and sugar to taste.

Note: Duck sauce is a kind of chutney, used especially for roast duck. It was used for pork in the old times. Now it is used for any kind of meat or salad; also with rice.

429. SAUCE FOR FISH (*Hoy-Seng Ding*)

A. 5 cups soy beans
B. 2 tablespoons garlic
C. 2 tablespoons boiled red rice
D. 1 tablespoon salt
E. 1½ tablespoons sugar

COOKING

Pour ¾ gallon boiling water into large pot or heavy kettle. Add all ingredients. Bake in oven, or steam in heavy kettle 3 hours, or until ingredients are soft. Mash fine, put in airtight bottle and keep in cool place for one month.

Note: This sauce is good with steamed fish or mixed with mustard for hot savories and salads.

430. SUBGUM SWEET AND SOUR VEGETABLE SAUCE (*Sip Gum Tien-Soon Wu*)

A. 1 cup water
B. ¾ cup sugar
C. ½ cup vinegar
D. 1 can imported mixed pickles, shredded fine
E. 1 tablespoon cornstarch
F. 1 teaspoon heavy soy sauce

PREPARATION

Mix E, F with ½ cup water. Stir well before using.

COOKING

1. Put A in saucepan; heat until boiling.
2. Add B, C and cook until sugar dissolves.
3. Add D and cook 2 minutes.
4. Add prepared mixture and cook until sauce thickens.

Note: Shredded fresh tomato, green pepper, carrot or mixed American sweet pickles may be used instead of the Chinese pickles.

431. SOY BEANS AND RICE JAM (*Dow-Ding*)

A. 5 cups soy beans, roasted and mashed
B. 4 cups cooked rice
C. 2 tablespoons sugar
D. 1 tablespoon salt
E. 1 tablespoon each leek and scallions (white part only), chopped
F. 2 cups rice wine

PREPARATION

Mix ingredients thoroughly and form a cake, like a hamburger. Dry in sun or under heat. Put in jar. Cover and let stay about 1 week. Add boiling water to about level with cake; then add 2 cups rice wine or pure alcohol. Keep in airtight jar 6 months or longer.

Note: This jam is very good with steamed pork, poultry or fish.

432. PURE SOY BEAN JAM (*Mien-Shee Ding*)

A. 3 cups soy beans
B. 2 tablespoons sugar
C. 3 tablespoons salt

PREPARATION AND COOKING

Mix A, B, C together in boiling water 3 inches over beans. Cover and cook 2 hours; add more boiling water if necessary. Preserve in airtight jar for 6 months or longer.

Note: This jam is often used with lobster, Chinese style, instead of black bean sauce. Also good with pork, lamb, poultry or fish.

433. LIGHT SOY SAUCE (*Yuen You*)

A. 10 cups soy beans
B. ½ cup salt
C. 6 gallons water

COOKING

Mix all ingredients together and cook until boiling. Lower heat, simmer 5 hours (about 5 gallons of water should be left). Strain. Pour in 5-gallon glass jar. Seal airtight. Keep, if possible, on roof or window ledge, facing the sun, about 1 year or more. The liquid is light soy sauce. The beans could be used to make Soy Bean Jam (No. 432) or used as a cooking sauce for fish.

434. BLACK SOY SAUCE (*Chow You*)

Use same method and ingredients as in recipe No. 433. After **6** months, strain off the beans and add 1 quart of molasses and 1 **cup** rice wine or alcohol. Seal jar again. Let age another 6 months **or** longer. (*Make sure it has lots of sunshine.*)

Note: This sauce is served with a meal as a substitute for salt; it is not used in cooking.

435. HEAVY SOY SAUCE (*Chee You*)

Use same method and ingredients as in recipe No. 433. After 6 months add one gallon molasses to each gallon of soy sauce and age for another 6 months or longer.

436. OYSTER SAUCE (*Hoo You*)

A. 1 gallon fresh oysters
B. 3 tablespoons cooking salt
C. 4 cloves garlic, mashed
D. 4 slices fresh ginger
E. 2 fresh leeks (white part only)
F. 2 gallons water
G. 2 cups light soy sauce
H. 2 tablespoons sugar
I. ½ cup cornstarch
J. 1 tablespoon seasoning powder

COOKING

1. Put A, B, C, D, E, F in a large pot. Bring to a boil. Reduce heat and simmer 5 hours (about 1 gallon water should be left).
2. Mix G, H, I, J together with 1½ cups water; stir up well and add to oyster sauce gradually. Cook another 20 minutes. Strain, reserving oysters.
3. Pour sauce in airtight bottle and keep in cool place.

Note: Dry oysters in sun, or heat thoroughly; you will then have dried oysters for future use. This sauce is used for cooking meat, fish or poultry; it is also used at table as a salt substitute.

437. CHINESE HOT SAUCE or CHINESE CHILI SAUCE (*Lard-Dew Din*)

A. 5 cups red chili
B. 4 cups apricots
C. 2 tablespoons preserved lemon
D. 2 tablespoons garlic
E. 10 cups water

PREPARATION AND COOKING

Put A, B, C, D through meat grinder. Cook in E to boiling point, then lower heat and let simmer 1½ hours. Pour in airtight jar and keep in a warm place (facing sun, if possible) for 3 months or longer.

Note: This sauce is good in salads, sweet and sour vegetables, fish, pickled vegetables; or may be cooked with salted or spiced cabbage, etc.

Note: Another sauce that is mentioned throughout this book as a cooking ingredient is shrimp sauce. During the second World War, many Chinese here tried to make it with American shrimp, without success. Imported shrimp sauce may be bought at any Chinatown grocery store.

438. CHINESE BROWN GRAVY

A. 4 cups water or super soup stock
B. 1 teaspoon salt
C. 1 tablespoon seasoning powder
D. 1 teaspoon heavy soy sauce
E. 1 tablespoon cornstarch

PREPARATION AND COOKING

Heat A in deep saucepan until boiling. Mix B, C, D, E with ¾ cup water and add to A. Cook until translucent; keep hot until ready to use.

TEA

There are two kinds of tea in China—black or green tea. Influenced by the foreign demand, the Chinese producer has developed several kinds of red tea which are becoming popular in domestic trade and export to foreign markets.

Tea is the most common beverage in China—found in every home, shop and office. The Chinese drink tea instead of water, morning, noon and night. The price of tea ranges from ten cents to a hundred dollars a pound, and teapots range from fifty cents to astronomical figures. The longer a teapot has been in use, or the older a teapot is, the greater its value. A good teapot is always put into a beautiful basket lined with wadded mufflers to keep the tea hot.

We introduce here a few of the most popular teas which you can purchase in this country.

Green Teas: *wo hop* tea—most Chinese restaurants use this.
     oolong tea—most common for popular family use.
     loong soo tea (dragon's whiskers)—one of the popular teas.
     sui sing tea—also a popular tea.
Black Teas: *kee-mon* tea (black)
     pu-nei tea
     look on tea—all three are popular.
Red Teas: *lichee* tea
     kee-mon tea (red)—both are popular.
Fancy Teas: *soo-hing* jasmine tea (tea with Jasmine added).
     goat-far loone ding (dragon's well—tea with Chrysanthemums).
     To these two sugar and lemon may be added.

WINE

There are as many kinds of wines and liquors in China as in France ad the U.S.A. combined—wine made of fruits, melons, game, herbs and even snakes. Some are similar to brandy or whisky. Some are rather strong, some are milder, but wine and liquor is not usually drunk in China for a pleasure drink, at parties and banquets. It is used as a medicine as well as a food. Snake wine with herb cures rheumatism and poor blood. We have tiger bone and melon wine; deer's horn and tail, with herb, wine; pheasant, tiger and snake wine, etc. These wines all have to be aged for years (from five to fifteen years).

We shall not go into the detail of all Chinese wines, but shall list a few that you can purchase in Chinese liquor stores in the U.S.A.:

     rose wine—*amoy qur low*
     ng ga pai (made of herbs)
     pear wine—*shot lee low*
     orange wine—*chang-far low*
     rice wine—*mei-dew*
     glutinous rice wine—*noo-mei dew*
     tiger bone and melon wine—*foo-good mok-qur*

INDEX

BEEF (*continued*)
    with gravy, 102
    with green pepper, 103
    with luto's roots, 106
    with mushrooms, 103
    with mustard greens, 104
    with new gingers, 106
    with oyster sauce, 103
    with pea pod (snow pea), 104
    with pickled mustard greens, 104
    with preserved sweet pickle and gingers, 107
    with salted Chinese cabbage, 107
    with string beans, 106
    with tomatoes, 103
    with tomatoes and green peppers, 104
    tong-yan yoke-par, 112
    vermicelli with, 109
    with Chinese turnip soup, 32
    with curry, 108
    yer-toy far chow gow-yoke, 105
BIRD'S NEST
    chicken stuffed with, 140
    duck stuffed with, 164
    yen-wor chun guy, 140
    yen-wor chun op, 164
bitter melon chicken soup, 14
BLACK BEAN SAUCE
    chicken saute with, 132
    chow tien-low, 202
    dow-shee guy lok, 132
    dow-shee pai-good, 100
    dow-shee see-doy, 246
    dow-shee wong-har, 196
    fried shrimp with, 196
    pork spare ribs with, 100
    saute potatoes with, 246
    saute snails with, 202
black mushroom duck soup, 26
black mushroom sweet root soup, 29
black soy sauce, 260
boiled boneless chicken, yoke ling style, 132
boiled chicken with soy sauce, 136
boiled eggs with soy sauce, 239
boiled eggs with tea, 240
bok far guy, 133
bok opp soong, 168
bok suey yu, 221
bok you guy, 136
bok-far fish's maw chicken soup, 18
bok-far gaw guy tong, 18
bok-toy chow gee-yoke, 65
bok-toy chow gow-yoke, 104
bo-lo chow gee-yoke, 73
bo-lo tiem-shoon hong-lor, 200
boneless chicken garnished with 100 flowers, 133
boneless chicken with cream sauce, 133
boo-loo dep suey, 121
boo-loo guy din, 142
boo-loo guy kew, 126

boo-loo guy pan, 145
boo-loo leong ben op, 160
boo-loo loong-har kew, 177
boo-loo tiem-shoon har kew, 190
boo-toy par op, 153
bow-yu dong-koo tong, 34
braised
    beef northern style, 112
    conch with mushrooms, 197
    duck with mushrooms, 160
    duck with sweet bean curd sticks, **161**
    fish with black mushrooms, 224
    pork with Chinese red cheese, 86
    pork with Chinese turnips and red cheese, 86
    pork with bean sticks, 93
    pork with jade bamboo shoots, 92
breaded boneless duckling with **almonds** and sweet sauce, 163
BROCCOLI
    diced cut pork with, 97
    guy-liang chow gow-yoke, 105
    kai-leang chee-yoke din, 97
    kai-liang chow har, 194
    kai-lun chow gee-yoke, 74
    stir-fry beef with, 105
    stir-fry pork with, 74
    stir-fry shrimp with, 194
BROWN BEAN SAUCE
    mien-shee jing yu, 222
    steamed fish with, 222
but-bor chun op, 157
but-chen chun op, 155
butt-bor chow-fan, 55
butt-chen chow-fon, 57
BUTTERFLY SCALLOPS, 210
    with bacon, 210
    with vegetables, 211
BUTTERFLY SHRIMP, 183
    with bacon, 184
    with vegetables, 184

CABBAGE
    bok-toy chow gee-yoke, 65
    bok-toy chow gow-yoke, 104
    chung-toy chow gow-yoke, 107
    chung-toy jan gee-yoke, 88
    fish ball, soup, 33
    steamed pork with salted, 88
    stir-fry beef with Chinese, 104
    stir-fry beef with salted Chinese, **107**
    stir-fry Chinese, with pork, 65
    stir-fry, with pork, 75
    yer-toy chow gee-yoke, 75
    yu-yen-shou-toy tong, 33
Cake, *see* Cookies and Cakes
caul fat wrapped shrimp with **Chinese** bacon and ham, 188
CAULIFLOWER
    stir-fry, with pork, 71
    stir-fry beef with, 105
    yer toy far chow gee-yoke, 71, 105